THE LONGEST CON

ALSO BY JOE CONASON

Man of the World:
The Further Endeavors of Bill Clinton

It Can Happen Here:
Authoritarian Peril in the Age of Bush

Big Lies: The Right-Wing Propaganda Machine and
How It Distorts the Truth

The Hunting of the President: The Ten-Year
Campaign to Destroy Bill and Hillary Clinton

The Raw Deal: How the Bush Republicans Plan to Destroy
Social Security and the Legacy of the New Deal

THE LONGEST CON

HOW GRIFTERS, SWINDLERS, AND FRAUDS HIJACKED AMERICAN CONSERVATISM

JOE CONASON

FOREWORD BY GEORGE T. CONWAY III

ST. MARTIN'S PRESS
NEW YORK

First published in the United States by St. Martin's Press, an imprint of
St. Martin's Publishing Group

 Printed in the United States of America. For information, address St. Martin's Publishing Group, 120 Broadway, New York, NY 10271.

www.stmartins.com

Designed by Kelly S. Too

The Library of Congress Cataloging-in-Publication Data is available upon request.

ISBN 978-1-250-62116-0 (hardcover)
ISBN 978-1-250-62117-7 (ebook)

Our books may be purchased in bulk for promotional, educational, or business use. Please contact your local bookseller or the Macmillan Corporate and Premium Sales Department at 1-800-221-7945, extension 5442, or by email at MacmillanSpecialMarkets@macmillan.com.

First Edition: 2024

10 9 8 7 6 5 4 3 2 1

Dedicated to Elizabeth Newhouse, Ann Gund, and Barbara Landreth, for all the reasons they know

CONTENTS

FOREWORD

It's a big part of the story. An essential one.

If you're wondering how it came about that one of the two major political parties in the United States of America—the once Grand Old Party, the party of Lincoln—now stands ready to nominate as its presidential candidate a soulless, conscienceless, quadruply-indicted, twice-impeached pathologically lying conman (not to mention an adjudicated rapist) who tried to overthrow American democracy once, has proposed terminating the Constitution, and today openly promises that, if elected, he'd use the powers of the presidency to jail his opponents and to quash a free press, then this book is for you.

To be sure, there are many threads to the sorry tale, and long after we know how it ends, and long after we are gone, historians, political scientists—and psychologists—will still be pulling all of them. Teachers will teach them, students will study them. Cultural and demographic change, economic discontent, racism, xenophobia, authoritarianism, narcissism, disinformation, foreign influence from malign state actors, technology—so many angles may be found from which to view our nation's current kaleidoscope of political dysfunction.

But there's one engine that helped drive all of these factors to the fore, one force that pulls them together, one element that illuminates how so many people who knew better became—and remain—complicit in spreading these cancers on the body politic.

And that's grift. Profit.

As Joe Conason so ably—and relentlessly—describes in these pages, the story of Trumpism, the decay of conservatism, is in no small part a story of money in politics. But not the story that's normally told: of moneyed interests paying off politicians with campaign contributions, or even straight-out graft, for tax or regulatory breaks or government contracts. That's out there, to be sure, and Joe touches upon some of it. What this book is really about is hucksterism, on an ever-expanding scale.

It turns out that lies sell. Anger sells. Hatred sells. Conspiracy theories, libels, imaginary enemies—they all can be manufactured, at minimal cost, and marketed, from coast to coast, at a handsome markup, to the masses, including many people who probably can't afford the price. You don't even have to be that smart or skilled to get into the business: What economists call barriers to entry are low. Anyone can play the game, if they're shameless and greedy and dishonest enough.

As Joe explains, it didn't start with Donald Trump. There's a remarkable throughline to the story, recounted skillfully in this book. Remember Roy Cohn, the lawyer whom Trump has idolized and lionized as a model of ferocious advocacy? Turns out Cohn and a (special?) friend led the high life, gallivanting around Europe, sleeping in while keeping intimidated American diplomats waiting, all on the government dime on a hunt for communists on a list (Senator Joe McCarthy's) that didn't really exist. Cohn was the master; Trump later the apprentice. Now Trump is the master, for the moment.

But there were so many other bad actors along the way, and so many more in the pipeline. People who discovered, and monetized, the fact that the rubes who send money to people who peddle lies do so over and over again. Those lists—mailing lists—were real, and they were worth fighting over, stealing, and litigating about. At first they were lists of names and street addresses. Now they're electronic addresses, with extensive data describing which pitches work for which donors to boot. Hey, do you want to help President Trump build the border wall he said Mexico would pay for? Enter your Mastercard number here, and send your hard-earned money to me, Steve Bannon, at WeBuildTheWall.com! Don't like the election result? Well, that's because it was stolen! You can help by sending me, billionaire Donald Trump, money to bring lawsuits against everyone everywhere! Is something else upsetting you? We've already checked the recurring donation box for you!

And let's not forget—Joe's book doesn't—the preachers for profit, who market salvation (along with self-enrichment, of course) in much the same way, to many of the same people. Want the Lord on your side? Tithe to my church, so I can buy me that Mercedes-Benz. We needn't bother Him. Oh, and let us all pray for Donald Trump, man of God.

So it didn't start with the Orange Jesus, and no doubt it won't end with him, either. We see the metastasis of the disease today in Congress, where a Republican majority in the House is controlled by members who care not a whit about policy or legislating in the public interest, but who serve only themselves by sticking to a reliable and endemic formula. Get on Fox News, or Newsmax, say something outrageous (and untrue), then have someone (on the payroll!) send out the blast email solicitation. Collect cash. Rinse. Repeat. No wonder the Republican Speaker of the House worried that it might be imprudent to expel George Santos, whose crimes amounted merely to carrying out, to its logical conclusion, what others have been doing all along.

Never did I think I—a charter member, if I may say so myself, of Hillary Clinton's "vast right-wing conspiracy"—would write a foreword to a book by Joe Conason, praising him and his work. I was once a subject of his sharp words. But here we are. You can believe, in good faith, that the public interest is served by this policy or that, by more government or less. But if you believe that there is a public interest, and that public servants should serve that interest, and that facing raw truths is essential to that end, then you should care and learn about the toxic industry of mendacity that Joe so unsparingly describes here.

—George T. Conway III

THE LONGEST CON

Introduction

The most appropriate way to introduce *The Longest Con* is by paying homage where it is owed. The inspiration for this book's title—and much of what you will find in its pages—was a magazine article written more than a decade ago by Rick Perlstein, the historian of modern conservatism whose skill, integrity, and commitment have been widely celebrated across our nation's political divide.

"The Long Con" appeared in the November 2012 issue of *The Baffler*, a bimonthly journal of culture and politics that melds a left-leaning perspective with a surly temperament and a deft style. Published on the eve of a national election that pitted President Barack Obama against former Massachusetts governor Mitt Romney, Perlstein's essay amusingly dissected the Republican nominee's prevarications as an object lesson in right-wing chicanery. But then, as any serious historian is called to do, he delved far deeper.

Peering through the scrim of Romney's falsehoods and beyond his deceptive campaign, Perlstein described a highly developed, very profitable system that marketed lies in many forms to millions of gullible American conservatives—and had mined that vein for a long time. He recalled subscribing some years earlier to several right-wing periodicals online, a decision that soon filled his email inbox to overflowing with fervent pitches for miracle "cures," get-rich-quick "investments," and assorted additional examples of "important information" from what an earlier generation would have called snake-oil salesmen. Their messages promised to cure heart disease, reverse arthritis, end diabetes, ensure a secure retirement, provide thousands of dollars a month for little or no effort, and more—all endorsed by the trusted celebrities and outlets whose pronouncements are conservative gospel.

Meanwhile, a kindred horde of entrepreneurs had built dozens of political-action and issue-oriented committees, raising millions of dollars that would supposedly result in an end to abortion, a shutdown of the United Nations, a clampdown on labor unions, and an apocalyptic rout of liberals everywhere. What they didn't mention, at least not in any legible typeface, was that only tiny fractions of the funds donated would be deployed for any campaign, cause, or candidacy; in fact, the proceeds were almost entirely destined for "overhead" or "prospecting." Which meant in practice that nearly all the remainder swelled the accounts of those who had solicited the money.

It was not a coincidence, in Perlstein's view, that direct-mail and online swindlers overlapped so heavily with right-wing con artists and often were identical with them. To an expert who has devoted his professional life to exploring and exposing modern conservatism, those motley scams suddenly seemed less a comic distraction than a central feature. Partisan chroniclers who look away from such low-brow phenomena in recounting conservatism's heroic narratives are hiding from a fundamental truth.

His verdict was unequivocal in warning that "this stuff is as important to understanding the conservative ascendancy as are the internecine organizational and ideological struggles that make up its official history—if not, indeed, more so. The strategic alliance of snake-oil vendors and conservative true believers points up evidence of another successful long march, of tactics designed to corral fleeceable multitudes all in one place—and the formation of a cast of mind that makes it hard for either them or us to discern where the ideological con ended and the money con began."

That harsh judgment has been confirmed repeatedly since the rise of Donald Trump and the unabashed grifting that he embodies. But the evidence, which could fill the pages of many books, was piling up and spilling over well before Trump even showed up. As the author of *Before the Storm*, the definitive history of Barry Goldwater's 1964 presidential campaign, Perlstein detected the "infrastructural" roots of the grift in that movement. He was not wrong, as this book's retracing and elaboration of those connections will show. (Nor was he wrong about Romney, although the retiring senator from Utah has improved his image considerably since that ill-fated presidential race.)

With Trump as the new paradigm, however, there is a powerful reason to trace the story back still further, to the days when Roy Cohn made his scandalous national debut as an assistant to Senator Joseph R. McCarthy. The brazen young attorney—who would become Trump's mentor in mendacity—demonstrated how a conspiracy theory could be used not only to advance a far-right agenda but to glom unearned benefits for himself and a male companion.

The premise of Cohn's rip-off, recalled in chapter 1, was a bogus threat to national security from supposedly leftish books in United States Information Service libraries across postwar Europe. Vowing to stamp out this alleged literary subversion, he and his strapping pal David Schine indulged themselves in a tour of five-star hotels from London and Paris to Rome and Berlin. Compared with the multimillion-dollar depredations of Trump and his ilk, that junket now looks quaint and faintly comical, but it was a ruthless exercise in self-promotion that harmed the reputations of innocent individuals and damaged American prestige overseas.

Subsequent chapters outline the template for right-wing grift that followed in McCarthy's wake, when various charlatans prospered by exploiting amplified anxiety over the "Red Menace" among middle-class Americans. While some overlaid the message with fundamentalist religion and others emphasized partisan political themes, all of them aimed to trigger irrational fear and popularize the myth of an impending communist takeover.

By creating such an atmosphere of utter dread—and then promising that they alone could prevent America's doom—they induced thousands of suckers to hand over large wads of cash. Their mercenary antics and vacuous lectures enraged FBI director J. Edgar Hoover, who had his own racket to protect. Even Hoover understood that insofar as communism posed a challenge to the West, those con men had no idea how to oppose it and could only discredit its adversaries.

Out of that environment of delusion and paranoia emerged the Goldwater movement and its leaders—and with them came direct-mail dynamo Richard Viguerie (who had served as an early fundraiser for Billy James Hargis and his Christian Crusade). The commercial and political success of Viguerie's enterprises stimulated scores of imitators as the grift metastasized continuously into different forms—the New Right, the Moral Majority, the Tea Party movement, the prosperity gospel church, and today Trump's MAGA movement, which encompasses a whole series of subsidiary swindles and scams, though none as potent as those overseen by Trump and his family.

What remained consistent in each succeeding variation was the reliance on exaggeration, deception, and fabrication, frequently permeated with racial apprehension and hostility, as well as a remorseless drive to squeeze every penny from the dupes. None of this appeared suddenly in 2015, and its impresarios have profited exorbitantly for a very long time.

Indeed, literature tells us that grifting was an abiding feature of human society for centuries before the advent of modern politics. The history of cons, scams, and rackets in America dates back to the dawn of the Republic and no doubt earlier; frauds of every flavor have proliferated over the past century or more, growing in scope, complexity, and damage. More than once, those cons have inflicted terrible consequences, whether in the financial crash of 2008 or in the anti-vaccine uproar that left so many unnecessary dead from the COVID pandemic.

There may or may not be something inherent in right-wing ideology that encourages dishonesty. Conservative philosophy demands civic virtue and moral rigor—and yet Americans who call themselves conservative are undeniably more susceptible to the multiplying varieties of politically tinged fakery, from phony charities and direct-mail boondoggles to cancer and COVID "cures," watered penny stocks, overpriced gold, and useless dietary supplements.

While such con artists have come to play a dominant role among the

Right—where rejection of government and science leave the gullible unprotected—it is only fair to acknowledge there are and always were crooks identified with the Left. The most notorious example in recent years was the national leadership of the Black Lives Matter movement, whose sincere donors were dismayed to learn of the gross mismanagement of nearly $100 million since 2020, with vast sums squandered on luxury real estate, big payouts to the relatives of its officials, first-class travel, and other insider abuses.

A more complicated case is Robert F. Kennedy Jr., the most prominent voice of the anti-vax movement, with all its attendant sleaze and profiteering from human misery. Kennedy has always represented himself as a man of the Left, trading on his family's illustrious liberalism, despite his now extensive and evidently warm connections with the extreme Right both in the United States and Europe. His rhetoric and name also drew in a cohort of disgruntled liberals and may well continue to attract them—along with many millions of dollars. Charlatans can work both sides of the aisle.

Still there are fundamental distinctions in outlook between Left and Right that make one side more vulnerable than the other. It doesn't seem accidental that the principal Democratic campaign fundraising website, ActBlue, is a nonprofit organization that only takes money for credit card fees and operating costs, while WinRed, the main Republican fundraising site, is run for private profit—and announced in 2023 that it will be raising prices during the next presidential cycle. There have been a few scammy political action committees on the Democratic side, but there have been dozens that fleeced Republicans. If your ideology dictates that profit is the highest aspiration, you will probably try to wring surplus value from everything and everyone—and your moral character may well deteriorate in that process.

I will confess that my own political orientation has led me to grimace (and sometimes laugh) while writing this book. But it isn't only liberals like Perlstein and me who have noticed rampant swindling on the Right. Prominent conservatives have issued the most damning indictments, a budding genre of essays that bemoan grifting as a spreading stain on their movement. In *National Review*, Jim Geraghty has written scathing, heavily documented columns about the abusive practices of right-wing "scam PACS" and kindred outfits. His colleague Kevin Williamson has denounced the "steady stream of surprisingly lucrative grifts of diverse and sundry kinds" in those pages. The same complaint has been voiced by Jonah Goldberg, Rod Dreher, Matt Lewis, and Erick Erickson, among many others.

The tone of those condemnations is often anguished and even bitter, particularly among those who have observed the sharp uptick of politicized larceny under Trump. When Geraghty first broached the subject in 2019, he wrote, "I'm just sick and tired of so many of our brethren averting their eyes from the big, glaring, worsening problem that rips off so many decent, hard-working folks."

Erickson, a gun-loving religious rightist and hard-liner who rejected Trump in 2016, has often called out what he sees as grifting on both sides. He publicly quit the corrupt NRA and repeatedly trashed his movement for betraying its donors. In September 2023, he returned to the troubling topic that has preoccupied him for years—and nothing had changed for the better.

"I've seen senior members of the [conservative] movement decide it was time to cash in and grift out," Erickson told his podcast listeners. "I've seen young hucksters wrap the label of conservatism around themselves and prey on retirees for cash, showing fabricated results in return. I'm so old, I remember when CPAC was a gathering of actual conservatives and not a grift operation with a gay cruising scene on the side," referring acidly to a sexual harassment scandal that embroiled Matt Schlapp, the Conservative Political Action Conference chairman.

Does Erickson sound angry? For honest conservatives, that sense of disappointment and cynicism, tinged by fury, is now a routine state of being with no prospect of relief. In the pages that follow, we examine how American conservatism sank to such a degraded condition—and why that should matter to all of us.

1

The Role Model

On a Saturday morning in April 1953, a mismatched pair of political hustlers descended from an American military transport aircraft onto the tarmac of Orly Airport, just south of Paris. They wore expensive suits and carried fancy luggage.

An observer glancing in their direction might first notice David Schine, tall, handsome, and endowed with the smiling confidence of status and wealth. But his shorter companion, a dark figure with a pugnacious expression and a distinctive scar on the bridge of his nose, was in command of this expedition. He was Roy Marcus Cohn, counsel to Senator Joseph R. McCarthy's communist-hunting subcommittee back in Washington, DC.

Both men were in their midtwenties, but it was Roy Cohn who had already helped send the convicted Soviet spies Julius and Ethel Rosenberg to the electric chair. (A newly admitted lawyer, he had won the merciless decree through a series of secret and highly unethical conclaves with the sentencing judge.) Impressed by that grisly achievement, McCarthy had recruited Cohn only a few months earlier to assist him in cleansing the United States government of subversion of all kinds, from left-wing sympathizers to suspected homosexuals.

Not long after he was hired, Cohn had persuaded McCarthy to employ Schine. They had been introduced at a nightclub in New York by George Sokolsky, the right-wing Hearst newspaper columnist. Cohn presented the rich but intellectually underdeveloped Schine to his new boss as an "expert on communism," which was a gross deception. Schine's father, a hotel magnate, had somehow gotten him into Harvard University (much as real estate mogul Charles Kushner would do for his son Jared decades later). But when Schine arrived at Harvard Yard, he had immediately hired a secretary to attend his classes, which he too often failed anyway, while he swanned around town in a chauffeured black limousine.

Evidently, he didn't learn much. The sole evidence supporting Schine's expertise on the Red Menace was a six-page pamphlet titled *Definition of Communism* that he was said to have written for distribution in the family hotels, where it was placed in every room alongside the Gideon Bible. Even a glance at this brief opus betrayed his comical ignorance, for Schine had gotten the dates of the Russian Revolution and the founding of the Communist Party wrong, while badly confusing the identities of Stalin, Trotsky, Lenin, and Marx.

The whip-smart Cohn, a graduate of Columbia University and Law School, surely knew the Schine pamphlet was garbage (if he ever actually looked at it). How little Cohn or Schine cared about their ostensible mission was exposed years later by the anti-communist author Freda Utley, who dismissed him and Schine as "unscrupulous careerists." As a McCarthy adviser and confidante, she had prepared his would-be investigators with a list of important anti-communist books that were "missing from the shelves" of United States Information Service (USIS) libraries. But as the outraged Utley later recounted, the careless duo had misconstrued her list as a compilation of "pro-communist" books.

Their fact-finding mission was merely a cynical boondoggle. McCarthy's callow emissaries plainly understood that public service could present outstanding opportunities for what we would now recognize as scamming—and they took full advantage.

SHORTLY AFTER HE and Schine landed in Paris, Cohn issued a peremptory command to US Information Service personnel in the French capital that he expected to meet with them in their offices the next morning—which happened to be Easter Sunday—at 8:00 a.m. sharp. No doubt resentful of this imposition on the holiday, which they had expected to celebrate with their families, the loyal American civil servants nevertheless arrived on time, just as Cohn had demanded. But neither he nor Schine showed up.

That introductory debacle was recounted in a 1991 oral history interview with Julia Child, who had studied cooking in France when her husband, Paul, was among the American diplomatic employees there:

"Cohn and Schine had arrived in Paris and of course they went out to all the nightclubs and so forth, and it happened to be during Easter, and on Easter Sunday they had called a meeting that everyone was to go there at eight o'clock a.m. at the USIS office," Child recalled acidly. "Of course, they didn't appear. It turned out that when [USIS officials] finally got hold of them, they were sleeping off a night at Montmartre," the city's fabled cabaret district.

This inauspicious debut in no way daunted Cohn, whose sense of entitlement was matched only by his duplicity. Several days later in Frankfurt, he and Schine pulled an even more embarrassing stunt.

Having ordered public affairs staffers of the High Commission for Occupied Germany to appear for another 8:00 a.m. meeting, they arrived three hours late. Before the meeting could even begin, Schine "announced that he had put on the wrong trousers" and dispatched a driver to their hotel to pick up the right ones. Then he realized that he had also left behind his notebook and returned to the hotel with Cohn to retrieve it.

In the hotel lobby, according to a Frankfurt newspaper, Schine was observed "batting Mr. Cohn over the head with a rolled-up magazine." Both men then "disappeared" into Schine's room for several minutes. Later, the hotel maids reportedly found ashes and cigarette butts strewn around the room, amid the overturned furniture.

With all this peculiar behavior, it wasn't surprising that hints of a homoerotic relationship between Cohn and Schine soon proliferated in the press—even as the two tough guys mocked the supposedly limp-wristed diplomats they were investigating. The Washington columnist Drew Pearson reported deadpan that "they seemed unusually preoccupied with investigating alleged homosexuals." The nasty whispers enraged Cohn, who would spend a lifetime attempting to conceal his own promiscuous homosexuality beneath a veneer of overbearing masculinity. With McCarthy's collaboration, he pioneered what would become a chronic syndrome on the American Right: the political victimization of gays by closeted "conservatives" like himself.

In the decades that followed, sexual hypocrisy became an indelible right-wing brand, from the moralizing politicians who hounded Bill Clinton while concealing their own adulterous affairs, to the "conservative" preachers and online activists who condemned homosexuality while molesting teenagers and even children. The more loudly they condemned pederasty, the more pedophiles seemed to pop up in their ranks. But Cohn had discovered the secret of diverting attention from his own conduct by stirring up paranoia and stoking hatred. He had learned that he and Schine could "own the libs" while enjoying a taxpayer-funded jaunt across Europe—and that with enough bluster, they could escape any real consequences.

Over the following weeks, Cohn and Schine brought their sinister vaudeville to Bonn, Berlin, Munich, Vienna, Belgrade, Athens, and Rome, then back to Paris, and finally to London, spending little more than a day in any city. They conducted perfunctory interviews with the Americans they purported to investigate and then invariably hosted press conferences where they entertained reporters with arrogant and ill-informed denunciations of "subversive literature" in the USIS libraries. Following their appearance in Rome, the *Manchester Guardian* published a scathing review that mocked "their limited vocabulary, their self-complacency, and their paucity of ideas, coupled with the immense power they wield, [which] had the effect of drawing sympathy for all ranks of the United States diplomatic service who had to submit to this sort of thing."

The US embassy press attaché in Paris, a future *Washington Post* editor named Ben Bradlee, set up a press conference for "the boy Commie hunters," inviting all the resident British correspondents, "who were particularly outraged by the 'little wankers' thinking they were going to investigate the BBC," and the fifty or sixty American journalists, making certain the event would be on a Sunday, ruining their time "lunching in some romantic moulin." Bradlee stationed his pal Art Buchwald of the *New York Herald Tribune* in the front row and called on him to ask the first question. But it was the Reuters correspondent, "in a clipped British accent," who inquired, "Mr. Cohn, Mr. Schine, are you happy in your work?" "And," recalled Bradlee, "things went precipitously downhill from there." He secured their itinerary and alerted the British press to greet them at Heathrow Airport in London, "and their visit crashed around their ears."

In 1953 dollars, the estimated cost of the ten-day trip was $8,500, not counting military transportation—a price that would approach ten times that amount in current dollars. No report of its findings or results was ever released, nor was any information that they gleaned ever cited at a subcommittee hearing. Needless to say, perhaps, Cohn found no communists lurking in the US information offices abroad.

Ridiculed as buffoons and "junketeering gumshoes" in the international press, the McCarthy team inflicted serious damage on American prestige. Their threatening demeanor—and the fear struck in the civil service by their raging boss—had caused enough turmoil in the ranks that dozens of books were pulled from USIS libraries, and a few were even burned, causing deep embarrassment to the United States when European media outlets reported those incidents. Competent and loyal officials were forced to end their careers ignominiously. Those few weeks were an ugly snapshot of McCarthy's reign of terror.

WITH HINDSIGHT, THE most striking aspect of Cohn's European spree—his "ludicrous, destructive crusade," according to Bradlee—and indeed his entire career with McCarthy's "witch-hunt," was its hollow fraudulence. McCarthy's campaign against communist infiltration of government and society had commenced in February 1950 with a dramatic Lincoln Day dinner address in Wheeling, West Virginia, where he brandished a scrap of paper that he described as a "list of 205 members of the Communist Party" who supposedly worked in the State Department with the full knowledge of the secretary of state. The senator had no such list, because none existed, and his accusation was essentially baseless. Yet that speech, and a series that followed across the country, eventually ignited a conflagration of hysteria that burned destructively for years. By the time Cohn showed up, McCarthy's popular crusade had made him seem invincible. And yet within a year, Cohn's self-serving mendacities would bring down the whole show.

While the European escapade with Schine was exciting and fun, Cohn later confessed that it was a political flop—and it was later seen as the beginning of the end. He blamed its failure on hostile media coverage and the left-wing enemies of McCarthyism, but his basic assessment was even more accurate than he knew. The misconduct of the two young clowns heralded the ignominious end for McCarthy—after Cohn brazenly shook down the highest officials of the United States Army for Schine's benefit.

The history of Cohn's and McCarthy's interventions with the army on behalf of Schine is a convoluted tale. At its center was a cynical abuse of political power and demagogic propaganda for personal gain. In essence, Cohn and McCarthy wielded their ongoing investigation of supposed leftist influence in the US armed forces to extort special treatment for Schine, who was subject to the draft during the bloody closing months of the Korean War.

The surreptitious campaign to spare the hotel scion from military service—and when that failed, to ensure for him the softest possible duty—was especially ironic in light of McCarthy and Cohn's alleged populist disdain for "elites." When the scheme was completely exposed during the famous Army-McCarthy hearings of 1954, its sheer effrontery left the nation wondering whether to laugh or weep.

On the day after Schine was declared fit for military service in July 1953, McCarthy and Cohn told an army congressional liaison that Schine should immediately receive a commission as an officer. The army's rejection of that preposterous demand only provoked further pressure: Schine had to be assigned a duty post near New York City, said Cohn, or to the CIA so he could continue working with the subcommittee; and the army had to give him special weekend passes, and cut short his basic training, and even provide him with filet mignon, squab, and other fancy fare not served to the infantry.

Schine soon enjoyed all kinds of special pampering and privileges. But Cohn wasn't particularly appreciative. When he heard that his special friend might be posted overseas, he threatened to stage congressional hearings to "show the country how shabbily [the army] is being run," adding ominously, "We'll wreck the Army."

That threat exposed the fraudulence of Cohn's loudly proclaimed patriotism—and McCarthy's, too. Throughout his life, particularly in troubled moments, Cohn would wave the flag incessantly, warble drunken choruses of "God Bless America," and furiously denounce the disloyalty he claimed to perceive in others. Mounting a rearguard assault on the armed forces in the middle of a war, strictly for personal gain, left Cohn vulnerable at the televised Army-McCarthy hearings. When McCarthy questioned the use of a photograph of Schine, asking about its possible origin from a "pixie," Army counsel Joseph Welch explained, "a pixie is a close relative of a fairy." And when McCarthy attempted to smear Welch's young law colleague as a communist, Welch famously remarked, "Have you no sense of decency, sir?"

The absurdity, malevolence, and self-aggrandizement of the episode epitomized McCarthyism as a campaign of smear and falsehood that only served to undermine the values it pretended to defend. Communism represented a potential danger to American democracy, although it had diminished to almost nothing on the home front by then. Nearly all the actual spies in the US government had been apprehended by the Truman administration and the FBI years before the Wheeling speech. The abusive tactics of McCarthy and Cohn only undermined liberty by casting a free society as authoritarian, indecent, and unfree. With every assault on American institutions, from the government to the universities, from the military to the churches, those ideological termites advanced the objectives of their supposed enemies.

At long last, the Army brass, supported by President Dwight Eisenhower, hit back hard.

Offered the chance to fire Cohn and let the dispute fade away, McCarthy refused—and by the spring of 1954, he was facing a Senate inquiry into rampant misconduct by him and his staff. Unfortunately for the Wisconsin demagogue, top Army officials had kept copious records that incriminated Cohn and Schine as well as McCarthy himself. In no small part, it was Cohn's wildly corrupt conduct—and his refusal to admit wrongdoing—that led the Senate to pass a bipartisan censure resolution in December 1954 condemning McCarthy, who never recovered his reputation and died three years later, a lonely alcoholic.

The aftermath of the hearings damaged Cohn, too, but he had lied brazenly with no legal or professional repercussions. Guilty of the boldest fraud ever perpetrated by a Senate staffer, he escaped accountability, absorbing instead the lesson that he was exempt from any constraints. Nobody in the Republican administration, least of all his close friend and promoter, FBI director J. Edgar Hoover, would ever pursue his offenses.

From his experiences with McCarthy, Cohn developed the philosophy of impunity that he lived and taught his acolytes, who would shape right-wing politics in the decades to come, even beyond his death. It was not only possible but admirable to lie, cheat, swindle, fabricate, then deny, deny, deny—and get away with everything. He remained consistent in purveying untruth and contesting the incontestable. Rather than acknowledge what he had cost McCarthy—or that McCarthy had lost the confidence of the Senate—he would insist throughout his life not only that he and McCarthy had acted righteously but that they were always the victims of a liberal conspiracy.

Cohn's feigned outrage, voiced in his 1968 biography *McCarthy*, strikes a chord that is all too familiar today. The senator's critics "have to fall back on picayune things about whether he drank and had a liver condition, usually with a total distortion of the facts," Cohn wrote. "They talk about the innocent people he destroyed. I have yet to have them give me one name. I have a standard answer—'name one.' They usually come up with someone who came before some other committee, or Hollywood, or something which was never a focus of a McCarthy investigation." McCarthy, and not his targets, was the true victim.

WITHIN WEEKS AFTER the hearings, Cohn quit the McCarthy subcommittee and left Washington for New York, where his father was a Supreme Court judge and Democratic political boss. His mother had inherited wealth, and he moved into her Park Avenue apartment, where he continued to live with her for over a decade. Thanks to his pampered upbringing and the mutually beneficial relationships he had long cultivated with powerful friends in the press, business, and government, Cohn gradually acquired what the writer Ken Auletta dryly described as "innocence by association."

Cohn established his law practice in Manhattan by purchasing a dormant firm with the hilariously Waspy name of Saxe Bacon, which he operated from the disorderly town house where he lived. Although he aspired to the eminence of white-shoe firms that represented major corporations, the reputational damage he sustained in Washington made that impossible. But he attracted an influential, diverse, and often gamy clientele.

Unscrupulous and belligerent as well as skillful, Cohn became prominent in New York society as a "legal executioner" who would stop at nothing to win. He had big clients—George Steinbrenner, owner of the New York Yankees, Cardinal Spellman and the Catholic Archdiocese, and later, the press lord Rupert Murdoch. His specialty was in representing Mafia bosses, mobbed-up real estate moguls, and the aggrieved wives of very wealthy men. He became known among his peers as a lawyer for whom the law was something in the way and to be trampled. It was far better, he often told associates, to know the judge than to know the law.

Among his most active and profitable clients were top organized crime figures, beginning with Moe Dalitz, a legendary fifties gangster who was among the early developers of Las Vegas, and eventually including Anthony "Fat Tony" Salerno, Thomas and Joseph Gambino, Carmine "Lilo"

Galante, and John Gotti, along with dozens of less celebrated hoodlums. He was known to host meetings of gangsters in the East Side town house that served as the firm's offices, to shield them from government surveillance.

In a city where real estate is a dominant industry and too often a corrupt racket that thrives on abusive practices, tax chicanery, and political favoritism, Cohn also represented several of the leading landlords. By far, his favorite was a flashy and ambitious developer from Queens named Donald J. Trump, for whom Cohn was not just counsel and friend but also the single most influential mentor. What the awestruck younger Trump saw in Cohn was an all-powerful public figure who had lived, until then at least, a life of lying, bribing, cheating, stealing, swindling—and never apologizing—without any lasting consequences. The lesson Trump learned was that he could get away with anything.

Cohn lived like a prince of the city, tooling around in a chauffeured black Rolls-Royce or a Cadillac convertible, maintaining an estate in Greenwich, Connecticut, and a yacht named *Defiance*, but reporting almost no taxable income. While he bragged endlessly of his skill in avoiding taxes, he didn't only cheat the Internal Revenue Service. Cohn stiffed creditors large and small, including the state of New York, a tailor, a locksmith, a mechanic, a stationery store, a travel agency, a button shop, even temporary typists, all of whom obtained judgments against him in city courts. Trump learned that, too.

Never content with the proceeds of his legal career, Cohn also pursued a side hustle as a corporate raider and penny stock promoter. His prolific activity on the shady side of the financial world, as he sought to take over companies and small banks in byzantine deals, brought him into proximity with some of that era's most notorious stock market crooks. He organized a group of investors to take over the Lionel Corporation from a relative who had founded it. But under Cohn, Lionel neglected its original niche to acquire other companies, and he soon drove the beloved toy-train maker into bankruptcy.

The newspaper columnist Murray Kempton, who knew Cohn well, recounted a hair-raising version of one of his alleged financial schemes, with McCarthy himself as the mark. In 1957, Cohn and another hustler were marketing uranium penny stocks and allegedly approached the Wisconsin senator with a deal. After McCarthy purchased $30,000 of the securities, Cohn and his partner sold off tranches of shares on the strength of the senator's endorsement. Within weeks of this marketing coup, however, the Cohn syndicate dumped the worthless stock, driving down the price and wiping out McCarthy and the other rubes—and then refused to answer McCarthy's panicked phone calls.

Observing Cohn's frenetic manipulation of companies large and small—and his legal maneuvering on behalf of the crooks he represented—federal prosecutors finally indicted him in a fraud case that involved an infamous financial felon named Alexander Guterma. The Manhattan federal grand jury charged that Cohn had obstructed justice to shield four Guterma associates in a stock-swindling conspiracy and then committed perjury when he denied the charges. The case ended in a mistrial, and when Cohn was retried the following year, he won an acquittal.

The US attorney who prosecuted Cohn was Robert Morgenthau, a highly accomplished prosecutor who believed firmly that Cohn had violated securities laws and worse. In both cases, Cohn got of, while loudly protesting that Morgenthau and attorney general Robert Kennedy were engaged together in a "vendetta" against him. Whatever the prosecutors' motivations, their failures left Cohn virtually unindictable, at least in New York.

Despite escaping criminal penalties for bribery, conspiracy, and filing false reports with the Securities and Exchange Commission, Cohn got scalded when the same offenses came under civil court scrutiny three years later. That court said Cohn had misused corporate funds for his own benefit and enjoined him from violating securities laws—a warning that should have been grounds for disbarment in most states. A year later, he was indicted again in Illinois for secretly seizing control of two banks, whose funds he then misused for the benefit of himself and his law firm. Somehow, he skated on those charges, too.

Even better than knowing the judge is fixing the case in advance, reportedly Cohn's aim in raising money for the 1968 presidential campaign of Richard Nixon (an old friend whose autographed photo he displayed in his office). According to *Life* magazine, he handed over

$40,000 worth of checks at a fundraising luncheon for Nixon in Manhattan's exclusive Lotos Club, which featured Maurice Stans, the Nixon finance chairman later convicted of accepting illegal donations in the Watergate prosecution.

Cohn preferred Nixon to his Democratic opponent, Hubert Humphrey, for all kinds of reasons. But above all, he believed that Nixon could be bought. He bluntly told Stans and the other Nixon aides present that if their candidate won, he wanted Robert Morgenthau and SEC chairman Manuel Cohen to be fired immediately. Whether at Cohn's behest or not, Nixon disposed of both within months of entering the White House.

The man who eventually became his most famous client was fascinated by Cohn's apparent immunity from the consequences of his acts. In *The Art of the Deal*, published a year after the lawyer's death, Donald Trump recalled an intimate teaching moment.

> I don't kid myself about Roy. He was no Boy Scout. He once told me that he'd spent more than two-thirds of his adult life under indictment on one charge or another . . . I said to him, "Roy, just tell me one thing. Did you really do all that stuff?" He looked at me and smiled. "What the hell do you think?" he said. I never really knew.

WITH HIS CLIENTELE of boldface New York names, from the Catholic Church to the impresarios of the legendary Studio 54 nightclub and sex den, Cohn was the toast of the town. He was fashionable if not entirely respectable. His power extended deep into the news media, where he represented and influenced the titans S. I. "Si" Newhouse of Condé Nast and Rupert Murdoch. He could likewise rely upon old friends like William F. Buckley Jr., the editor and publisher of the conservative *National Review*, and *New York Times* columnist and former Nixon staffer William Safire, who wrote a fulsome letter to the New York State Bar Association attesting to Cohn's upstanding character in a vain attempt to prevent his disbarment. Cohn squired Barbara Walters around the club scene, ridiculously claiming they were engaged.

Yet even some of his most prominent and wealthiest clients were not safe from his baroque flimflams. Among those he victimized was Lewis Rosenstiel, the multimillionaire founder of the Schenley Industries liquor empire and an associate of multiple organized crime figures, including the legendary Meyer Lansky. Cohn and Rosenstiel had bonded over their shared paranoia in the fifties, when both were closely linked with FBI director J. Edgar Hoover. The liquor magnate had hired the lawyer to represent him in a couple of his four divorces.

When Rosenstiel lay dying and semiconscious in a Florida hospital in 1975, Cohn appeared in his room with a typed codicil to the old man's will, naming Cohn as a trustee of the huge Rosenstiel estate. The same document also named Rosenstiel's granddaughter and her husband, both of whom happened to employ Cohn, as estate trustees—with little effort to conceal the self-serving sham. In a decision voiding the new will, a Dade County probate judge accused Cohn of tricking Rosenstiel about the document to which he had affixed a shaky signature.

Such public embarrassments didn't seem to affect Cohn's relationships with his other clients, who liked to brag about their tough-guy lawyer's intimidation of potential opponents and his ability to magically "fix" their legal problems. Nor did his scrapes with legal authorities diminish his political power, which his reputation for treachery only seemed to enhance.

Although he cultivated his image as a swashbuckling right-winger, Cohn was less an ideological partisan than an influence peddler, a fixer in pursuit of graft and grift. His politics revolved around money and power more than policy or philosophy. Of course, he never abandoned the "conservative" posturing that had lifted him into the limelight during the fifties. Baiting liberals and flapping the flag were intrinsic to the bullying persona that undergirded his business.

Forever identified with the right wing of the Republican Party, Cohn in fact had been raised in New York City's Democratic Party political culture, from which he inherited powerful connections to the local party machinery. During his heyday, the boss-dominated Democratic organization was just as colorfully corrupt as during the reign of Boss

Tweed. Cohn could call any of the county leaders of either party in the five boroughs for favors. And they knew in turn that he would provide legal counsel for any crooked pol indicted by prosecutors, just as he did for his Mafia clientele.

Cohn didn't just know the judges, he knew the party bosses who anointed them. For nearly a decade before his death, he feasted on judicial patronage from Manhattan Surrogate's Court, where lucrative appointments to oversee trusts and estates were handed down. Having surreptitiously financed surrogate Marie Lambert's primary campaign, for instance, he was repaid in the debased coin of her realm—specifically, cash fees reaped from handling the estates of those who die without wills and the finances of the young or incapacitated.

Lambert's crooked operation of the court provoked numerous investigations by bar groups and law enforcement, including the United States attorney for the Southern District of New York, yet she, too, always escaped prosecution.

The power wielded by Cohn reached its zenith in the boss-dominated mayoral administration of Abe Beame, with municipal bankruptcy just over the horizon. In city hall, Cohn's favors and contracts were overseen by Stanley Friedman, a cigar-chomping machine pol who ran the Bronx Democratic Party and served as Beame's deputy mayor. It was Friedman who ensured the city bureaucracy's approval of an obscene $400 million tax abatement in 1976 that essentially financed Donald Trump's first big Manhattan project, the renovation of the old Commodore Hotel as the Grand Hyatt, a few years after he became a Cohn client.

The Beame administration's lucrative and illicit indulgences to Cohn predated the Trump deal. As deputy mayor, Friedman had facilitated a scheme that secretly siphoned hundreds of thousands of dollars from city-owned parking lots into shell corporations operating out of the Saxe Bacon law firm. That money was delivered to Cohn's office every week in cash, providing a reliable source of funds for the lawyer, while he reported no taxable income to the IRS. When Beame was ousted after a single disastrous term, Friedman turned up as a newly minted partner at Cohn's firm. Ten years later, only months after Cohn's death, the former deputy mayor went to prison in a massive corruption probe involving the city's Parking Violations Bureau, along with a long list of other city officials. (Ironically enough, they were brought down by none other than Rudolph Giuliani, then a crusading federal prosecutor and not yet a Trump crony or a criminal suspect himself.)

COHN'S REPUTATION FOR sleaze never alienated his more reputable friends, especially on the Republican right. Among his most ardent champions were such eminences as William F. Buckley Jr., the founder of *National Review*, and William Safire, the *New York Times* columnist, bestselling author, and Pulitzer Prize judge. Both Safire and Buckley had known Cohn since the McCarthy era, and both certainly knew what he had become.

It was Bill Buckley who led the toasts at a black-tie gala dinner honoring Cohn in 1973, attended by hundreds of judges, lawyers, journalists, business executives, politicians—including President Nixon and Mayor Beame—and probably not too many of his Mafia pals. Cohn had "triumphed over his tormentors," Buckley intoned in his clipped, mid-Atlantic style, "and he deserves the credit we are here to give him so enthusiastically." He didn't mention the boat loan that Cohn had arranged for him ten years earlier from a bank that the lawyer and his cronies controlled.

Asked about his own connection with the tainted attorney, Safire once explained that "over the years, when he needed me I was there; when I needed him he was there . . . I would go to a big gathering of his in New York or something and I would get up and say, 'I'm here because I like unpopular causes.' And that would get a big laugh and a lot of people who were uncomfortable about it being publicized felt better. That's what I could do for him." (The *Times* columnist wouldn't disclose exactly how Cohn reciprocated.)

For Republicans like Buckley and Safire, and clients like Trump, what Cohn represented was the will to dominate, in smirking disregard of the rules and norms that govern society. The respectable right-wingers didn't want to be associated with dirty tricks or bribes or any of the shadier aspects of politics in America, at least not in those days, but they understood the uses of a skillful thug. Cohn not only didn't mind his notoriety, he enjoyed and promoted it, but he performed most of his political hatchet work out of the public view. Both Richard Nixon and Ronald Reagan found their uses for him.

That was how Cohn came to mentor a young political operative named Roger Stone.

When Cohn first ran into him in 1979 at a Manhattan dinner party held by the Republican socialite and heiress Sheila Mosler, Stone had been recruited by the Reagan presidential campaign to oversee its 1980 campaign in New York, New Jersey, and Connecticut. He was a past president of the Young Republicans, but he, too, had a claim to real notoriety—a brush with the Watergate grand jury, which had investigated his role in Nixon's dirty tricks squad during the 1972 presidential campaign.

Ostensibly working as a scheduler, Stone had perpetrated some amateurish skullduggery, like writing a $135 check from the "Young Socialist Alliance" to the campaign of Representative Pete McCloskey, a liberal Republican running a protest campaign against Nixon in New Hampshire. Then he dropped an anonymous letter containing a receipt for the contribution to the *Manchester Union-Leader*, which dutifully published a negative story. He also sent a spy into the George McGovern campaign in California. The Watergate prosecutors found nothing on Stone that rose to the level of indictment, but *The Washington Post* reported his bit part in the scandal—which in no way diminished his stature in the party.

Cohn invited him to breakfast at the law firm's town house office, where Stone found him in a bathrobe, wrapping up a meeting with the Genovese crime family chief Anthony "Fat Tony" Salerno. (The lawyer and the mob boss had known each other since at least 1959, when Salerno secretly financed and Cohn promoted a heavyweight title rematch between Floyd Patterson and Ingemar Johansson.)

After listening to Stone's pitch for Reagan, Cohn made a fateful decision. "You need to see Donald Trump," he said. "I will get you in, but then you're on your own." Stone persuaded Trump, who arranged

$200,000 in checks from his father Fred's account. The Trumps also arranged rental of an office for Reagan's state headquarters on West Fifty-Second Street in Midtown, next door to the iconic 21 Club, where Cohn often had lunch in his favorite red leatherette booth.

The mark of Cohn's malign influence was unmistakable thereafter in the intersecting careers of Stone and Trump, whose impact on American political life remains so pestiferous today. Indeed, both men boasted of their connections with Cohn and his influence. "Where's my Roy Cohn?" Trump famously cried whenever he grew impatient with the more conventional lawyers surrounding him in the White House. Visible at first only as a small speck, the legacy of Roy Cohn, the role model, grew into an exceptionally colossal cancer on conservatism.

He was long gone before the political ascent of Trump even began. At the height of his power in the Reagan era, when his Washington connections even garnered for him an Americanism Award from the same United States Information Agency he had once persecuted, Cohn's seemingly permanent reprieve came to a sudden end. Infected with HIV/AIDS, which he publicly insisted was "liver cancer"—avoiding the gay stigma to the very end—he visibly wasted away until his terrible death in August 1986. Despite secret and privileged access to experimental treatment arranged for him by the White House at the National Institutes of Health, Cohn couldn't be saved.

Those special treatments prolonged his survival, however, just long enough for the New York Bar Association to complete its lengthy disbarment proceedings against him, based on his gross misconduct in the Rosenstiel case and three other cases when he had cheated clients. Those proceedings featured a long line of witnesses attesting to his good character, including Donald Trump, George Steinbrenner, Barbara Walters, and Alan Dershowitz, as well as Safire and Buckley. They left little impression on the court, and less than two months before his death, Roy Cohn lost his license to practice law in New York State. The state's highest appellate court denounced his behavior as "unethical" and "particularly reprehensible." And finally, the IRS closed in, too, seizing $7 million worth of property to cover the taxes and penalties he had owed for decades.

SETTING ASIDE THE dishonesty and dissembling during his years with McCarthy, perhaps Roy Cohn really feared communism as a mortal threat to the United States. He said so often enough, and even predicted in his gloomier moments that the communists inevitably would take over the world. Somehow, though, he didn't seem troubled when the presidents he admired, Nixon and Reagan, reached agreements with the Russian and Chinese governments. He may or may not have truly believed in the dangers of communism, but he absolutely believed in the Red Scare.

Whatever threat communists posed at any particular moment in history, he knew they served as an enduring symbol of terror—and thus of all the political manipulations that such fear can accelerate. Over the decades that have ensued since Cohn helped to orchestrate the McCarthyite purge, the Republican Right has never stopped stirring the same dread—and a catalogue of attendant hatreds—to mobilize masses of angry Americans. And, not incidentally, to strip those paranoid masses of as much money as possible. Although the shape of the terrifying threat may shift over time, the concept remains fundamental. And its exploitation has only grown more varied and lucrative since the earliest days of the right-wing grift, when anti-communist preachers roamed across America, scaring impressionable rubes by the thousands while relieving them of large wads of cash.

2

The Profits of Paranoia

For a nation that emerged from history's most destructive war with an unconditional victory over fascism and a rapidly growing economy, the America of the early fifties was strangely demoralized and apprehensive. Having brushed aside fear itself to overcome the Depression and the Axis, Americans were unable to resist the panic over communism that enabled the rise of McCarthy and his cynical henchman Cohn. The McCarthyites hyped the Red Menace for their own political and personal advancement, encouraging a wave of hysteria that long outlasted the Wisconsin Republican's meteoric career. Every day, Americans were warned that rising communism threatened their way of life, not only overseas but everywhere, from the schools and universities to the churches, the military, and even the movies.

Looking back, it's not easy to determine how much of this political offensive was spurred by genuine concern over the Kremlin's attempts to subvert democracies. Very often, it was advanced by far-right forces aiming to discredit liberals, labor unions, minority groups, intellectuals, and anyone identified with the Democratic Party—and never mind that those liberals were far more effective in opposing communism, both at home and abroad, than their right-wing critics. When McCarthy publicly slandered General George C. Marshall—whose aid and reconstruction program had played a critical role in brushing back Europe's Stalinist parties—as an instrument of the "communist conspiracy," the petty partisan motive was plain. McCarthy was trying to smear not just Marshall himself but his boss, President Harry S. Truman—a zealous anti-communist whose "loyalty" programs were an assault on First Amendment freedoms.

Many of the prominent Far Rightists who promoted mythical plots in the postwar years were the same figures whose isolationism and hatred of the New Deal had aligned them with pro-Axis seditionists before the war. McCarthyism's authoritarian bullying damaged America's reputation, while providing a convenient propaganda topic for the Kremlin. Such strategic considerations never troubled the Right when there was money to be made.

Confrontations between East and West played out on the global stage, but by the time McCarthy gave his Wheeling, West Virginia, speech warning of Red conspirators in government, the communist movement in the United States was moribund if not dead. By 1950, the tiny cadre of Russian spies in Washington were apprehended and facing prosecution. The Communist Party (CPUSA) had been decimated by federal prosecution of its leaders during the late forties, in a spasm of legal repression that sent dozens to prison and menaced hundreds more with potential prosecution under the Smith Act. And as the monumental crimes of Stalinism emerged, an intense disillusionment gripped party members and sympathizers. The remnant of a few thousand diehards posed no threat to anybody but themselves.

Yet once launched, conspiracy theories tend to fester and spread, without respect to reality, as we have seen in recent years—especially when their cultivation still sustains a profitable enterprise. Decades before social media turned conspiracy-mongering into an online industry, the impresarios of the Far Right found many ways to monetize the "communist conspiracy," as they exaggerated its dimensions beyond absurdity.

These "professional anti-communists" pioneered the exploitation of "fake news" and disparaged traditional news sources, spreading stories that overstrained credulity. They found the niche audiences that not only believed their far-fetched warnings of imminent doom but would spend good money to hear the bad news. For well over a decade, nearly any speaker who inspired dread of the Red Dawn would draw a paying crowd, no matter how implausible the tale.

In 1962, for instance, rumors quickly spread that Operation Water Moccasin, a military training operation run by the US Army in rural Georgia, was secretly a rehearsal for a United Nations plot to seize power in the US, spearheaded by "barefoot" African guerrillas. (The appeals to racial anxiety were never subtle.) The same nefarious scheme was also said to involve a huge contingent of Chinese Communist troops over the border in Mexico, where they eagerly awaited the signal to invade. Incredibly, the hysteria over this entirely fabricated scenario reached a crescendo across the South that forced the Pentagon to cancel the exercise entirely. A CBS News special investigation later found that panic over a UN takeover had begun when a radio evangelist started the rumor, which gained velocity after a far-right congressman from California, the aptly named James B. Utt, picked it up. By then, of course, the phony story had achieved its principal purpose: to intensify fear and alienation among the targeted audiences.

As a vocation, anti-communism had provided a substantial living and a measure of fame (or infamy) to a host of government informants, industrial consultants, writers, and public lecturers for many years, dating back to the first Red Scare that followed the Russian Revolution. But as the CPUSA declined, so did the prosecutions, congressional hearings, and other platforms that had sustained "experts" on communism, principally former party members who snitched on their ex-comrades. Opportunities in that once-flourishing field were evaporating by the early fifties. But a cohort of bold grifters with a fresh angle—"anti-communist education," pitched to the suburban masses—was about to show up.

THE BUSINESS OF "educating"—or more precisely, scaring—Americans about the problem of communism began as a means of market expansion for a few entrepreneurial Christian evangelists. The original practitioner was an Australian physician named Frederick C. Schwarz, founder of the Christian Anti-Communism Crusade. He first arrived in the United States in 1951 at the invitation of the Reverend Carl McIntire, a Protestant fundamentalist radio preacher from New Jersey who had been expelled from the mainstream Presbyterian Church and earned national notoriety for his anti-Catholic, anti-Black, and ultra-right sermonizing.

When he embarked on his new career, Schwarz was a balding, bespectacled man in his forties, with a ruddy face and enormous personal energy. His folksy speaking style and strong Aussie accent charmed American audiences, and he so impressed McIntire and the other preachers who hosted him that they invited Schwarz to return the following year. At the conclusion of his second tour, a prominent Iowa radio preacher signaled the beginning of a new career for the provocative doctor, who would soon abandon medicine altogether:

> A group of Christian men have felt the need of alerting the nation as to the perils of communism. God has raised up Dr. Fred Schwarz from Sydney, Australia, as a special messenger on this vital subject. We are organizing the Christian Anti-Communism Crusade.

Ostensibly a charitable endeavor, the Crusade was incorporated as a nonprofit. And during the first year or two, it didn't earn much. Schwarz's lectures were booked by Rev. James Colbert, a former truck driver turned Baptist preacher, who became his partner. At first, Colbert had to pull together a schedule of lecture dates for Schwarz the hard way.

"Jim would go to a chosen city and exchange a five-dollar bill for nickels, the cost of a phone call, and sit in a hotel lobby with a phone book, tracking down the program chairmen of listed clubs," Schwarz recalled in his memoir.

By 1956, however, Schwarz's lectures were bringing in enough money to relocate the Christian Anti-Communism Crusade from an Iowa church basement to offices in San Pedro and then Long Beach, California. Schwarz moved his wife and three children there from Australia, but soon, they wearied of the West Coast and returned to their homeland, where they remained. Moralistic as he was, the busy crusader managed to visit his family briefly in Sydney only twice a year.

Like the preachers who introduced him to American audiences, Schwarz was in show business, but unlike them, he had to develop his own version of fire and brimstone to draw crowds and inspire donations. As the actual threat from communists and communism diminished, he learned to amplify the supposed peril to monstrous and even fantastic proportions—a perennial style of persuasion among the purveyors of conspiracy.

As an "expert" on communism and Marxism who had never visited the Soviet Union or any other communist country, Schwarz felt free to invent the most lurid and menacing stories he could imagine—and to heighten the sense of urgency among his listeners with predictions of a Red triumph just over the horizon. The Soviet plan to annihilate Western civilization, according to him, would reach fruition in 1973, although he occasionally revised that forecast. "The hour of their final conquest draws near," he told an audience in Phoenix, Arizona, in 1961. "I think my prediction of world conquest for the communists for 1973 was too conservative. They are running ahead of schedule."

Whenever that fateful day arrived, he warned his largely middle-class and middle-aged fans, they would face a grisly end. Voice rising, Schwarz would step to the edge of the stage and remind them that communism's principal aim is "to liquidate the bourgeoisie," meaning middle-class Americans like them. "If you own shares of common stock, it means you!" he bellowed. "If the Reds win, it means the gallows!" On other occasions, he would narrate the terrible finale with a softer, more insinuating tone: "When they come for you . . . on a dark night, in a dank cellar, and they take a wide bore revolver with a soft nose bullet, and they place it at the nape of your neck . . ."

In Schwarz's worldview, the communist takeover would be accompanied by an almost unimaginable bloodbath. At that very moment in Russia, he claimed, children were being forced to watch mass executions. "Communists believe they must put about half the world's population to death," he told one audience, according to the *Chicago*

Daily News, "and the children are being conditioned for their role as adults."

Sometimes he confided even more detailed knowledge of the Kremlin's plans, which included establishing the headquarters of the world communist dictatorship in San Francisco, specifically at the renowned Mark Hopkins Hotel. Any San Franciscans not dumped in the bay, he said, would be exiled "to the Nevada desert, which is quite handy." If communism took over, the commissars' bloodlust would be "unrestrained. People will be animals, to be disposed of. Imagine them coming for you."

AS HIS CRUSADE drew bigger audiences and amassed more funds, Schwarz expanded its events to feature additional speakers—including former investigators for congressional committees and federal agencies, FBI informants, and even retired military officers. Among the better-known of these guest lecturers was Richard Arens, a onetime aide to Joe McCarthy and former staffer on the House Un-American Activities Committee.

Arens was an old-fashioned racist who moonlighted on quack studies designed to prove the genetic inferiority of Black Americans. He also demonized immigrants, informing Crusade audiences that between three and five million "illegal immigrants" were living in the US, all of them "criminal communists." According to Arens, there were no fewer than "nine million communist agents in Africa, and the House committee knows for a fact that some African witch doctors have been taken to Moscow, trained and returned to Africa, loaded with a new and terrible Soviet drug from which there is no point of return."

None of their fearsome fairy tales had any factual basis at all. The truth about communism was damning but familiar and relatively dull, and not the kind of terrifying infotainment that brought out checkbooks.

Appearing with Schwarz on many of these occasions was Helen Birnie, a former Communist Party activist who had repudiated her old comrades and hired on as a staffer with the Crusade. "Of all the ex-communist speakers I have heard in the US," he once said, "she is far and away the best," and was said even by critics to possess a "dramatic and commanding manner." Dramatic she certainly was, telling audiences at American Legion posts, Kiwanis clubs, and churches that many of the nation's teachers in both primary and secondary schools "were strategically placed there by the [Communist] party in order to capture the minds of little children" and that the Boy Scouts of America had been completely infiltrated by the Reds. If that weren't sinister enough, she warned that the communists had "900 million Asiatics being scientifically educated and prepared to be the executioners of the boys and girls of America."

To emphasize the educational character of these hair-raising yarns, Schwarz usually described his public events as "schools" or "seminars." At the conclusion, having sufficiently spooked his "students," he conveyed the reassuring message that they could defeat the Red scourge by donating funds to his Crusade. In return, they could expect to receive publications and taped speeches to continue the learning process and indoctrinate friends and family.

Full of bromides and aphorisms, Schwarz would often declare that "knowledge is power" and, in a related vein, "We must pay the price for knowledge." That price was not low, although corporate backers of the Crusade, such as Richfield Oil or Schick Safety Razors, would often sponsor whole classes of high school or college students for a Saturday seminar. The gate for the single most successful "school rally," held at the Los Angeles Memorial Sports Arena in August 1961, brought in over $310,000, with expenses just over $96,000, leaving a tidy surplus that would equal nearly $2 million now. When the California attorney general examined the items listed for sale at Crusade events in 1962, he found that buying one of each available tape and booklet would cost nearly $700, the equivalent of $6,250 today. ("No wonder this whole movement has been called 'Patriotism for Profit,'" he remarked acidly.)

With the Crusade's increasing visibility, Schwarz was able to put together a spectacular rally in October 1961 at the Hollywood Bowl, presented in prime time on West Coast television stations, boasting sponsorship by Schick and Technicolor. The three-hour program featured major stars like John Wayne, Dale Evans, Pat Boone, and Ozzie and Harriet Nelson, as well as a B-list actor named Ronald Reagan.

Within seven years of its shoestring launch, Schwarz's nonprofit was raking in over $1.2 million annually in total gross income, as reported to the Internal Revenue Service, or the equivalent in current dollars of $11 million. The Christian Anti-Communism Crusade was then the largest single-issue right-wing organization in the country, with a low budget and a small full-time staff. Or as Schwarz himself put it, in presenting the organization's audited 1960 financials, "From our inception in 1953, the story has been of increase by geometric progression. . . . Never in our moments of greatest hope could we have conceived that such a growth would take place. It is truly wonderful in our eyes what the Lord has done." For the first few years, the IRS had declined to approve tax-exempt status for the CACC, but that changed in 1956 and greatly enhanced its fundraising, especially from right-wing high rollers.

Even as the political fortunes of the Far Right waxed and waned, Schwarz continued to importune his followers for funds, whether at lectures and rallies or via direct mailings to his ever-growing list. "The Lord loveth a cheerful giver," he assured them in a 1967 mailing, as he beseeched donors to cover the "extra $50,000" cost to sponsor "special summer schools of anti-Communism" for students in Washington, DC, and on the West Coast. In other mailings, he would ask for funding to subsidize taped anti-communist lectures—"What Is Communism?"—for college radio stations, or public service announcements for television, featuring an "anti-communist folk singer."

The monthly appeal could always use a fresh gambit—or a new opportunity to promote Schwarz's book, *You Can Trust the Communists (to Be Communists)*, which eventually sold over a million copies. Filled with the same kind of sensational horror stories and ominous predictions as his lectures, it portrayed communism as "a movement which is frightening in its superb organization, strategy, mobility, and universal program." But his book's highly emotive, semi-fictional contents were wholly inadequate as a guide for the perplexed citizen.

Despite his zeal to "save America" from evil leftists, Schwarz remained an Australian citizen for his entire life and maintained his personal residence in Sydney. As a result, he was often asked during media interviews why he chose to "educate" Americans—already strongly hostile to communism—rather than his fellow Australians. When a reporter from a California paper suggested he was out to "take lots of money from lots of communities" in the US, he bristled at first, then said, "The United States saved Australia from Japan at the beginning of World War II. . . . It was then that I decided to fight communism with the base set up in the United States."

The less uplifting but more plausible explanation is that the residents of Oz showed no interest in what Schwarz was selling. Although he set up a Sydney branch of the organization—mainly as an excuse to provide income for his neglected family—it relied wholly on subsidies from the US headquarters. His infrequent visits to his homeland went ignored there. When he held a lecture in Sydney, according to an American reporter, only two hundred people attended and the donations amounted to seventy dollars, "not enough to pay the meeting expenses." The sheep were much easier to shear in North America.

To keep the money flowing, a truly professional anti-communist had to keep the paranoia growing. Toward that end, the Christian Anti-Communism Crusade's curriculum was highly effective. When a group of Stanford University social scientists studied the organization and its followers, they discovered the startling power of its propaganda, which they analyzed in a report to a 1963 conference of the American Political Science Association. The adherents of the Christian Anti-Communism Crusade were mostly not alienated loners or losers but included many individuals with substantial status and income, who were able to pay the exorbitant fees for its seminars, pamphlets, and tapes. A majority were college graduates and fell into the "business or professional" category.

The alarming revelation was what Schwarz and his ilk had persuaded this affluent and highly educated cohort to believe. Most of them presumed that a large proportion of their fellow Americans were secretly communists, which led them to fear the chimerical "enemy within" far more than any foreign adversary. Up to 90 percent believed that "communist professors" wielded enormous authority in the United States.

Fifty percent thought that communists maintained significant influence in the Democratic Party. (Twenty percent suspected communists were also steering the Republican Party.) Unsurprisingly, the social scientists' analysis showed that both Schwarz and the "faculty" who joined his seminars were exponents of right-wing extremism on many issues. The core of their teaching was that the most innocent-seeming American institutions—the Camp Fire Girls!—were thoroughly penetrated by communist influence.

This penchant for stoking distrust of traditional American institutions proved to be an enduring moneymaker and remains a pervasive theme on the right, which today targets not just Democrats, diplomats, and academics but schoolteachers, scientists, doctors, Hollywood stars, Girl Scouts, and ultimately even FBI agents.

How these toxic delusions affected real people was only too clear to the residents of communities that Schwarz and his campaign passed through. After inflaming baseless suspicions of their neighbors—from members of the mainline Protestant clergy and labor union leaders to college and high school teachers and other "intellectuals," a category he particularly hated—the Crusade often left polarization and division in its wake.

From time to time, a local union official or clergy member would speak up in dismay, as the Catholic Archdiocese of Indianapolis did on October 25, 1963:

> Dr. Fred C. Schwarz is coming to town Monday to save us from Communism again. He and his road show will be in Indianapolis just in time to compete with the goblins to make Halloween interesting. . . . Schwarz is the slickest of the far-rightists who have fatted themselves on the deep concern among Americans about Communism. . . . He just says everything is a mess, collects a lot of money from the well-to-do, and hurries on to the next town. Schwarz is nothing if he is not a potent force for community divisiveness, distrust, and confusion.

Surprisingly, perhaps, the clergy he targeted weren't the only skeptics of Schwarz's sincerity. The dedicated adversaries of communism at the FBI privately held a very low opinion of the Australian crusader, too.

At his public events, Schwarz often quoted J. Edgar Hoover—venerated by conservatives as the ultimate authority on communism—and sold Hoover's book *Masters of Deceit*. But within the FBI, Schwarz was seen as the master of a different brand of chicanery. FBI assistant director Alan H. Belmont set down his unflattering view of Schwarz in a March 1961 memo to chief inspector William C. Sullivan, one of the bureau's top experts on communism.

"As we know, Dr. Schwarz is an opportunist and we are not having anything to do with him and his activities," Belmont wrote. "It might be added that such people as Dr. Schwarz are largely responsible for misinforming people and stirring them up emotionally to the point that when FBI lecturers present the truth, it becomes very difficult for the misinformed to accept it. In my opinion, Schwarz and others like him can only do the country and the anticommunist work of the Bureau harm."

What troubled other critics was how many of the speeches delivered by Schwarz were tinged with partisanship. For a resident alien with a religious tax exemption, any intervention in electoral politics was worse than inappropriate. He would sometimes claim, deceptively, to be working with the United States Information Agency or other government agencies, yet he freely criticized President John F. Kennedy and his administration while talking up the far-right opposition. A few months before Kennedy's assassination, at a Schwarz appearance before the Long Beach Women's Club, a man stood up and shouted, "We need to elect a different president, like Barry Goldwater!" As the audience hooted its approval, Schwarz replied loudly, "I would say Amen! Amen! Amen!" In fact the Goldwater campaign in 1964 would draw the entrepreneurial extremists like Schwarz into the Republican Party as it began shifting inexorably further rightward.

WATCHING SCHWARZ HARVEST the financial bonanza that poured into the Christian Anti-Communism Crusade during the decade after McCarthy's demise inspired more than a few imitators, often flourishing a gimmick of some kind to attract funds. Perhaps the most ostentatious, and certainly the most successful, at least for a while, was an outfit with a confusingly similar name: the Christian Crusade, fronted by Rev. Billy James Hargis of Tulsa, Oklahoma. The ostentatious Hargis had his very own tics and gimmicks, as well as a colorful life story that swiftly dispelled any confusion between him and Schwarz.

Hargis liked to call himself "doctor," too—but unlike the Australian physician, his academic credentials were highly suspect. The basis for his title was an honorary doctor of divinity degree awarded by the Defenders Theological Seminary in Puerto Rico—an outfit established by the Reverend Gerald B. Winrod, an anti-Semitic rabble-rouser from Kansas who became infamous during the thirties as the "Jayhawk Nazi." (Although Hargis didn't traffic in anti-Semitism, his close associates included many prominent anti-Semites and Nazi sympathizers, including Willis Carto of the Liberty Lobby, Pedro del Valle of the National Economic Council, and Allen Zoll of American Patriots Inc., an organization whose connections with foreign fascists led the Justice Department to list it as "subversive.")

Hargis also boasted a bachelor of theology from a degree mill called Burton College and Seminary of Manitou Springs, Colorado, and a doctor of laws from Belin Memorial University, another degree mill located briefly in Chillicothe, Missouri. The president of Belin Memorial University, a certain Dr. Clyde Belin, wound up in federal prison on six counts of mail fraud. The actual postsecondary education of Dr. Hargis ended after one year at Ozark Bible College in Bentonville, Arkansas, when at eighteen he was ordained a minister in the Disciples of Christ church and dispatched to a pastorate in rural Oklahoma.

By the time he was twenty-five, the ambitious Billy James had started a radio ministry and left the church behind to incorporate a new religious nonprofit known as Christian Echoes National Ministry Inc. From his new pulpit, he soon reached thousands of listeners across middle America with his propulsive and petrifying exhortations about the Communist conspiracy. In his first year on the air, Hargis brought in donations topping $70,000, which left a hefty "nonprofit" surplus of $33,000, or roughly $300,000 today.

He also enjoyed some high-level assistance as he launched his business. The fundamentalist firebrand Rev. Carl McIntire, who had helped to promote Fred Schwarz and the Christian Anti-Communism Crusade, took note of Hargis, giving him a burst of publicity with a stunt that sent Bible verses into Eastern European communist countries via balloon. Hargis also benefited enormously from the public relations and marketing guidance of two professionals.

The first was a resourceful public relations expert named L. E. White, who had transformed the Oklahoma Methodist preacher and faith healer Oral Roberts into a national phenomenon and a multimillion-dollar industry. The second was a young marketing genius named Richard Viguerie, then a devotee of McCarthyism and segregation who would go on to build a legendary career in direct-mail consulting.

Hargis was a prodigious fundraiser and a pioneer of persuasive techniques, in personal appearances, on the air, and via direct mail, that have become standard practice. In 1964, the authors of *Danger on the Right*, a book-length report on American political extremism, described his "unique ritual of backwoods, fundamentalist exhortation and loud prayers to the Lord to open the eyes, hearts, and wallets of his listeners." Observing him at the Crusade's third annual convention, they watched how he swiftly pulled pledges worth nearly $40,000 (about $350,000 today) from an audience of rapt followers. The specific aim, he said, was to buy radio time on the Mutual Network.

"I pray to God for one man to sponsor this program for six months," Hargis called from the stage. "I know that man exists in this audience. Will he stand up?" Nobody stood up. "All right then, we will divide this burden. I need four men who will accept God's challenge and give $10,000 each to sponsor this program." Two men rose. "Give us four, oh God, who would give $5,000 each. Quickly! Two thousand?" Another stood up.

At each level, down to $100, his listeners rose singly or in groups until he had raised $38,870, or just enough to get his Mutual deal. It was, as *The New York Times* noted later, essentially a "prayer auction." And the auctioneer was a highly skilled professional with "the Bible in one hand and a cash register in the other."

The Christian Crusade's direct-mail appeals were also exceptionally effective, employing the combination of urgency and sappiness that could make checks fly through the mail. In those mail pieces, too, Hargis was an innovator whose little touches became commonplace. "Shall I quit now?" would appear scrawled across the top of a letter, in what looked like his own handwriting. His wife, Betty Jane, wrote to donors, too, as she did in a 1962 letter featuring a heartfelt family pitch:

> I have always tried to keep the children mindful of their Daddy. . . . Only recently we have felt the need to tell them why he is not liked by everyone. This is hard to explain to little ones but. . . . I thought they should be prepared if they hear something unfavorable about their Daddy at school or at play. . . . He is pictured by the liberal press as heartless and greedy, "out" for money and publicity and doing our country more harm than good. . . . Recently, because of illness, I have not been able to visit the office as often as I like, but I know the work is in great financial need right now. . . . Won't each of you help to relieve this pressure with your contributions?

Mrs. Hargis also offered a "brand new" booklet, titled *American Socialism—Moving America Downhill!* that Billy himself had told her was "the best thing he ever wrote exposing all American Liberals." Upon request, she would also send "a snapshot of Billy and the children." Even in the early days of Christian Crusade, Viguerie sent pleading letters to two thousand potential donors every day.

While their orientation was similar, Hargis was more blatantly ideological than Schwarz. Neither a partisan Democrat nor Republican, he admired both Strom Thurmond, the segregationist South Carolina Democrat (who would soon switch parties), and Barry Goldwater, the ultra-right Arizona Republican. Hargis despised labor unions, the United Nations, Ivy League universities, the NAACP, and the mainstream media, which he often accused of "aiding the Kremlin."

His favorite theme on the podium and over the airwaves was the impending communist takeover of the United States, abetted by the perfidious liberals in Washington and New York. In fact, he would explain that every economic and political reform measure dating back to the New

Deal was an artifact of the rapidly accelerating Marxist conspiracy. Like almost every leading "conservative" of that era, he was also an ardent segregationist, who believed that Black Americans would be perfectly happy with their condition except for the agitation of "pro-communist" civil rights activists. In his view, God had ordained the separation of the races; only communists and their liberal "dupes" disagreed.

Not only were the Reds preparing to attain full control of American society, as Hargis warned at a Texas speech in early November 1963, but when they did, it would mean the abolition of our most cherished traditions. "This coming Thanksgiving," he wailed, "may be the last legal one we Americans will celebrate!" Undoubtedly aghast, his audience whipped out wallets and checkbooks.

With such primitive but reliable methods, Hargis achieved an astounding level of success, eventually appearing on hundreds of radio stations and attracting more than 130,000 subscribers to his monthly Christian Crusade magazine. By the early sixties, the Crusade's annual income exceeded $800,000 (roughly $8 million today). Many of his donors were, as Daniel K. Williams noted in *God's Own Party*, the venerable old ladies and struggling pensioners who "scraped together funds to support his ministry," making an average donation of four dollars.

Hargis had a pitch for potential marks of every age and background. When he had accumulated enough capital, he purchased the Grand View Hotel in Manitou Springs, Colorado, a nineteenth-century structure with sixty-eight rooms at the foot of Pikes Peak, planning to turn it into an anti-communist educational institution for "America's youth." Aiming to inoculate students against "the liberal poison being spread in our high schools, especially in the metropolitan areas, by the National Education Association," the Christian Crusade's Summer Youth Anti-Communist University would train 150 selected young people every two weeks, "who will return to their high school and college campuses to fight communism." Between sessions, the property would operate as a vacation resort. (Unimpressed by Hargis's investment, a prominent pastor in nearby Colorado Springs remarked that "the nation is full of these radio preachers who prey on old people and collect millions.")

As his "ministry" expanded, Hargis relished the trappings of prosperity.

He traveled around the country in a leased Greyhound bus reportedly rebuilt to his specifications at a cost that would now exceed half a million dollars—including "mustard-colored carpeting," orange upholstery, a stainless-steel kitchen with refrigerator, a bathroom with shower, a mobile telephone apparatus, a radio broadcasting setup, and ample sleeping space for five passengers. The Crusade also held the title to a luxurious home in Tulsa—which would now sell for over $500,000—where Hargis and family resided and that he dubbed "the parsonage" (with a suitably expensive car parked outside).

While Hargis excelled at marketing and fundraising, he wasn't much of a theorist. After Joe McCarthy tumbled into his alcoholic abyss, the Tulsa evangelist quickly glommed on to the next big wellhead of conspiratorial mania—namely, the John Birch Society. Founded by a wealthy candy manufacturer named Robert Welch in 1959 and named after an American missionary and intelligence officer killed by Chinese Communist troops at the end of World War II, the Birch Society echoed McCarthy's claims and elaborated on them: American society was thoroughly infiltrated and manipulated by an elite seeking to impose world government and Communist control.

In its rococo version, Welch's theory held that this global "Insider" plot predated Karl Marx by centuries. Much of the conspiracy blather that pollutes the internet today is brazenly ripped off from Birch Society tropes. When Donald Trump's aides and followers rant against "globalists" and "elitists," or smear their opponents as "communists," they're recycling Birch Society rhetoric that went stale more than a half century ago.

According to Welch's demented worldview, most of the leaders of both political parties—indeed, most leaders of significant American institutions of all kinds—were either witting or unwitting tools of the conspiracy. Among the conscious agents of communism in Washington, Welch charged, was none other than President Dwight D. Eisenhower. Yet despite such outlandish premises, the Birch Society came to wield great influence on the Right and eventually within the Republican Party. Among its official endorsers was Hargis, who praised Welch as "a great American patriot." Schwarz was also a self-professed admirer of Welch and the Birch Society; he boasted that its members had been inspired to join by his Christian Anti-Communism Crusade.

When Welch's conspiratorial slurs against Eisenhower were exposed, however, Schwarz backpedaled at top speed—as did William F. Buckley Jr., who wrote a lengthy essay in his *National Review* denouncing Welch. Along with Barry Goldwater and other conservatives, Buckley tried to get Birch Society members to remove Welch from the society's leadership, without success.

Financed largely by top corporate executives, including the leadership of the National Association of Manufacturers, where Welch himself had served as president, the society didn't compete with organizations dependent on small donors like Christian Crusade. Oddly mirroring the old CPUSA structures, the Birch Society developed into a secretive group that relied on building local chapters, selling books and other literature, and collecting membership dues as well as corporate contributions. For years, Welch went out of his way to promote the campaigns of Hargis, Schwarz, and other far-right evangelists as part of his overall mission. He didn't seem to mind that their operations were long on grift and short on organization or results, so long as they conveyed the same conspiratorial message.

Even as the Birch Society's nutty extremism irritated more mainstream conservatives—and drew condemnation of Welch himself from the likes of Buckley—it attracted others to the Far Right. Prominent among them was a former US Army major general, Edwin A. Walker, who had been forced to resign his command in West Germany after the Pentagon discovered that he was propagandizing his own troops with Birch Society literature. Walker moved to Dallas, where he hobnobbed with right-wing oilmen and leaders of the segregationist Citizens' Councils, who saw in the lanky and laconic ex-general a potential "man on horseback" for their movement. He was a dull public speaker, however, and his 1962 campaign for Texas governor was a brief and dismal failure.

A few months later, however, Walker showed up at the University of Mississippi in Oxford, where federal marshals were confronted by local and state officials over a court order to admit the university's first

Black student, James Meredith. A few days earlier, the former general had issued a call to arms on the radio: "We have been pushed around by the anti-Christ Supreme Court. . . . It's time to rise. . . . Thousands strong from every state in the Union! Bring your flag, your tent, and your skillet! I will be there!"

On the night of September 30, Walker's appeals to "patriotism" helped provoke an armed mob gathered on the Ole Miss campus to launch a massive attack. Hurling firebombs and firing guns, the furious rioters injured scores of the marshals, burned many vehicles, and killed two civilians. Walker himself was arrested, held for psychiatric evaluation, charged with insurrection, and then released. (The Mississippi grand jury never charged him.) He returned to Dallas, where an enthusiastic crowd greeted him at the airport, waving Confederate flags and "Walker for President '64" signs.

That galvanizing incident, one of the worst public disturbances in American history, inspired Hargis. Despite Walker's awkward stage presence, he saw a glint of gold in the ex-general's renewed popularity with the Far Right. He drove down from Tulsa to Walker's home, where he proposed a national speaking tour, with the general as the main attraction. They would sell tickets, pass a bucket for extra donations, sell books, pamphlets, and recordings, and split the proceeds between Christian Crusade and Friends of Walker, an outfit that benefited several young ex-military men who lived at the bachelor general's house.

Walker swiftly agreed to join the tour, which Hargis dubbed Operation Midnight Ride, except that instead of British invaders, the duo would warn America against the liberal enemy within. With a substantial radio campaign and the support of the Birch Society, Hargis pulled together rallies in twenty-seven cities across seventeen states, beginning at the Dade Civic Auditorium in Miami, Florida, and winding up at the Shrine Auditorium in Los Angeles, with stops across the South and Midwest. FBI agents tracking its progress reported back to headquarters that its sponsors included front groups for the Ku Klux Klan. According to a detailed report in *Smithsonian* magazine, the tour featured "a nightly passion play, enacted on a stage set with as many as 40 American flags." Hargis was careful to speak first, often working up the crowd for as long as ninety minutes with a jeremiad against the churches, the schools, the press, and the entire federal government, whose "administrators have conspired in and collaborated with a demoralizing, degrading, and repulsive Satanic force." He would always make the pitch for money before Walker spoke, knowing that his partner's wooden, sometimes incoherent presentation might deflate the take. Often a local far-right celebrity joined them onstage. In Birmingham, Alabama, for instance, their special guest was the brutally violent Sheriff Eugene "Bull" Connor, famed for assaulting civil rights protesters with fire hoses and attack dogs.

Operation Midnight Ride was a huge success, attracting at least forty thousand and, according to Hargis's own estimate, as many as one hundred thousand paying attendees. On the first night in Miami, the audience put an additional $3,000 into the buckets ($26,000 today). The Shrine Auditorium rally that concluded the tour was the Crusade's largest, most enthusiastic event ever. Their month on the road had raised an amount in excess of a million dollars in today's currency. Almost as soon as the tour ended, he was ready to hit the road again, and so was Walker. They went out once more in May on a different itinerary, but with somewhat less success.

WHILE FRED SCHWARZ, Billy James Hargis, and their Crusades today appear retrograde and laughable, they were nevertheless among the earliest developers of a new style of politics that drew its power—and large sums of money—from its followers' distrust and rage. Their success blazed the political and financial trails that would soon be followed by the promoters of Barry Goldwater's 1964 presidential campaign, which brought an enormous opportunity to Hargis associate Richard Viguerie, making him a national force. (The Goldwater campaign wanted nothing to do with Hargis and Walker, tainted as they were by association with the Klan and other disreputable organizations.)

Both the preacher and the general tumbled into disrepute of a different kind in the following decade. In 1976, *Time* magazine revealed that Hargis had seduced three or four young men and a young woman at a religious college he had founded in Tulsa. He denied any wrongdoing—"I was guilty of sin, but not the sin I was accused of"—but was eventually forced to resign from his ministry. That same year, Dallas police arrested Walker for public lewdness after he made sexual advances to a plainclothes cop he had pursued into a men's room at a city park. The former general pleaded nolo contendere and was fined $1,000. Schwarz suffered no such personal scandal, but he, too, fell from prominence in the decades before his death in 2009. He had been assured of his place in history by far-right icon Phyllis Schlafly in a 1998 letter: "You were an indispensable factor in building the grassroots anti-communist movement, which became the conservative movement, which ultimately elected Ronald Reagan." By then, the conservative movement was turning into a more aggrieved, more aggressive, and more cynical phenomenon.

3

"Experts" and Patrioteers

The John Birch Society's version of "anti-communist education" was exceptionally influential—and, as a source of accurate information for perplexed and worried Americans, totally worthless. Its fixation on conspiracy in the highest places of government and its twisting of history made the society's members believe they possessed inside information. These delusions conferred a certain kind of expertise that could command top dollar from the society's affluent suburban fan base.

But there was a broader universe of inner knowledge. Great deference was paid to professional anti-communists who had formerly worked in government, especially for one of the congressional investigating committees or the FBI, headed by anti-communist idol J. Edgar Hoover. Most in demand were those whose résumés included the bureau or a branch of military intelligence. The proper credentials could transform the dross of rumor, slander, and suspicion into gold, even when those credentials were highly questionable.

A prime example was the checkered career of Edgar C. Bundy, director of the Church League of America. Started in 1937 by a Chicago advertising man to oppose the New Deal, the Church League waged a very long, nasty, and ill-founded Red-baiting campaign against mainstream Protestantism and the National Council of Churches, which it accused of conspiring to promote communism. Its religious concerns were a scrim behind which the organization pursued a more partisan mission, exemplified by its blatant campaigning against FDR's bid for a third term in 1940.

Before Bundy took over as the Church League's executive chairman in 1956, he had served as the president of the Abraham Lincoln National Republican Club, an ambitious far-right outfit that had nothing to do with President Lincoln. It aimed to gain control of the GOP by ousting the "Eisenhower liberals." Having served as an air force intelligence officer during the war, rising to the rank of major, Bundy on paper appeared to have impeccable national security credentials. He was also an ordained Southern Baptist minister, although he never pastored a congregation, lending him an aura of moral authority. He had worked briefly in journalism, too, as city editor of the Wheaton, Illinois, *Daily Journal*, which gave him experience in producing information that sounded like news. Most importantly, Bundy was a protégé and operative of Rev. Carl McIntire, the fundamentalist radio preacher with a legendary, obsessive hatred of mainstream Protestant churches. Bundy and the Church League also worked closely with Billy James Hargis, who had likewise been groomed and promoted by McIntire. At various times, its payroll included veteran congressional research staffers, notably J. B. Matthews and Karl Baarslag, both of whom had labored in the vineyards of conspiracy for Joe McCarthy.

The Church League's tax-exempt "educational" functions included the maintenance and sale of extensive files gathered on alleged "subversives." In those files were the names of a million or more individuals and organizations that were alleged to have in some way "served the communist cause in the United States"—not only current and former party members but perhaps as many as a million innocent people whose views supposedly made them "communist dupes." This sweeping category encompassed Democrats, liberals, union activists, civil libertarians, and anyone else who might qualify as politically impure by far-right standards. Specifically included, for instance, would be anyone associated with the National Association for the Advancement of Colored People, the nation's premier civil rights organization. This whole cohort—McIntire, Bundy, Hargis, the Birch Society, and the

Church League—deemed the civil rights movement and especially the NAACP to represent nothing more than a communist-inspired attack on the foundations of Americanism. Falling into the same category were the American Civil Liberties Union, the liberal (and strongly anti-communist) Americans for Democratic Action, and the renowned educator and pragmatic philosopher John Dewey, whose work it said "softens many intellectuals in America for the acceptance of Communism."

Bundy himself never became a barnstorming public figure or radio preacher like McIntire, Hargis, or Schwarz, but instead appeared at two-day "seminars" before local groups that could muster fifty eager "students" willing to pay $10 each (a total of $500 or roughly equal to $5,000 today). Anyone unable to afford the seminar could buy instead a do-it-yourself kit of tape recordings that featured Bundy droning on about "The Perils of the Social Gospel" or "The Communists Are After Your Churches." According to the authors of *Danger on the Right*, the Church League sponsored a seminar somewhere in the US almost every day by the early sixties.

Between 1956 and 1964, the Church League's budget swelled tenfold, and the organization built a handsome colonial-style mansion in Wheaton as its new headquarters. The organization also published a monthly newsletter as well as "special reports" (mostly newspaper reprints and pamphlets from other groups), available by subscription. Money also poured in from corporate sponsors, including Abbott Laboratories, Greyhound Corporation, Monsanto, and the Borg-Warner Corporation. Bundy hobnobbed with William F. Buckley Jr., Ronald Reagan, Barry Goldwater, and other conservative luminaries. Behind the rows of massive cabinets filled with derogatory files about liberal clergy and other wayward types, the nonstop radio and TV appearances, and the national fundraising apparatus lay a troubling secret: Edgar Bundy was a fraud—and, worse, the FBI was onto him.

Despite Hoover's well-deserved reputation as a fanatical Red hunter, the FBI director and his subordinates nevertheless were skeptical of the industry of "professional anti-communists" who profited from fear. As the presiding national oracle on communism, and subversion more generally, the FBI jealously guarded its preeminence against others who pretended to possess that same kind of authority—and for a profit. However right-wing and racist Hoover was, he also took a dim view of conspiracy-mongers, in the John Birch Society and elsewhere, who spread the idea that top US government officials were covertly in thrall to Moscow. The bureau's field offices kept a close eye on political organizations of all kinds, including radical Right outfits like the Birch Society, the Christian Crusade, and the Church League—and its agents regularly filed reports on their activities that grew into massive files. Many of those reports, only slightly redacted, are publicly accessible.

In 1961, special agents and top officials at the FBI's Washington headquarters filed a sheaf of blistering memoranda about Edgar Bundy.

After FBI chief inspector William Sullivan delivered a series of speeches in which he declared that the communists had failed to infiltrate American churches, Bundy protested angrily to Hoover, members of Congress, and others. Sullivan's remarks, he complained in a letter to the chair of the House Un-American Activities Committee, had "given the Communists, their sympathizers, fellow-travelers, and dupes among the clergy, the biggest assist against all of us who have been exposing Communist propaganda in church groups which they have ever received." Hoover sent back a curt reply: "I am fully aware of the speech Chief Inspector William C. Sullivan made in Cincinnati on February 23, 1961, entitled *Communism and Religion*. It is completely factual and has my unqualified approval." Bundy had made a strategic error. The FBI brass didn't take his insults lightly. In an August 1961 HQ memo to Sullivan, the Church League chief was described as "hysterical" and prone to "employ all the well-known tricks of the professional demagogue."

A contemporaneous memo written by Deputy Director Cartha "Deke" DeLoach, the bureau's third-ranking official, noted, "Our files are replete with information concerning the hypocrisy and falseness of one Edgar C. Bundy, who styles himself as the General Chairman of the Church League of America. . . . Bundy is a professional anti-communist whose only livelihood is creating publicity for himself so that he will be paid handsome sums for speeches and literature. . . . Naturally, any action that hurts Bundy's livelihood will cause him to turn in fury against his tormentor. . . . Speeches by [Sullivan] apparently have caused Bundy considerable worrying."

The bureau had first encountered Bundy years earlier, when he claimed on the lecture circuit that "my credentials are on file with the FBI in Washington and I have personal letters from J. Edgar Hoover." He also said that he "has frequently furnished information to the Bureau" and worked closely with agents in the field. None of that was true, and Bundy's stream of false assertions about his relationship with the FBI even provoked bureau officials to open an "impersonation file" on him. No charges were ever pursued, but top FBI leaders regarded him as a familiar breed of con man: "Bundy is typical of the irresponsible, irrational, 'professional' anticommunists who make a living touring the country and charging fees for their lectures."

By September 1961, FBI officials were sufficiently irritated by Bundy to make inquiries about his military service. What they learned was that he had been lying about that, too. He had been an air force intelligence officer, but his service was confined to a station in Alaska, rather than taking him to exotic foreign theaters. His professional experience involved "minor routine intelligence duties with the Alaska Air Command," not daring counter-subversive missions. According to an officer who had served with him, Bundy was merely "a disgruntled individual." Worse yet, the bureau learned that air force officials were likewise furious with Bundy, who had suggested publicly on many occasions that he had inside access to military intelligence information.

The gross exaggerations on his résumé included a claim of "19 years in the intelligence service of the US Air Force," when he had served only a little more than four years. Concerned air force brass had bluntly warned Bundy not to give the impression that his former service branch endorsed him or his opinions in any way. FBI officials were told confidentially that both the secretary of the air force and the air force chief of staff wanted to kick Bundy out of the reserves. They were unable to act against him, however, unless and until he explicitly disobeyed orders.

Yet another facet of Bundy's grifting irked the FBI leadership. Among the books, tapes, and other items he sold at seminars and lectures were pamphlets published by the bureau that its offices normally distributed free of charge. Indeed, Bundy had scooped them up for free from a Republican member of Congress who supplied him with such materials in bulk regularly. Bundy was selling *Communist Target: Youth*, a small masterpiece bearing Hoover's own byline, for twenty-five cents a copy. In 1961, two FBI agents warned him to cease the illegal sale of FBI materials he obtained gratis.

The darkest aspect of the FBI investigation of Bundy was the discovery that he was homosexual and in all likelihood a pedophile. The 1963 HQ memorandum to Sullivan contained a shocking revelation about the secret life of this married Southern Baptist minister, a biblical fundamentalist who professed strict conservatism on all matters sexual. After summarizing Bundy's contentious relationships with the FBI and the air force, and other derogatory reports, the memo reached a crescendo of indignation:

> For years, he has been engaged in an ostensibly patriotic crusade which actually constitutes a monstrous effort to destroy the members of his own profession—the clergy. The damage this man has done in the cities and towns throughout our country by his self-serving activities constitute a spike driven into the heart of this Nation.
>
> Most disgusting of all is [the] true nature of this pious hypocrite. He brags about being an ordained minister. He poses as a paragon of virtue for youth. He parades as a patriot. The disgusting truth is that Bundy is a sexual pervert. He has been for years and is the worst kind in that he particularly favors satisfying his perverted desires with young boys. Bundy's perverted sexual activities reportedly are well known to hundreds of ministers across the country.

Hoover's special agents had amassed a copious record of Bundy's homosexual activity, with special attention to young boys he had allegedly seduced, dating back to his years in the air force. The Cincinnati field office had even obtained a copy of a 1954 letter from Bundy to an unnamed youth, pleading for forgiveness (and begging him to stop talking about their furtive liaison). When other fundamentalist ministers in Carl McIntire's orbit learned about Bundy's sexual history, they demanded his ouster from any position of responsibility, including the Church League leadership. McIntire refused, and Bundy kept his job until 1982, when he was finally forced to retire. The Church League folded two years later, bequeathing its files to Liberty University, the institution of higher learning founded by another McIntire ally, the Reverend Jerry Falwell.

TODAY'S CONSPIRACY THEORIES, promoted ubiquitously everywhere on the Republican right from the QAnon cult to Fox News, owe much of their foundation and flavor to the mania of their forebears in and around the Birch Society. When figures like Tucker Carlson and Sean Hannity chatter on furiously about the "deep state" and the "globalizers," demonizing George Soros or Bill Gates, they are merely putting a new gloss on old far-right fantasies. The notion that America is under the thumb of malignant and secretive elites is a perennially profitable narrative.

Consider the pioneering career of a former FBI agent and Birch Society favorite named Dan Smoot.

It was Dan Smoot who popularized the notion of an "invisible government," operated by liberal Eastern elitists to guide America toward a communist future, when he published a book with that title in 1962. According to *The Invisible Government*, the United States was in fact secretly controlled by the Council on Foreign Relations, the reputable New York–based nonpartisan organization and publisher of *Foreign Affairs* magazine, which has boasted thousands of prominent Americans as members. In the book's introduction, Smoot laid out his thesis in stark terms:

> I am convinced that the Council on Foreign Relations, together with a great number of other associated tax-exempt organizations, constitutes the invisible government which sets the major policies of the federal government. . . . I am convinced that the objective of this invisible

> government is to convert America into a socialist state and to then make it a unit in a one-world socialist system.

However absurd that notion, Smoot's background in the FBI lent credibility to his loony speculations—and made him an exceptionally popular and influential figure on the far right during his heyday.

Dan Smoot grew up in Missouri and Texas, graduated from Southern Methodist University, and spent a few months as a teaching fellow at Harvard University before dropping out in April 1942. He then joined the FBI, which sent him to the Cleveland field office. Eventually, he was transferred to FBI headquarters, but after two years in Washington, the bureau transferred him to its Dallas office. There he met H. L. Hunt, the oil tycoon and sugar daddy of many far-right political operations in the fifties and sixties. The eccentric billionaire soon hired Smoot to work for a Hunt propaganda outfit called Facts Forum, which produced radio and TV programming and ran a free circulating library that featured books by Hunt favorites like Joe McCarthy. Smoot became a Facts Forum commentator, appearing on weekly television and radio broadcasts that aired on up to 350 stations with a combined audience of millions.

Hunt's own political philosophy was encapsulated in his conception of the perfect system of undemocratic government, in which "the more taxes you pay, the more votes you get." (Hunt, of course, employed a small army of accountants and lawyers to avoid paying taxes.) Smoot quickly adopted the values articulated by his boss, telling a Canadian audience that America's founders knew "a democracy is the most evil kind of government possible."

After a few years, Smoot struck out on his own as a far-right commentator, publishing a newsletter called *The Dan Smoot Report* and delivering lectures around the country as a professional anticommunist. His general approach was to lump FDR's New Deal, Truman's Fair Deal, John F. Kennedy's New Frontier, and Eisenhower's Modern Republicanism together with communism as systems that stood for "the total transfer of power from the individual to the Federal Government." Within a year of establishing his new business,

Smoot found a benefactor to replace Hunt. D. B. Lewis made a fortune producing Dr. Ross' Dog and Cat Food, based on rapacious hunting of sea lions off California, which ultimately spurred passage of the Marine Mammal Protection Act of 1972. The Lewis pet food companies sponsored *Smoot Report* programs on hundreds of radio and TV outlets. Support from that firm and others allowed Smoot to mail well over a million copies of his report every year to members of Congress, students, ministers, and others as "gifts."

Essentially a fearmonger in the same mold as Schwarz and Hargis, Smoot predicted the impending seizure of power by Reds who had supposedly infiltrated almost every American institution. He lectured audiences that a federal law permitting Alaska—then still a territory—to provide hospital and community care for its mentally ill residents was in fact a communist scheme to create a gigantic concentration camp on Alaskan lands. He regarded school integration as a communist plot, fostered by the "notorious NAACP," and bluntly accused the Methodist Church of harboring Red clergymen. Even as he developed a lucrative national presence on radio and TV, Smoot became a local nuisance in Dallas, which, as a community, suffered from the political rancor festering among its far-right residents. (The city's reputation as a nest of violent extremism was fixed for decades after the assassination of President Kennedy in November 1963.)

Drawing a bead on Smoot, the *Dallas Morning News* denounced "the professionals for profit who have found a remunerative field" as anti-communist agitators. "Patriotism is a justly venerated human quality. Patriotism for profit is just suspect. . . . If Mr. Smoot has not been around long enough to encounter it, the *News* has. When your daily mail includes such tripe as defining Communism as a Jewish conspiracy, a Catholic conspiracy, and an NAACP conspiracy, you can discern the hand of the patrioteer for profit. He exists. . . . The whole question is whether a man is out to make a fast buck or to serve the country." With respect to Dan Smoot, that question was answered conclusively by no less an authority than J. Edgar Hoover himself. Cited almost incessantly by propagandists on the far right, with great emphasis on his expertise and access to inside knowledge as a former FBI agent,

Smoot inevitably came to the attention of the unamused FBI director and his aides.

The FBI brass were annoyed when Smoot billed himself as a former "administrative assistant" to Hoover, and they conducted an internal investigation to ascertain whether anybody had ever held such a title. Nobody ever had, and the bureau released a statement to that effect, silencing Smoot's self-aggrandizing claim. In an internal memo to Deputy Director DeLoach about Smoot dated November 8, 1962, Agent D. C. Morrell wrote that such a title appeared in no documents pertaining to him or anyone else, but noted, "After Smoot left the Bureau, he was publicly described in newspaper articles as an Administrative Assistant to the Director. Files indicate he has continued to use this designation. . . . It appears obvious that Smoot is attempting to use his prior service with the FBI as much as possible. He is a professional '*anticommunist*' who is strictly out for money."

Smoot was fortunate that his former employer did not take the additional step of releasing the true story of his checkered FBI career and how it ended. He did not leave the bureau voluntarily and in good standing, as his references to his nine years on the job indicated. Three weeks before he resigned to embark on his career as an ultra-right huckster in 1951, Smoot received a harsh disciplinary letter of censure from Hoover, with a warning that he was on probation. He had run afoul of headquarters during an inspection of the Dallas office, when he was found to have concealed important information about an internal investigation, and to have undermined his superiors by spreading false information about them. He was issued a transfer from Dallas to the FBI field office in Savannah, Georgia, which was also a disciplinary measure. He quit instead and went to work for Hunt, who evidently was duped by his self-aggrandizing image as an intrepid G-man.

Several years later, when Hoover was asked about Smoot, his response was astringent:

> I welcome this opportunity to make it perfectly clear that former Special Agents of the FBI are not necessarily experts on communism. Some of them have sought to capitalize on their former employment

> with this Bureau for the purpose of establishing themselves as such authorities. I am firmly convinced there are too many self-styled experts on communism, without valid credentials and without any access whatsoever to classified, factual data, who are engaging in rumormongering and hurling false and wholly unsubstantiated allegations against people whose views differ from their own. Such activity makes more difficult the task of the professional investigator.

Whatever Hoover's own sins—and he committed many—the FBI director correctly pinpointed the unwholesome and destructive nature of the "anti-communist" grift perpetuated by Smoot, Hargis, Bundy, Schwarz, and others of their ilk. When profiting from smears and fables became a career path on the right, the certain to proliferate—and they did.

4

The Wizard of Id

In the years leading up to the epochal election of 1964, nobody stirred the fervor of the American Right like Barry Goldwater. Preceded by the debut of William F. Buckley Jr.'s new conservative journal *National Review*, and the founding of Young Americans for Freedom, another Buckley enterprise, the Arizona Republican's presidential campaign drew together the elements of a coalition that would grow (and mutate) for decades.

Much of Goldwater's appeal could be attributed to the man himself, a square-jawed stalwart from the western prairies who rejected the compromising taint of "establishment Republicans" such as President Dwight Eisenhower. Ike's role in the Allied victory over fascism meant little to the Far Right, which had promoted isolationism or worse before the war and smeared the moderate president as a "conscious agent of the Communist conspiracy"—the inside story as told by the John Birch Society's delusional Robert Welch. After four terms of New Deal Democrats, two terms of a self-proclaimed "Modern Republican," followed by John F. Kennedy's New Frontier and Lyndon Johnson's Great Society, then just coming to fruition, the right-wingers yearned for a revolution.

Goldwater's decision to run for president—after a fizzled attempt in 1960 that Richard Nixon had crushed—was greeted with euphoria by the Far Right, whose leaders saw in the attractive and energetic Arizonan a galvanizing figure for their movement. For admirers of Joe McCarthy and Strom Thurmond, his campaign promised to channel the resentments of decades into a powerful national movement. If it failed to achieve an electoral victory, then at least it might provide the momentum to seize control of the Republican Party and finally oust the traitorous moderates who had accommodated to the New Deal. Despite being tarred as an extremist, and pointedly declining to reject that label, however, the cool and sometimes diffident Goldwater was not the kind of strongman to instantly attract the more primitive right-wingers.

To the entrepreneurs of the Far Right, it was the racial resentment inflamed by the Kennedy administration's commitment to civil rights that represented an ideal marketing opportunity, as Billy James Hargis and General Edwin Walker had proved in 1963. Until then, Hargis had never seen any reason to identify the Christian Anti-Communism Crusade with either political party, and while he admired Goldwater, he felt even more drawn to Governor George Wallace, the segregationist Democrat from Alabama. He had envisioned an ultra-right third-party insurgency if a moderate Republican won the party's nomination. Both Hargis and Walker knew that Goldwater, despite his vote against the 1964 Civil Rights Act, felt discomfort and perhaps disgust with their racist and authoritarian rhetoric; indeed, the senator had refused to appear with Walker at a Madison Square Garden rally sponsored by Young Americans for Freedom in March 1962. That insult particularly irked Walker because he believed that Goldwater had invited him to speak at the rally, which drew tens of thousands and proved to be a landmark event for conservatism. Nevertheless, Walker endorsed the Republican nominee two years later, albeit in his own phlegmatic and inarticulate way. The retired general said he approved of the movement that had "put Senator Barry Goldwater where he is," and hoped that his victory in November would bring the White House "back in a position of America first."

Goldwater's campaign was controlled by longtime Republican operatives like F. Clifton White and Phyllis Schlafly, with histories in the Robert Taft isolationist wing that had opposed the party establishment and the candidacies of Wendell Willkie, Thomas Dewey, and Dwight Eisenhower. Characters like Hargis and Walker were bit players on the margins, out for a grift. Dan Smoot, the former FBI agent turned radio personality and author, felt more enthusiasm for Goldwater from the beginning, although he, too, detected a little softness in the senator's positions—and openly challenged him during the campaign over his support for NATO, a "globalist" outfit that required excessive cooperation with European social democratic parties and other suspect entities. Dr. Fred Schwarz, leader of the Christian Anti-Communism Crusade, was far less reserved, despite being unable to vote, as an Australian citizen, in the United States. What American communists feared most, Schwarz told *The New York Times*, was the election of Barry Goldwater.

In the 1964 election, neither American communists nor anyone else disturbed by Goldwater's extremism, including his casual attitude toward the use of nuclear weapons, had much real reason to fear him. Johnson steamrolled Goldwater, amassing over forty-three million votes, or more than 61 percent, and winning forty-four states, plus the District of Columbia, which gave him 486 electoral votes. Goldwater won his home state and five states of the old Confederacy, for a total of 52 electoral votes. Measured by the popular vote alone, the election represented a crushing defeat for the Republican Party, on the order of Alf Landon's legendary rout by Franklin Delano Roosevelt in 1936. The Republican establishment, which had warned against nominating Goldwater, saw the ruinous margins, which swamped GOP candidates all the way down the ballot, as a sign that the "conservatives" must never be allowed to nominate a national ticket again. It would take a few more cycles before the moderates lost control permanently.

But in those same dismal numbers, the Right saw their own form of vindication. For the first time, Republicans had nominated a "movement conservative" for president. Despite Goldwater's overwhelming defeat, they found encouragement and a portent of ultimate victory. The twenty-six million voters who had chosen Goldwater—and those who would seek to lead them—realized that they weren't a mere fringe.

After losing four battles for the nomination with Taft, they had captured the citadel of the party. Their hero Goldwater had lost, but a new hero emerged at the end of the campaign with an electrifying television appearance: Ronald Reagan.

Political scientists and pollsters sifting through the data coldly dismissed the right-wing spin, noting that the bulk of those Goldwater ballots were cast by habitual Republican voters, not true believers, a cohort estimated by at least one academic analyst at no more than three million. No matter what the polls said, however, the Far Right's publicists fiercely laid claim to every single Goldwater voter. Within a couple of weeks, the Louisiana-based Conservative Society of America began to distribute an orange bumper sticker that screamed: 26,000,000 AMERICANS CAN'T BE WRONG! To them, those millions of voters represented a source of potential support—and money—that was an order of magnitude larger than they had ever imagined.

According to the arithmetical logic of Dan Smoot, the 1964 campaign multiplied the support of the right-wing cause by a factor of at least fifty-two, because Goldwater had won fifty-two times as many votes as T. Coleman Andrews, the Virginia accountant who had run in 1956 as the candidate of the States' Rights Party. The ultra-right Liberty Lobby, operated by an obscure Nazi sympathizer and anti-Semite named Willis Carto, estimated that there had only been a million right-wing Americans when the Goldwater faction seized control of the GOP. By Carto's estimate, that plucky one million "had convinced 25 million in four months," a feat that promised unlimited vistas over the horizon. Fanciful calculations aside, Billy James Hargis was undoubtedly correct in his own more measured reaction. "In the past several months," he said, "the conservative message has received unprecedented exposure." Arnold Forster, who had coauthored *Danger on the Right*, a book-length research project on right-wing extremism published that year by the Anti-Defamation League, agreed with Hargis. "The radical right organizations are correct in claiming 1964 as a year of victory despite the devastating rebuke the voters gave Goldwater," he wrote. "By insinuating themselves into the Republican party machinery they achieved a degree of prominence, cohesiveness, and public acceptance they never had before."

THE RIGHT-WING ENTREPRENEURS who won by losing with Goldwater included a young activist from Texas named Richard Viguerie, who had spent most of the previous few years toiling as a lowly employee of Young Americans for Freedom. It was a job that primarily entailed fundraising, a craft that Viguerie learned from Marvin Liebman, a middle-aged right-wing organizer associated with the Buckleys, who had whipped up various postwar conservative crusades. Among those efforts, he was most notorious for claiming that he had gathered a million signatures opposing the admission of "Red China" to the United Nations, hence the "Committee of One Million" that became a major direct-mail platform. (Nobody ever saw the million signatures, which Liebman claimed were stored in a New Jersey warehouse.) Liebman and William Rusher, then publisher of *National Review*, recruited Viguerie to help run YAF in 1961 after he dropped out of law school. What that job actually required was to serve as an account executive for Liebman's small New York public relations firm.

Viguerie already had gained experience in raising money via direct mail from his previous work with Billy James Hargis's Christian Crusade. Hargis had blazed an early direct-mail trail with such innovations as the "wife letter" pitch, which proved exceptionally lucrative. Like Hargis, Viguerie was an admirer of Joe McCarthy. But he was interested in the business of conservatism, not the ideological arguments in *National Review*. Eager and quick, he learned the art of parting fervent believers from their cash on a repeat basis. Viguerie's New York apprenticeship taught him to treat truth in marketing as an obstacle, not a principle. According to historian Rick Perlstein, Liebman immediately informed Viguerie, "YAF had two thousand paid members but that in public, he should always claim there were 25,000." From such minor falsehoods, big lies could grow.

At his initial meeting with Liebman, Viguerie recalled in his 2004 book, *America's Right Turn*, the veteran publicist showed him a set of file cabinets filled with thousands of three-by-five index cards. Each card listed a donor to a cause promoted by Liebman's outfit. "All you had to do was ask," Viguerie wrote, recalling his astonishment at this display, "and these people would give money!" It was as though he had struck an oil gusher. The facile Viguerie soon discovered that while he disliked asking for money in person, he could instead send fundraising letters, the basic tools of the direct-mail campaign. He did not much bother with conservative philosophy or right-wing journalism but assiduously studied the past masters of commercial promotion, including the legendary admen David Ogilvy and Bruce Barton. By trial and error, Viguerie determined which pitch inspired donors to pull out their checkbooks. He focused "on becoming the best marketer I could be."

The main hindrance to Viguerie's marketing career in those years was a dearth of lists with the names and addresses of confirmed conservatives, beyond the paltry files maintained by Liebman, *National Review*, YAF, and a few other tiny organizations. Only a new source of names could refresh and grow a nascent movement. Then, late in 1964, with a flash of insight, Viguerie realized that the failed Goldwater campaign had created exactly what he needed. For the first time, a Republican presidential campaign had attracted a large contingent of small donors, rather than relying on the usual big corporate contributors. Required to register the name and address of every person who gave more than fifty dollars, the campaign had dutifully filed its full donor list with the clerk of the House of Representatives as a public document. Bingo!

The young entrepreneur paid "a half dozen or so women" to go to the Capitol, where they copied the list in longhand on yellow legal pads. They succeeded in retrieving nearly the entire file before a nervous House clerk called a halt to the operation. "And that list was my treasure trove," Viguerie boasted, "as good as the gold bricks deposited at Fort Knox, as I started the Viguerie Company and began raising money for conservative clients. . . . I was now the sole possessor of the best list in the nation for raising money for conservative causes. I also knew what to do with that list." As Viguerie tells this story, he quit the YAF staff and took the group on as his first client; as others tell it, he was fired and then persuaded YAF to hire his firm. Either way, he was in business by January 1965 with thousands of potential contributors captured on the newfangled technology of magnetic computer tape. He began to purchase fresh lists of names wherever he could find them, especially conservative names, and eventually acquired Liebman's own list when the publicist moved to London for a brief and ill-fated sojourn as a theatrical producer.

As other conservative organizations engaged Viguerie's services, he developed a set of protocols for exploiting their resources to fatten his own business. To him, whatever grew the Viguerie firm would by definition enhance the growth of the Right. "My contract with any client would give both the client and me access to donors' names, which was critical in expanding the base of the conservative movement. It had the effect politically that free trade has economically—it made for easy access across borders (in this instance organizational borders) since I was, in effect, the NAFTA framework governing conservative lists. . . . Just as free trade dramatically expanded the world economy in the second half of the twentieth century, so my 'common market' of conservative names expanded the conservative universe."

Viguerie's analogy of his business to a "common market," however, doesn't truly describe a scheme overseen by one individual that centralized the resources of everyone else under his sole control and for his own profit. But, he explained, this monopolistic deal meant that conservative organizations "were able to prospect . . . at less expense, faster and with greater precision" for new supporters. It was all very efficient and would "keep that pie growing bigger and bigger." During the decade that followed, the Viguerie firm enjoyed broad domination over the field of mass right-wing fundraising, even as a select few of his employees took what they had learned from him and established their own ventures. Viguerie himself amassed a substantial fortune that included suburban Washington office buildings and an estate in the Virginia horse country. Without underestimating his own industriousness or creativity, his market position in those early days of conservative direct mail enabled him to set terms that were entirely to his advantage, transforming a lucrative business into a personal and political gold mine.

Viguerie's profits and influence were enhanced, ironically enough, by the effort to reform campaign finances in the aftermath of the Watergate scandal. The epic personal and partisan corruption of the

Nixon administration included massive corporate payoffs, in cash, to the Republican Party and the Committee to Reelect the President (or CRP, frequently mocked as "CREEP"). To curb that kind of crooked business, congressional Democrats passed a series of reforms in 1974 that set strict contribution limits, restricted corporate contributions, and created the Federal Election Commission to oversee candidate compliance. Though well intentioned, the new rules did little to remove the influence of money from national politics. While the new contribution limits temporarily reduced the power of individual fat-cat donors, they greatly amplified the power of Viguerie and other consultants who knew how to use mailing lists to mobilize thousands (and ultimately millions) of smaller donors. The same law encouraged the rapid expansion of political action committees, or PACs, the federally sanctioned groups that pull together donations from individuals to finance candidates and causes.

Viguerie boasted that direct mail became the "secret weapon" behind the resurgence of the Right. By the time his Richard A. Viguerie Company, or RAVCO, reached its high-water mark in the late 1970s, he controlled no fewer than three hundred mailing lists, employed more than 250 people, and sent more than one hundred million pieces of mail annually from a computerized system that ran twenty-four hours a day, seven days a week. While that ever-advancing machinery of communication made Viguerie's operations highly productive, his secret weapon's ammunition was not technological but emotional. What he sent forth was a carefully calculated mixture of fear, anger, and resentment, usually including at least a hint of racial hostility. The way to get self-styled "conservatives" to write a check, as Viguerie and his imitators learned in short order, was to enrage them against the liberal "enemy." In one letter, the lurking menace might be labor unions ("union bosses"), while for another it might be government officials ("federal bureaucrats"), assertive women ("radical feminists"), or gay people ("homosexual activists").

That messaging, aimed at the politically alienated, achieved its best results with the pitch and volume cranked up to the shrillest level. No middle ground existed, no concessions or compromises could be accepted, and the twilight of liberty, morality, and the American way of life loomed over the horizon. The inescapable conclusion was that only a donation—five dollars, ten dollars, fifty dollars—could forestall the triumph of evil. It was a small price to pay for saving America.

WHILE REFINING HIS methods for separating enraged conservatives from their money, Viguerie knew that whatever his letters promised to do for the groups he promoted, he would not be precluded from keeping much of the loot. Thus, beyond the boundaries of electoral politics was spawned a vast landscape of ostensibly nonprofit organizations mounting constant emotional appeals to right-wing small donors.

The growth of the nonprofit sector during those decades included an array of ideological and cause-oriented "charities" whose directors felt they could safely ignore the nonpartisan strictures of the Internal Revenue Code. Neither the IRS nor any other regulatory body, such as the US Postal Inspection Service, commanded sufficient resources to police direct-mail entrepreneurs. Most of the responsibility for overseeing charitable solicitations fell to the states, usually through their attorneys general, who might or might not seek to aggressively enforce laws against fraud and duplicity. The stiffest state sanction would rarely amount to more than a small fine and a few days of bad publicity, neither of which interfered much with business as usual.

Among Viguerie's earliest nonprofit clients was an outfit called Citizens for Decent Literature (CDL), established in 1956 by Charles Keating, a Cincinnati lawyer and devout Catholic, to promote the censorship of books and films he deemed pornographic. More than two decades later, Keating's name would become synonymous with the looting of the savings and loan industry and the congressional corruption surrounding that scandal.

In the early 1970s, when Keating first approached Viguerie, CDL had expanded to hundreds of local chapters, boasted one hundred thousand members, and its founder had finagled appointment by President Nixon to the United States Commission on Obscenity and Pornography. Unlike his bluenose predecessors, Keating took a modern approach to stamping out "smut." His organization's most popular propaganda product was *Perversion for Profit*, a titillating short movie that offered outraged citizens an opportunity to watch snippets of porn in the guise of education, while a voiceover recited statistical evidence about the damage such images inflicted on innocent youth. "A flood tide of filth," the narrator intoned, "threatens to corrupt an entire generation." Keating later acknowledged that he had simply invented most of the data cited in the film. It was just a preview of more sinister deceptions that would eventually send him to prison.

Under Viguerie's guidance, what began as Keating's crusade against sexually explicit art turned into an even more cynical enterprise. The operating budget of Citizens for Decent Literature reflected the change, with nearly 90 percent redirected toward administration and fundraising rather than efforts to impose censorship, the group's ostensible goal. By far the largest share of the proceeds from its direct-mail fundraising was retained by RAVCO; over a period of three years, the CDL mailings brought in nearly $4 million, of which slightly more than $600,000 went to program activities. Lawyers in the New York State attorney general's charities fraud division and their counterparts in several other states tried to bar CDL from raising money within their borders. Keating's self-dealing went still further, however, when he began to invest large sums from the nonprofit CDL accounts in American Financial Corporation, the holding company where he was then vice president—the beginning of his greatest fraud in the mammoth savings and loan scandal that made him infamous.

THE ENDLESS OUTPOURING of commercialized fury into the mailboxes of citizens across the nation provoked dismay among some honest conservatives, who regarded this toxic hucksterism as a stain on their cause. The more they learned about the conservative direct-mail business, the more embarrassed they became. Interviewed by disillusioned conservative Alan Crawford after he left the industry he had helped to create, a shocked Marvin Liebman described Viguerie and the imitators he spawned as "an entire army of hustlers!" The *Washington Post*'s conservative columnist George Will described Viguerie and company as "quasi-political entrepreneurs who have discovered commercial opportunities in merchandising discontent."

Compared with the hysterical tone of current email fundraising, the mailings dispatched in those early days appear almost tame. But they were replete with dire predictions of what would transpire if the enemies of America were permitted to run amok. Union bosses ordering firefighters to let your house burn down. Gay teachers turning your children into homosexuals. The United Nations forcing you to pay your own kids minimum wage for household chores. Pointy-headed diplomats negotiating arms control in abject surrender to the communists. In short, your world was ending—so send money now!

Viguerie explained that the nuances of discourse and the questions of philosophy that had seemed to matter to the conservatives around Buckley were no longer relevant to the new wave of "aggressive" and "proactive" conservatives. Like him, they were more concerned with "winning the election . . . and gaining power . . . than winning the debate." What this meant in electoral politics was the promotion of the most extreme and ideological candidates, who perfectly suited Viguerie's sales methods. More than once during his political career, the direct-mail guru would renounce the Republican Party and declare his preference for a far-right alternative such as the American Independent Party, whose vice presidential nomination he once sought. At every turn, the money rolled in.

In 1968, he brushed off an opportunity to work for Richard Nixon's presidential campaign. The former vice president represented the Republican establishment and wasn't sufficiently hard-line. Nixon didn't drive traffic. Viguerie felt a far stronger affinity for George Wallace, a "true conservative." Wallace and the Dixiecrat Strom Thurmond, Viguerie stated, "had opposed most of the civil rights legislation of the '60s on constitutional grounds, only to find themselves smeared as racists." They had drawing power. Ka-ching! When Wallace ran for president again in 1972, his bid ended in an attempted assassination that left him in a wheelchair and his campaign sunk in debt. But his ambitions survived, and the following year, at the urging of Billy James

Hargis, a Wallace aide approached Viguerie to raise money so that the Alabaman could run yet again in 1976. With three-million-plus names on the Wallace list to expand his direct-mail database, Viguerie gladly agreed.

Taking on Wallace as a client marked another departure from the traditional conservatives. Political writer Frank Meyer had warned in *National Review* that the Alabaman's populist belligerence represented "the radical opposite of conservatism" and threatened to poison "the moral source" of the movement. But Wallace had the lists that Viguerie wanted, and the quibbles of "old-line conservatives" like Meyer didn't concern him. With his disdain for the philosophical virtues that had once defined conservatism, and his eagerness to stimulate passionate anger rather than intellectual debate, Viguerie appealed to the dark underbelly of the Right. In Freudian psychology, then still ascendant, Viguerie could be defined as the instinctual, aggressive, and even primitive element, while the eggheads like Meyer stood for judgmental and even sanctimonious standards. They were the superego of the Right, struggling vainly to contain the id unleashed by Viguerie.

With a flurry of mailings over a period of two or three years, the Wallace campaign's 1976 list brought in millions of dollars for Viguerie. But that massive direct-mail barrage exposed certain questionable aspects of the RAVCO business model. To get those lists of Wallace supporters, Viguerie started mailing long before the campaign could pay his bills—and continued to mail for years as the payments lagged. Campaign finance lawyers questioned whether this huge extension of credit constituted an illegal corporate donation to Wallace from Viguerie. Such questions probably didn't occur to Wallace donors, who never displayed much regard for pointy-headed "good government" reformers. What might have irked them more, if they had known it, was the fact that most of their donations weren't going to support Wallace's campaign against liberal elites but would end up instead paying for the campaign's enormous direct-mail expenses (including Viguerie's substantial profits).

This was the dirty little secret of the direct-mail business. According to an investigation published by *The New York Times* in May 1975, almost two years after the Wallace for President direct-mail campaign began, the net results were underwhelming, at least from a donor perspective. The average check of $9.70 from a Wallace donor fell considerably short of the cost of reaching each new donor, which amounted to $11.40. Only repeated mailings to the same names could defray those expenses and accrue a surplus, which also turned out to be rather unimpressive. Despite sending out an estimated ten million pieces of direct mail, the Wallace campaign had banked only about $212,000 after paying its own minimal expenses. As *Times* reporter Christopher Lydon noted, "Even that balance of cash on hand would apparently have been reduced to nothing, or a debt, if the Wallace campaign had been required to pay its fund-raising bills up to date." In other words, the campaign still owed the Viguerie firm more than its mailings had earned. Although this was plainly a scam, there was little reason to feel sorry for Wallace himself. The cynical Alabaman had found a neat way to exploit his devoted donors by quietly diverting a portion of the proceeds into his personal bank account.

Among the tried-and-true methods employed by direct-mail experts to stimulate larger donations was the marketing of cheap, glitzy merchandise, often tied to a personality. For the most devoted fans of George Wallace, this campaign offered various kitsch items, including a George Wallace wristwatch and, for twenty-five dollars or more, a shiny silver-plated George Wallace medallion from the Franklin Mint. To license these reproductions of Wallace's image, his campaign paid the candidate a "royalty" on each doodad shipped. Fundraising letters described the Wallace medallion as "a lasting tribute every patriotic American will be proud to own and display to friends for years to come," but didn't mention that the candidate would profit from each sale. It was a new mode of campaign grift perfectly suited to Wallace's cult of personality—and would continue to be exploited to perfection decades later, on a much grander scale, by Donald J. Trump. (Trump commemorative coins are gold-plated, like all things Trumpish—and far more expensive.)

Even though Viguerie did not ultimately recoup all the money owed him by the Wallace campaign, the deal was nevertheless highly profitable. In addition to all the little checks, those millions of letters had brought in hundreds of thousands of new names to mine—all of which were filed and henceforth controlled solely by RAVCO. Immediately, the Viguerie firm started mailing other solicitations to the Wallace supporters and would continue to solicit them for years, banking solid returns on the initial investment. The aggrieved white working-class George Wallace donors never realized that instead of "standing up for America," as the campaign slogan promised, their dollars were propping up Richard Viguerie's business. Few if any of them had ever heard of Viguerie, even as they enriched him.

A mark was simply a mark, whether the con was "political" or "charitable."

As Viguerie's methods gained traction, so, too, did his political style. After the Nixon presidency collapsed in the Watergate scandal, many Republicans and conservatives felt more cheated than chastened. They responded to the slash-and-burn political style popularized by Viguerie, which in turn became the animating spirit of a new wave of right-wing activism. Featuring a cast of characters who would become notorious, from Jerry Falwell and Jim Bakker to Lee Atwater and Roger Stone, this crowd billed itself as the New Right—and would find new ways to sucker the ever-credulous base that Viguerie had mapped. The populist rage of the Right, which seemed to expand in every election cycle, was pure gold.

5

Nixon's Avaricious Avengers

The multifarious crime spree that became known as Watergate hung over Washington for years after Richard Nixon's unceremonious departure in August 1974, its stench provoking a reformist zeal among congressional Democrats and even a few old-fashioned Republicans. They knew that the corrupt schemes overseen by Nixon and his henchmen had oozed far beyond the "third rate burglary" of the Democratic National Committee headquarters into outright bribery and money laundering on a massive scale, implicating some of America's most powerful corporations.

The true history of the Nixon administration was a pageant of sleaze that had commenced no later than 1969, when the president's top aides set up a secret multimillion-dollar slush fund—run out of a back room in a town house basement near Washington's Dupont Circle—that funneled cash payments to Republican congressional midterm candidates. By the time Nixon was running again in 1972, the town house operation had metastasized into several major bribery schemes connected to the Committee to Reelect the President, or CREEP as it came to be known. The ITT Corporation, to take just one of the more notorious cases, coughed up $400,000 for the Republican National Convention to "settle" a Justice Department antitrust probe. (Nixon can be heard on a 1971 White House tape discussing the proper timing of the ITT bribe: "Now this is very, very hush-hush, and it has to be engineered very delicately, and it'll take six months to do properly.") Dairy producer lobbyists agreed to donate at least $2 million after Nixon sent Treasury secretary John Connally to "shake them down," as the president himself put it. The Committee to Reelect the President was also illegally hauling in many millions of dollars from corporations, many of which felt pressured into making contributions.

The record of corporate donors was so tightly held that it was kept in a locked drawer in the desk of Rose Mary Woods, Nixon's White House secretary. The list—which came to be known as "Rose Mary's Baby"—wasn't released until Fred Wertheimer of the citizen group Common Cause broke it loose with a class-action lawsuit. Emblematic of the big corporate names found on the list was William Keeler, the chief executive of Phillips Petroleum, who pleaded guilty, during the post-Watergate prosecutions, to making an illegal corporate donation. (He was fined $1,000.) When added up, the list showed that Nixon's gang had collected $20 million—roughly the equivalent of $140 million in current dollars—from about 150 executives seeking "access" to the president. After that, nobody could deny the stunning level of corruption in presidential campaign finance.

Neither Nixon's corrupt fundraising extortions nor his repeated violations of federal law and constitutional precedent troubled the Republican Right, whose most zealous leaders had long disdained him as too moderate and too opportunistic. But the exposure of his authoritarian offenses suddenly made those right-wing critics appreciate Nixon as a kindred spirit. To them, his forced resignation represented not a victory for the rule of law but the triumph of everything and everyone they hated. He had asserted the will to power and the ideology of the Right against the liberal enemy, whose names he had actually compiled on an enemies list. For a time, he had defied the Democrats in Congress, the courts, the national media, and the "Eastern establishment." Many on the Republican right came to view him much more favorably after Watergate than before—and at least a few weren't ashamed to say so publicly. "If I'd known he'd been up to all that stuff," said the veteran right-wing editor and activist M. Stanton Evans, "I'd have been for

Nixon all along." As Evans told historian Rick Perlstein at a Princeton University symposium, "I didn't like Nixon until Watergate."

NIXON'S RUTHLESSLY AMORAL politics were admired, too, by a young Republican from suburban New York named Roger Stone, who was involved in CREEP's "ratfucking" dirty tricks—and would eventually have Tricky Dick's smirking likeness tattooed between his shoulders.

YET AMONG DEMOCRATS, who maintained a controlling majority in the House of Representatives that would expand by fifty seats in the 1974 midterm, CREEP's abuses inspired an insistent demand for change. Two months after Nixon resigned, his successor, President Gerald Ford, reluctantly signed the Federal Election Campaign Act of 1974, after protracted negotiations over its complex provisions, including public financing for candidates and party conventions, the creation of the Federal Election Commission, and strict limits on contributions, which permitted individuals to donate no more than $1,000 to a candidate for federal office. Any improvement in public integrity achieved following Watergate was soon eclipsed, however, by the formation of enormously powerful political action committees—which enabled the Far Right, liberated by Nixon's removal, to resume its crusade for control of the Republican Party.

Indeed, the most consequential and ironic aspect of the Election Reform Act was the empowerment of PACs. These political entities, not exactly new but revitalized under the new law, quickly dwarfed individual citizen donors. The faction best positioned to exploit the PAC explosion were the Goldwater veterans and other ultraconservative elements that were armed with the extensive mailing lists nurtured by Richard Viguerie and his acolytes. Within a few years, their political and financial resources would vault them into a position of enormous influence within the GOP.

As the Far Right prospered, Republican moderates began their gradual descent toward oblivion. Seeming to gain power when Vice

President Gerald Ford took over from Nixon and then named as his own vice president Nelson Rockefeller, the former New York governor demonized by the Right, the moderates enjoyed a brief reprieve. The right-wingers quickly came to despise Ford, regarding him as a conservative turncoat who had not only elevated the hated Rockefeller but supported the feminist Equal Rights Amendment and amnesty for Vietnam draft resisters. The Right coalesced around a challenge to Ford by former California governor Ronald Reagan, their new champion, who almost succeeded in toppling the incumbent president at the Republican National Convention. When Democrat Jimmy Carter drove Ford from the White House in November 1976, right-wing Republicans didn't mourn, they celebrated. And they were already prepared to take over.

More than a year before Ford's defeat, Viguerie had joined with other Goldwater campaign veterans to launch the New Right—a political initiative seen at first merely as a reaction to the Rockefeller nomination and the perception that Ford had moved leftward—which moved quickly to promote and exploit the Reagan primary candidacy. What soon became clear was that the younger operatives around Viguerie were far more aggressive, both politically and financially, than the Republicans of earlier generations. Despite its ideological roots in the Old Right and the Goldwater campaign, the heavily hyped New Right resembled a corporate conglomeration more than an organic political movement. The publicity-conscious political professionals of the New Right chose their moniker to distinguish what they were doing from the older conservative outfits around William F. Buckley Jr., which they had come to view as effete, ineffectual, and weak—an indictment that Buckley validated by endorsing Ford's choice of Rockefeller for vice president.

Centered around a handful of Washington-based organizations, the New Right was heavily if not wholly dependent on Viguerie's fundraising machine. It operated under varying labels and rubrics, including the Conservative Caucus, a grassroots outfit run by former Nixon administration official Howard Phillips; the Committee for the Survival of a Free Congress, run by former Republican Senate staffer Paul Weyrich; the Heritage Foundation, an ideological think tank launched by Weyrich with money from Colorado beer baron Joseph Coors; the National Conservative Political Action Committee, or NCPAC, overseen by John T. "Terry" Dolan, a former College Republican leader; and a vast array of single-issue organizations such as the anti-union National Right to Work Committee, the antiabortion American Life League, and the anti-feminist Eagle Forum, led by the redoubtable Phyllis Schlafly.

Branding themselves as a refreshing alternative to the tired old politics was somewhat deceptive, since most of the New Right leaders were depressingly familiar. They had been around for decades—and more than a few had indulged in various kinds of disreputable extremism. Schlafly, for example, was a Fifties-vintage activist and author whose ultra-right credentials dated back not merely to the Goldwater campaign but to the early days of the John Birch Society (although in public she always denied her secret membership). Viguerie and Weyrich had met while working for the arch-racist George Wallace and promoted his American Independent Party as a far-right alternative. Phillips had quit the Republican Party and would eventually move beyond the Wallaceite fringe to found a political party based on "biblical principles," which apparently included death by stoning to punish gay sex, among other sins.

Still, there was no denying the renewed energy on the right, which fed off the anger and fear of middle-class Americans and siphoned away their money to finance still more propaganda that fed those resentments. They created a vicious cycle that left the country's social fabric badly tattered but clothed the New Right "populist" operatives in luxurious bespoke suits. Many of the older conservatives around Buckley and *National Review* viewed these political upstarts with the same distaste they reserved for the nouveau riche. If the Buckley crowd had supported Joe McCarthy and Barry Goldwater and later favored Southern segregationists over civil rights marchers, they remained unabashed elitists, repelled by Viguerie's populist pretensions and vulgar appeals. They detected worrying traits among the self-styled New Rightists, who struck them as crude, hateful, anti-intellectual, rabble-rousing, and insatiably greedy.

Reflecting the free-market credo that "greed is good," Viguerie scarcely bothered to conceal his avarice. At a meeting of right-wing financiers and activists at an inn in Middleburg, Virginia, in March 1976, he famously quipped: "My political principles? That's easy. M-O-N-E-Y."

Not everyone in conservative circles found this attitude amusing. Having trained Viguerie back when they both worked at the Buckley-inspired Young Americans for Freedom, Marvin Liebman became one of the harshest critics of the New Right's ethics, or lack thereof. As the New Right's wealth and influence swelled, Liebman told Alan Crawford—a longtime conservative activist and author who wrote the 1980 exposé *Thunder on the Right*—that he abhorred Viguerie's "hideous" business methods, which "raped the public." Those methods, as well as the self-serving philosophy behind them, were becoming harder for the Buckley crowd to ignore. Another conservative critic who remained anonymous told Crawford, "There are two kinds of people involved in these scams. There are those who climbed on board, and those who pretend it doesn't go on."

M. Stanton Evans, the longtime Buckley associate, explained exactly what troubled him about the fundraiser's enrichment schemes. "As far as I am concerned, the real difference between the two elements ['Old' and 'New' Right] is fundraising. Richard Viguerie and the group with which he is associated believe in massive direct-mail campaigns, involving millions of dollars in overhead and mailing costs to give away thousands." Evans suspected the New Right direct-mail operators were defrauding small donors by promising to spend the money on candidates and causes while glomming most of the revenue for "expenses," which meant high salaries and big profits for themselves.

"We're creating an entire conservative welfare class in Washington alone—people who cannot do much else who are doing very well off the $10 checks of little old ladies on Social Security," observed another dismayed right-winger.

Essentially, the same indictment could have been lodged against any of the groups whose financing relied on Viguerie and his direct-mail juggernaut. In a typical year, for instance, Paul Weyrich's Committee for the Survival of a Free Congress would raise nearly $1.7 million (or almost $8 million in current dollars), and transfer less than $300,000 to the candidates that its little-old-lady donors thought they were sending money to support. If Weyrich raised less the following year, he would send an even smaller percentage to candidates—while splitting the rest between his outfit and Viguerie's companies.

The ostentatiously pious Weyrich evinced a trace of guilt when Crawford questioned him about the con perpetrated by Viguerie on his own organization's small donors. He knew that those people, none of them rich, had sent their checks because they assumed the money would go to candidates who upheld their values. "Look, if I had given money and I heard the figures, I'd be disturbed," Weyrich admitted. But, he pleaded, "we spend money to recruit candidates, to train campaign managers, to analyze every vote cast in the House and Senate, to publish newspapers and weekly reports, and none of this is reflected in the financial reports." Nor was it reflected in the disclosures to the gulled donors, he forgot to add.

Whatever moral qualms Weyrich felt would have been summarily dismissed by the syndicate of operatives that profited from the creation of NCPAC: Terry Dolan, the brash operative who signed on to lead NCPAC in 1975; Charlie Black, an aide to North Carolina's race-baiting senator Jesse Helms; Arthur Finkelstein, a furtive Boston-based pollster; and Finkelstein's protégé, the ubiquitous Roger Stone, then fresh from his Watergate dirty tricks (which had been exposed in a Jack Anderson column, leading to his abrupt dismissal from Senator Bob Dole's staff).

Often profiled in the media as NCPAC swiftly rose to prominence in Washington, Dolan made no secret of his organization's reliance on the Viguerie money machine and on the sponsorship of Helms, its other principal patron, who had provided mailing lists from his own powerful fundraising arm, the National Congressional Club. During the first few years of NCPAC's existence, Dolan credited Viguerie with raising "90 percent of our money."

Where did all that direct-mail dough end up? As with Weyrich's organization—and Howard Phillips's Conservative Caucus—the cash flooding into NCPAC went mostly to "expenses," not candidates or campaigns. "Huge amounts of money have been raised by the New Right PACs," Crawford wrote, "but relatively meager amounts have actually been received by the candidates for whom the money was raised." Like Viguerie, NCPAC's Dolan measured his success by the amount of money he raised, and his outfit raised more than any of the other right-wing PACs. During its first full year in business, NCPAC brought in $2.5 million, or roughly $10 million in today's dollars, but disbursed less than $400,000, or about 16 percent, to candidates. Two years later, it raised $1.5 million and spent only $212,000 on candidates.

But as Crawford pointed out, there was a convenient yardstick available to measure the way New Right organizations spent their money—namely, the balance sheets of other conservative political action committees that raised funds through direct mail. In 1976, the Conservative Victory Fund, a PAC operated by the old-line American Conservative Union, raised $231,000 and contributed $101,000, or nearly half its receipts, to candidates. Two years later, the fund brought in $440,474 and donated $252,000 to candidates, or 57 percent. Comparing receipts and expenditures for the same year, the Conservative Victory Fund raised only a third as much as Weyrich's group—but donated almost twice as much to candidates.

Something was very wrong with Viguerie's pie chart.

There were no internal audits or ethical boundaries imposed on the operations of the New Right organizations, beyond what government regulators required, which wasn't much and which NCPAC, in particular, openly defied. The tight connections between the New Right organizations and their fundraising partners ought to have set off alarms from the very beginning. Several of these operatives even held positions overseeing New Right organizations while they were simultaneously on Viguerie's payroll—a conflict of interest that would have been forbidden by any nonprofit or corporation adhering to normal fiduciary rules. Viguerie himself effectively controlled the Conservative Caucus, which was "always in debt" to his companies. In another cozy arrangement, the Richard A. Viguerie Company leased offices in an Alexandria, Virginia, building owned by Dolan, Stone, and two top aides to Ronald Reagan, who was another Viguerie client then preparing to run for president.

Roger Stone's then wife, Ann E. W. Stone, worked for Viguerie and learned the fundraising business while her husband served as NCPAC's treasurer. Decades later, long after an amicable divorce from Roger, Ann Stone was still working the same racket—except this time as a "pro-choice Republican." Setting up a PAC called Republicans for Choice, with herself as chair, she raised millions via direct mail that she paid to her own consulting company, her own list brokerage, and herself. The PAC also separately reimbursed many of her personal "travel and entertainment" expenses, in addition to phone bills, auto repairs, gas costs, and even parking tickets. What Ann Stone didn't spend much on were the moderate Republican candidates she professed to admire. In 2005, Republicans for Choice spent more than $967,108, but only $5,420 went to federal or state candidates or committees, or just over one-half of 1 percent. Clearly, she had learned well from the master, but she was even more cynical than Viguerie. Ten years later, her "pro-choice" commitment didn't discourage her from organizing Women Vote Trump in 2016 or advising a pro-Trump super PAC—despite his repeated promises to appoint Supreme Court justices who would overturn *Roe v. Wade*, as he did by naming three who then tossed out half a century of pro-choice precedent.

MILLIONS OF DOLLARS flowed into NCPAC, as millions of deceptive letters flew out in envelopes from Viguerie's suburban Virginia offices. In typical style, an early NCPAC fundraising letter highlighted a shocking claim to fleece the rubes:

> Your tax dollars are being used to pay for grade school classes that teach our children that cannibalism, wife-swapping and the murder of infants and the elderly are acceptable behavior.

That letter was signed by Jesse Helms himself, who presumably knew there was no truth to its alarming description of public schools, a mash-up of conspiracy theories that prefigured the Trump-era paranoid fantasies about prominent Democrats and celebrities engaging in pedophilia in the basement of a Washington, DC, pizza parlor. But it is likely Helms never saw the letter and simply let his name be used, which was the common practice. These apoplectic screeds, replicated thousands of times in the copy-writing sweatshops of Viguerie and his imitators, were products of another New Right innovation: the permanent negative campaign. American politicians have routinely defamed and demonized their opponents, of course, dating back to the scandals that enveloped Alexander Hamilton and Thomas Jefferson in the revolutionary era. But the most vicious political attacks were often launched anonymously, or at least deniably, the way Roger Stone defamed Senator Edmund Muskie for CREEP as a "socialist" and worse in the 1972 New Hampshire Democratic primary. Muskie was the strongest possible candidate against Nixon. When he denounced the smears, the press characterized him as overly emotional, compounding the damage. Mission accomplished: Muskie soon withdrew from the contest.

YET FOR NCPAC, the defamatory attack was no longer shameful but a token of pride. In the worldview of Stone and company, the purpose of direct-mail and TV advertising was to "define" and destroy the opponent at the earliest possible moment. "Groups like ours are potentially very dangerous to the political process," Terry Dolan boasted to Myra MacPherson, who profiled the "short, slim, and mustachioed" operative for *The Washington Post*. "We could be a menace, yes. Ten independent expenditure groups, for example, could amass this great amount of money and defeat the point of accountability. . . . We could say whatever we want about an opponent of a Senator Smith and the senator wouldn't have to say anything. A group like ours could lie through its teeth and the candidate it helps stays clean."

The *Post*'s report cited numerous examples of smears in NCPAC's ferocious 1980 crusade against a half dozen Democratic senators. Its ads fabricated votes that had never occurred, attributed issue positions that the senators had never adopted, and lied with populist gusto about the senators' personal lives. NCPAC told voters that Senator Tom Eagleton of Missouri had voted to give $75 million to the Marxist government of Nicaragua, when he had voted against that aid package. NCPAC told voters that Senator Frank Church of Idaho had voted to give himself a pay raise, although he never did. NCPAC told voters that Senator George McGovern of South Dakota favored "a gas tax that could reach 50 cents a gallon," which he did not. When confronted about these lies, Dolan might issue a late "correction," or more likely, he would just snicker.

What the victimized senators and many others viewed as NCPAC's sleazy tactics seem fairly mundane in hindsight, but Dolan and his team were in the vanguard of the vicious tactics that increasingly came to polarize American politics. The chairman of the Republican National Committee at the time, William Brock, a Ford appointee from Tennessee, objected to independent right-wing outfits like NCPAC because their focus on "emotional social issues" obscured the "American dream issues" of tax reduction, job creation, health care, and housing.

Dolan's retort? "He's frustrated by jealousy. We're raising the funds. We're on the cutting edge of politics. . . . Brock should have been fired long ago." Paul Weyrich, not a fan of the flamboyant Dolan, nonetheless agreed with his assessment of the moderate Brock. When Weyrich approached the party chairman with a proposal to organize evangelical voters behind Republican candidates in the 1978 midterm, "he didn't understand what I was talking about. . . . It was so foreign to him that it didn't make any sense."

In that pivotal year of Reagan's victory, with the Senate suddenly flipping to the Republicans, Dolan's outfit raised more money than the Republican National Committee and achieved more success in defeating incumbent Democrats because he understood what Brock did not. On the right, the way to raise money and the way to move voters coincided neatly. "Make them angry and stir up their hostilities," Dolan boasted. "The shriller you are, the easier it is to raise funds." The path to victory was paved with slander.

Understanding what motivated their base, Dolan and his colleagues chose from a long menu of issues to vibrate the nerves of right-wing donors. The Supreme Court's 1973 legalization of abortion rights in the *Roe v. Wade* decision became the basis of a lucrative industry tarring liberal politicians as "baby killers." The uproar raised by Anita Bryant, the Oklahoma beauty queen and pop singer with her antigay Save Our Children crusade, incited paranoia over "the homosexual agenda" and the sinister rumor that gay teachers were secretly "recruiting"—or eventually, "grooming"—innocent schoolchildren, a perennial right-wing theme and fundraising winner. The favorite themes of NCPAC mailers and advertising campaigns were cultural issues that polarized and divided—and brought in waves of donations.

What NCPAC did with that money, in addition to skimming heavily for profit, was to stoke open hatred. Such invitations to unvarnished loathing, shorn of any pretense to civility, were until that point rarely seen in mainstream postwar politics outside the Ku Klux Klan and never acknowledged proudly and publicly. (Joe McCarthy had used those tactics, not only against communist subversion supposedly lurking within the federal government but also against a supposed gay menace in government, and only after he attacked the US Army did he suffer the censure of his fellow Republicans. The NCPAC gang, including Viguerie, loudly lionized the demagogue as a hero and martyr.) Ratcheting up the rancor, without a trace of discomfort, was the stock-in-trade of Dolan and his colleagues. Mean-spirited politics became a big business.

"We want people to hate Birch Bayh without even knowing why," Dolan said, describing NCPAC communications strategy against Democratic candidates as the 1980 campaign began. (Roger Stone would later refine that corrosive attitude into one of his "rules" of politics: "Hate is a stronger motivator than love.") With voter frustrations rising during the late seventies, an era of stagnating employment and soaring inflation—and the hapless Democratic administration led by President Jimmy Carter seemingly incapable of solving the problems—the New Right weaponized anger into a potent force and a money machine.

In November 1980, with the defeat of four of the six Democratic senators it had targeted, NCPAC cemented its reputation as a giant-killer. But more importantly, it helped to elect Ronald Reagan to the presidency, which had been a principal aim of NCPAC from the group's inception. "It's my fervent hope," Viguerie said in 1975, the year NCPAC was founded, "that George Wallace and Ronald Reagan will team up as the ticket of a new party next year." Reagan's primary challenge to Ford in 1976 nearly wrested the nomination from the incumbent, a moderate Republican president. It was a crossroads for the Republican Party and a vista of seemingly unlimited opportunity for the New Right hustlers. During that 1976 contest, the former California governor had signed one of the first fundraising letters for NCPAC, and its leadership had all signed on a few years later with his 1980 campaign. Dolan's brother, Tony, became a Reagan speechwriter; Stone, who had led Youth for Reagan in 1976, was the Northeast regional campaign coordinator; and NCPAC pollster Arthur Finkelstein did polls for Reagan, too.

The electoral victories of 1980 marked a high point for NCPAC and the New Right that it epitomized. While the organization continued into the Reagan era, its ultra-right constituencies soon grew suspicious of the new president's compromises with traditional Republicans—not to mention congressional Democrats and the leadership of the Soviet Union. In a democratic society, the revanchist yearnings of "the base" were destined for frustration. But led by Dolan and Viguerie, NCPAC retained the capacity to manipulate those same restless right-wing voters. No matter what disappointments ensued during Reagan's presidency, the Democrats and liberals would always serve as lucrative scapegoats. Besides, Reagan himself remained an icon of conservative admiration, even as he cast aside his own ultra-right assumptions. The fundraising business continued as usual, and so did its most misleading marketing practices.

For Reagan's 1984 reelection campaign, NCPAC raised almost $20 million, roughly equal to $50 million today, which doesn't sound like much but was the largest haul of any political action committee during that election cycle. Given the incumbent president's landslide victory—he won 525 electoral votes, nearly 60 percent of the popular vote, and took every state except Minnesota, the home of Democratic candidate Walter Mondale, and the District of Columbia—those millions looked like money well spent, until someone examined the data more closely. Of that nearly $20 million, according to Federal Election Commission files pulled by *National Journal* and campaign finance scholar Michael Malbin, NCPAC allotted almost $9 million to general overhead, meaning salaries, rent, office supplies, and other costs. And of the $10 million left for its "independent expenditure" supporting Reagan, a bit more than $9 million went to mailing and printing to raise more money. Which left around $800,000 devoted to television advertising, a paltry sum for a national campaign even in those days and a tiny fraction of that original $20 million. NCPAC's direct-mail appeals had promised something quite different to the millions of donors who received its letters: "A $250 contribution will pay for a minute of commercial TV time and cover the costs of sending over 120 pro-Reagan letters to voters." As *The Washington Post* noted in a tart editorial, only $10.26 of every $250 check in fact funded television advertising for the GOP nominee. But those urgent mass mailings had the desired result. During the 1984 cycle, NCPAC added over one hundred thousand new, responsive donors to its computerized lists, so the grift could go on.

THE NCPAC GRIFT went on for several years, but things were never the same after 1984. The salience of NCPAC declined and so did its fundraising capacity, with receipts halved in 1982 and falling to a mere $1 million by 1986. It owed at least four times that amount to its creditors, including a million to Viguerie himself. The direct-mail pioneer's own greed had led him to overreach, too, resulting in millions of dollars in lawsuits and demands from disgruntled clients—notably including NCPAC itself, which had lost enormous amounts during the Reagan reelection campaign by following his advice. Forced to sell off properties and holdings, including his cherished *Conservative Digest* magazine, Viguerie was on the cusp of bankruptcy.

The collapse of NCPAC arose from moral crisis as well as financial troubles. Its fortunes declined even more rapidly following the death of Terry Dolan in December 1986, when he finally succumbed to AIDS. His closeted existence, unavoidable for any homosexual leader in the conservative movement, didn't protect him any more than it protected Stone's mentor Roy Cohn, who died from AIDS several months later.

The grotesque irony of Dolan's secret life and concealed cause of death, which he and members of his family persisted in denying, was that NCPAC had long profited from attacks on gays and lesbians, and from promoting politicians such as its patron Senator Jesse Helms, who exploited the antigay panic. Republicans supported by NCPAC formed the core of the Senate's most fervent antigay caucus, and Helms himself had campaigned on the issue in his 1984 reelection campaign against Democrat Jim Hunt, then North Carolina's governor.

"Let's talk about the homosexuals, labor union bosses, and crooks that support Governor Hunt," urged a Helms TV ad. A NCPAC letter for Republican congressman Phil Crane, an Illinois conservative, went much further: "Our nation's moral fiber is being weakened by the growing homosexual movement and the fanatical ERA pushers (many of whom publicly brag they are lesbians)." Although Dolan later disowned that letter, the truth was that NCPAC billowed with gay-baiting propaganda that was aired on behalf of dozens of Republican candidates. While Helms may have been the most prominent, his rhetoric typified the line taken by all the candidates supported with NCPAC funding. The "homosexual movement," he said, "threatens the strength and survival of the American family."

The hypocrisy of NCPAC's gay-bashing campaigns was further underscored by the presence of Arthur Finkelstein, the pollster who had been among its founders and who profited hugely from its fundraising as a consultant to its candidates. Finkelstein had a secret life, too. He was a closeted homosexual who lived with a man whose identity he concealed by registering in hotels under false names and never permitting himself to be photographed. It was Dolan who raised money for the gay-bashing ads, but Finkelstein who oversaw their production and media placement, earning a percentage at every turn. As he churned out homophobic propaganda, Finkelstein and his partner Donald Curiale enjoyed a lavish lifestyle with their two adopted daughters among the horse-and-hunt set in Ipswich, an affluent town on the Massachusetts coast. Eventually, they married.

The sanctimonious cruelty of right-wing "pro-family" ideology would play out again and again with the exposure of closeted antigay homosexuals in the conservative movement. So often did these scandals erupt on the Republican right that they became a political cliché—and yet the party base, especially white evangelical Christians, continued to follow like sheep and, most importantly, to send money. As for Dolan, despite the front erected by colleagues and friends, his sexual preference was scarcely a deep secret. In Washington's gay community, the truth about him was suppressed from becoming public knowledge by a taboo against involuntary "outing." They all knew while pretending not to know.

Well before his death, however, the "rumors" cited by New Hampshire senator Gordon Humphrey, a Republican he had helped to elect and who unequivocally despised gay people, had spread throughout the conservative movement and the Republican Party as well. For his part, Dolan denied those stories, including whispers that he had AIDS. When he resigned from NCPAC six months before he died, he falsely claimed to be suffering from anemia and diabetes.

Maintaining the profitable grift of NCPAC in the face of Terry Dolan's sad death demanded a truly stupendous effort of denial. Nothing captured that deceit more pointedly than the way he was ushered out of this world, in not one but two separate Washington memorial services. At the first, hosted by his family in a Dominican seminary, gay-baiting Republican luminaries like Humphrey, Senator Orrin Hatch of Utah, and former White House communications chief Pat Buchanan eulogized his service to the conservative cause—without any mention of his sexual identity or the cause of his death. The second, held in a local cathedral by a few dozen friends, was officiated by a well-known gay-friendly priest who had ministered to Dolan during his illness. Quite a few of his friends were too fearful to attend the more honest service, which even his brother Tony, a Reagan White House speechwriter, shunned.

Dominated by cynical figures like Viguerie, Dolan, Stone, and Finkelstein, the double-dealing conservative movement had been corroded to its core. Policy concerns and debate were supplanted by the deployment of "issues" designed for emotional manipulation, not legislation. Even such bedrock right-wing principles as limited government had proved expendable—because there was simply too much money to be made in Washington's company town of lobbyists. Feeding deep in the murk of what came to be known as "the swamp" were the same ideological con artists who had vowed to clean it all up.

6

Feeding the "Conservative" Hogs

The animating principle of the Reagan administration, as advertised by the publicists of the New Right, was its zeal for conservative reform of government across every agency and function. The determination to undo decades of Democratic rule in Washington—and the welfare state that it had spawned—was expressed concretely in a massive set of policy recommendations issued by the Heritage Foundation, then the capital's premier right-wing think tank, and titled *Mandate for Leadership*. With the blessing of Edwin Meese III, top adviser to Ronald Reagan since the latter's two terms as governor of California, the new Republican cabinet adopted Heritage's three thousand pages of specific plans as their official policy blueprint, covering everything from urban "enterprise zones," tax cuts, and acquisition of a modernized air force bomber to reductions in food stamps and school lunches. The blitz of proposals and schedules lent an air of intellectual energy and ambition to the Republican Right, suddenly touted as the "party of ideas." Within the administration's first year, boasted the Reagan White House, more than half of the Heritage policies were already on their way to implementation.

Well before the anniversary of Reagan's inauguration, however, Americans got a bracing glimpse of Republican governance as it really existed, rather than on the pages of a glossy think tank brochure. In the fall of 1981, word began to leak of a stunning story in *The Atlantic* magazine about the most important figure in the White House, aside from the president himself. In "The Education of David Stockman," *Washington Post* reporter William Greider revealed in Stockman's own words the deceptions and delusions at the core of the administration's economic program, which was itself so central to the Reagan presidency.

When Reagan named Stockman, a young Republican congressman from Michigan, to head the supremely powerful Office of Management and Budget, his sudden ascent was hailed as a triumph for "supply-side economics." By slashing taxes, spending, and regulations, according to the self-styled supply-siders, a titanic wave of growth would not only lift every American's income but produce more tax revenue than before. Contrary to what had seemed obvious for decades if not centuries, they argued that cutting tax rates would create surpluses rather than deficits.

To make a long story short, this scheme did not work out as envisioned by the ideologues. And the narrative of events as related by Stockman raised hard questions about whether anyone in power had ever honestly believed in the supply-side mythology. When the hard budget numbers showed alarming deficits rather than gleaming surpluses—which portended grave consequences in financial markets—those numbers were fudged or concealed. Equally disturbing was the cynical way that Republican special interests, the wealthy few inhabiting the corporate and financial sectors, had used supply-side rhetoric to camouflage their customary pursuit of self-enrichment at the public expense.

Under the new Reaganite dispensation, everyone supported or remunerated by federal expenditures ought to have been treated alike and denuded of their entitlements for the greater economic good—whether they were oil executives glomming tax advantages or single mothers surviving on food stamps. But the world worked that way only in the supply-side fantasy. In real life, as Stockman confessed to Greider, the markup of Reagan's monumental tax legislation represented a triumph of corporate power, not smaller government—and a brisk resumption of business as usual, with Republicans seeking to cut taxes for their wealthiest constituents while screwing everyone else. What was proclaimed to be a populist departure from traditional conservatism turned out, on closer examination, to be nothing but the same old order of privilege.

During a series of breakfast interviews at the Hay-Adams hotel near the White House, Stockman explained how the exciting buzzwords of Reaganomics were designed to deceive: "It's kind of hard to sell 'trickle down,' so the supply-side formula was the only way to get a tax policy that was really 'trickle down.' Supply side is trickle-down theory." In short, a brazen bait-and-switch on the white working-class voters, those "Reagan Democrats," who thought of "trickle down" as a rich snob urinating on them.

The kindest interpretation of Stockman's blunt confessional is that he and his cohort, including Reagan, were deceiving themselves as well as the nation. The failure of their theories was exposed in the form of unprecedented deficits, gross inequality, and growing unemployment. In its futile bids to reduce the deficit, the administration proposed further and deeper cuts in domestic spending; in perhaps the most infamous example, the conservative bureaucrats proposed to reduce the cost of subsidized school lunches by redefining ketchup as a "vegetable," even as the Pentagon budget continued to swell. The smiling face of Reaganism turned upside down into a hostile grimace.

But as Stockman himself observed, only those who couldn't engage lobbyists and dole out political donations were as disadvantaged as those hungry schoolchildren. For the monied and sophisticated denizens of Washington, the "supply side" moment was an unprecedented bonanza. Special deals brokered by both Republicans and Democrats smoothed the final passage of the tax cut bill, with big gifts to oil-lease holders and real estate investors.

No political virgin, Stockman had stopped concealing his disenchantment. While in Congress, for instance, he had routinely taken credit among his rural constituents for the same programs and projects he had opposed in Washington. "I went around and cut all the ribbons," he confided to Greider, "and they never knew that I voted against the damn programs." (Decades later, Republicans would present the same duplicitous pantomime when they voted to kill President

Biden's pandemic relief and infrastructure packages—and then issued press releases claiming credit for the benefits and projects that arrived months later.) Yet Stockman said that the eruption of avarice had astonished even him as he watched business lobbyists swarming the Capitol in the months after Reagan took office. "Do you realize the greed that came to the forefront?" he asked in a tone of shock. "The hogs were really feeding. The greed level, the level of opportunism, just got out of control." Lying just below the optimistic glint of Reaganism was a more candid expression of the Republican zeitgeist, articulated succinctly by Gordon Gekko, fictional financier and antihero of the hit movie *Wall Street*.

"Greed is good," Gekko said.

IF THERE WAS a singular, compact, and pure example of the avaricious excess that suddenly swept through Washington in the Reagan era, it was the little clique of ambitious young men who had founded NCPAC, the National Conservative Political Action Committee, just a few years earlier. Having helped to elect not only a conservative Republican president but also a Senate Republican majority at the dawn of the 1980s, the NCPAC gang swiftly adopted a new and far more profitable identity. The three kingpins of the operation—Charlie Black, Roger Stone, and Paul Manafort—reconstituted themselves as a wholly different kind of consulting firm that would provide both campaign and lobbying services, broadening their reach to encompass Republican politicians of all stripes, corporate clients, and even tin-pot foreign dictators.

Black, Manafort, and Stone became the true founders of what their own "populist" candidates and a certain unsavory real estate client mogul from Manhattan would come to denounce as "the swamp"—that nebulous nexus of legal graft and everyday corruption in a capital city overrun with unscrupulous special interests and their highly paid lobbyists. (Black, Manafort, and Stone later added Peter Kelly, a former Democratic National Committee finance chair, as a partner, to lend a bipartisan sheen and attract clients who were Democrats, and became known as BMSK.) When they heard Donald Trump's righteous vow to "drain the swamp," a line first uttered during the 2016 presidential campaign, Roger Stone and Paul Manafort must have been amused.

As a New Jersey casino owner seeking favors from government, Trump had been among the earliest clients of Black, Manafort, and Stone. Trump had been brought into Stone's orbit by their mutual friend and Trump lawyer Roy Cohn, the former counsel for Senator Joseph McCarthy who represented many powerful New Yorkers. Few industries required as much lobbying clout as the highly regulated gambling business, where Trump obtained state and local approval for his Atlantic City, New Jersey, operations despite his longtime connections with organized crime, and competed with Native gaming companies controlled by the Interior Department. The New York developer hired the firm to prevent the expansion of East Coast Indian casinos that might draw customers away from his Atlantic City gambling dens. He also used BMSK to exercise its clout to alter the scheduled operations of Palm Beach International Airport, whose jet noise he complained was disturbing members at his Mar-a-Lago beach club.

In Washington, from their lavishly appointed offices overlooking the Potomac, Stone and his partners quickly built a network of influence and patronage that overshadowed Washington's traditional lobbyists, who had mostly operated out of law firms. While Black and Manafort both had law degrees, Stone didn't even have a college diploma; he had dropped out after they all met in the College Republicans. Yet none of that mattered because BMSK represented a new style of influence peddling. After decades of Democratic dominance in both houses of Congress, the advent of Republican rule in both the White House and the Senate opened up lucrative opportunities that BMSK swiftly exploited. As *The Washington Post*'s Thomas Byrne Edsall explained, even lobbying firms with long-standing ties to Republican officeholders were tainted as "old establishment" and lacked the ideological right-wing outlook of the arriviste Reaganites.

But the BMSK partners had worked in Reagan's campaign and helped to elect key members of the new Senate majority through NCPAC. Ethical questions about lobbying the officials whose campaigns they had run did not give them the slightest pause. They scoffed at the apparent conflicts of interest and insisted that they were merely providing a service to their clients. "I think there is an advantage to the client and to the person in a position of authority to deal with someone they know and trust," Black blandly assured Edsall. BMSK instantly monetized their political network and signed big contracts with corporations and industries seeking goodies from the Reagan administration. Selling access gained them monthly retainers that could then top $20,000—or roughly $70,000 in 2023 dollars. The firm's partners were each clearing the equivalent of over $1.5 million annually.

Not all their former comrades in the conservative movement were impressed. To Paul Weyrich, who had worked closely with Stone and Black at NCPAC and helped to launch the Heritage Foundation, the whole enterprise reeked of opportunism. Regarding Stone, Weyrich said: "Every meeting I've had with the guy, I wanted to wash my hands three times afterwards." Weyrich spoke as a true believer in the conservative cause and a genuinely devout traditionalist Catholic. Stone claimed to be conservative, too, and he professed to be a Catholic until years later when he proclaimed himself "born again" after being indicted for his crimes in the Trump era. Weyrich sensed that Stone and his partners worshipped only money and power.

An early client of BMSK was Rupert Murdoch and his News Corp, a media conglomerate that became synonymous with breaches of journalistic and business ethics, and indeed was eventually the target of police investigations into its criminality in the United Kingdom. (In full disclosure I should note that Murdoch personally tried to fire me more than once from *The Village Voice* when he owned the paper.) Unsurprisingly, the connection with Murdoch was also forged by Stone's mentor Roy Cohn. Other major corporations that signed up for BMSK's services included MacAndrews & Forbes, the huge holding company owned by billionaire Ronald Perelman; GTECH, the worldwide (and heavily regulated) gaming and lottery giant; the automakers Chrysler and Mitsubishi; various aerospace and defense corporations; Salomon Brothers, then one of the largest and most profitable New York investment banks; and the Tobacco Institute, always aiming to block federal restrictions on marketing of its deadly products to teenagers. Gambling, investment banking, big tobacco, broadcast media, and Pentagon contractors—a mosaic of special interests that epitomized "the swamp."

Soon millions poured into the firm's accounts from a different sort of clientele. Numerous authoritarian regimes overseas hired BMSK to lobby both the State Department and Congress to increase their shares of American taxpayer largesse. Indeed, the worse their human rights records, the more those foreign dictatorships required the kind of persuasion that lobbyists could exercise. The roster of murderous despots whose remittances enriched Stone, Manafort, and company ranged from Asia and Africa to South America, which eventually resulted in BMSK gaining a reputation as "the torturers' lobby." The firm's foreign clients included repressive and corrupt governments like those that ruled Kenya and Nigeria, which spent millions on BMSK lobbying and reaped tens of millions in US foreign assistance.

An even more dubious client was the government of the Bahamas, then overseen by Sir Lynden Oscar Pindling, who had led the country from British colonial rule to self-government two decades earlier. Pindling needed BMSK after NBC News investigative reporter Brian Ross exposed his ties to the Colombian drug lord Carlos Lehder, who had paid him millions in bribes to allow cocaine and marijuana shipments to pass through the Bahamas on the way to the United States. The Justice Department prosecutors who eventually sent Lehder to prison presented evidence at his trial to substantiate the bribery allegations against Pindling, the subject of much boasting by the cocaine baron himself. In a twenty-page proposal that pitched the firm's services to improve Pindling's image in Washington, BMSK hyped "personal knowledge" of ranking figures in the Reagan White House and State Department, and promised to "upgrade a backchannel relationship" that would protect the Bahamas from its critics in Congress, law enforcement, and the media.

Pindling had been democratically elected, but the same could not be said for most of the firm's prominent foreign clientele, which, over the ensuing decades, included such brutal and corrupt autocrats as Mobutu Sese Seko of Zaire, Sani Abacha of Nigeria, and Jonas Savimbi, the terrorist leader of the UNITA rebel movement in Angola. Often seen sporting a leopard-skin hat, Mobutu was one of the most notorious warlords on the African continent. His theft of Zaire's resources and cash reserves, including US aid, has been estimated at no less than $5 billion. Manafort could boast that the Reagan White House had hosted Mobutu on three state visits, during which President Reagan praised the murderous authoritarian's "good sense and good will." For those emollient words and kind treatment, Mobutu forked over at least a million dollars in consulting fees to BMSK.

As the principal opponent of a postcolonial Marxist regime in Angola, Savimbi and his UNITA movement benefited enormously from Cold War priorities. With his forces financed by the US to fight a decades-long civil war—prolonged by BMSK's lobbying tactics—Savimbi stole truckloads of blood diamonds, as well as at least $40 million in US aid money. Human rights organizations documented Savimbi's horrendous abuses, from "witch" burnings and massacres to torture and cannibalism. Excusing that record in Washington was expensive: UNITA paid BMSK as much as $50,000 per month.

In Asia, BMSK was deeply involved in defending the indefensible rule of Ferdinand Marcos, kleptocratic dictator of the Philippines, under the same "anti-communist" rubric. Having ordered the killing in broad daylight of his principal political opponent on an airport tarmac, while imprisoning and executing thousands of political dissidents, and presiding over a crooked government that enriched him and his cronies with billions in stolen wealth, Marcos needed the best public relations firm money could buy. He was paying $950,000 a year. The BMSK gang, with Manafort taking the lead, were deeply involved in promoting and protecting Marcos up until the day he was forced by his own army to flee Manila on a plane to Hawaii—bringing suitcases of cash and strongboxes of gold bars along for the trip.

Without naming Manafort, the Republican consultant Ed Rollins later suggested that he had absconded with as much as $10 million that Marcos had secretly dispatched to the Reagan campaign as an illegal campaign donation. "I delivered the suitcase with the cash personally to him, and helped get it out of the country," he quoted a Philippines congressman confessing. Rollins told *Politico*: "I knew the lobbyist well and I had no doubt the money was now in some offshore bank." He asked Reagan's campaign treasurer whether any foreign money ever made its way into the campaign. "Absolutely not," was the reply.

Senator Paul Laxalt of Nevada, a personal friend of Reagan assigned to deal with the Marcos problem, said when he learned about the $10 million: "Christ, now it all makes sense." He explained that Marcos believed Reagan had double-crossed him when the US began applying pressure on him.

"I gave Reagan $10 million. How can he do this to me?" Marcos whined to Laxalt. "I didn't know what the hell he was talking about," said Laxalt later. "Now I get it." As for Manafort, whose propensity for lying and stealing was eventually proved to a jury of his peers, he retorted that the Marcos story was "totally fiction." (Philippine investigators claimed that Marcos funneled up to $57 million into the 1980 and 1984 Reagan campaigns.)

In a 2016 podcast, Stone boasted that "Black, Manafort, Stone and Kelly lined up most of the dictators in the world that we could find," even as he sought to justify the sleazy business practices that enriched him and his partners. "Pro-Western dictators, of course," he added. "Dictators are in the eye of the beholder." That final sentence, like so much of what Stone says, was simply false—dictatorship isn't so hard to define—but the flip remark gave a premonition of his support for Donald Trump's assaults on democracy in the United States.

While Stone, Manafort, and their partners would always insist their work for unsavory rulers abroad represented a public service to Western security, it is in fact hard to see how the United States benefited from propping up dictatorships that stole US aid and tarnished America's reputation abroad. What cannot be doubted is that tainted wealth, much of it ripped off from US taxpayers, ended up in the accounts of BMSK. Life at the top of the lobbying food chain was easy and luxurious, flaunted by the partners in newspaper and magazine profiles that were good for business. Portraits of Stone would inevitably mention his foppish wardrobe, which included custom Alan Flusser suits and Patek Philippe watches, and such over-the-top affectations as suspenders, homburgs, and spats. At the age of thirty-three, after only five years in the consulting racket, he had acquired expensive homes in suburban

Virginia and on the Maryland shore as well as a Jaguar and a chauffeur-driven Mercedes.

"He wants very badly to be a swell," observed Marvin Liebman, the longtime conservative and critic of New Right decadence. Paul Weyrich snapped that Stone's clothes and shoes "rival those of Imelda Marcos."

Stone could scarcely keep up with Manafort, whose self-indulgence shocked even his profligate partners. In addition to the standard Mercedes and the usual town houses and beach houses, he would show up at super-luxury spots like the Hôtel de Crillon in Paris, after popping over on the supersonic Concorde—and bill a client for the "expense." Manafort's high flying expanded as the years went by, until he had accumulated tens of millions of dollars in real estate along the East Coast, from Trump Tower to Palm Beach, filled with top-shelf antiques and fine Oriental rugs. His closets bulged with ridiculously pricey suits and casual wear, including a rare ostrich jacket—all of which federal agents eventually cataloged in a tax evasion indictment. Nothing was too good for the right-wing "populist."

These preening displays naturally excited the envy of rivals and competitors, who raised questions about what, exactly, the BMSK clientele had received for those fat monthly retainers. Republican lobbyist and activist David Keene, longtime head of the American Conservative Union and founder of the Conservative Political Action Conference, described the firm's modus operandi to *The Washington Post* with a touch of mockery. Billed as a "friend" of Stone, he noted that the firm's corporate clients were paying to maintain "access" to Reagan administration officials. "The further away a client is and the bigger he is," Keene explained, "the more likely he is to think that somewhere in Washington there's a button and if you push it, everything's going to be all right. He thinks that's the way the world works. You know there's probably nothing you can do for him. . . . If you're trying to get rich fast, that's not a bad way to do it. The dirty secret is, there is no button."

Major corporations like Murdoch's News Corp and GTECH would hire BMSK for a year or two, but they let the contracts lapse when no fabulous results materialized. The foreign dictators, far from Washington and largely ignorant of its realities, continued to pay and pay, using their people's stolen wealth or simply recycling US aid money into the consultants' accounts. Meanwhile, the BMSK partners—and their political consulting partner Lee Atwater, who ran Vice President George H. W. Bush's presidential campaign in 1988 and rose to lead the Republican National Committee—continued to oversee GOP political campaigns from the presidency to the Senate, ensuring their sway over congressional offices, federal agencies, and the White House. They ran campaigns vowing to slash foreign aid, reform wasteful spending, rein in gambling and other sinful businesses—none of which affected their lobbying practices, which junked all such promises without a second glance.

In his unpublished memoir, unearthed by *The New Yorker*'s Jane Mayer, Atwater offered a candid assessment of politics that would enlighten anyone who wondered how he and his cronies could pursue careers that were so brazenly dishonest. "I've always thought running for office is a bunch of bullshit. Being in office is even more bullshit. It really is bullshit," he wrote. "I'm proud of the fact that I understand how much BS it is." When Atwater was dying from brain cancer, he apologized for his political dirty tricks and racist smears. But Stone and Manafort never displayed a twinge of shame.

AT THE OUTSET of Ronald Reagan's presidency, he enunciated the guiding credo of his administration. "Government is not the solution to our problem," he said in his inaugural address. "Government is the problem." It was a prescient introduction to the Reagan era, though perhaps not in the sense he intended. The Reaganites' faith in the private sector's capacity to regulate itself, along with their disdain for many necessary functions of the modern state, encouraged grifting at all levels by cronies and crooks. Marked by burgeoning incompetence, corruption, and white-collar crime, Reagan's tenure saw a scandal epidemic unmatched before or since, until Donald Trump ascended to power a quarter century later.

Somehow Reagan's sunny disposition—and a pliant White House press corps—ensured that his reputation never descended to the level of earlier presidents associated with gross corruption. Most Americans didn't quite grasp how many Reagan administration officials were indicted, convicted, or expelled from their posts on ethics charges between 1981 and 1989. The evidence was fully available, with thousands of news articles that described the influence peddling, bribery, fraud, illegal lobbying, and myriad abuses that engulfed the Environmental Protection Agency, the Department of Housing and Urban Development, the Nuclear Regulatory Commission, the Justice Department, the State Department, the CIA, and the Pentagon, to name just the most notorious venues. But Americans' historical amnesia, a national affliction, protected the Reaganite reputation.

Estimates of the Reagan administration's venality depend on specific criteria: indictments, convictions, ethics investigations, resignations in disgrace. When the Poynter Institute's PolitiFact website compared the ethical records of recent administrations in 2019, its researchers found thirty-three indictments that occurred while Reagan was president, a handful more than Nixon's twenty-eight Watergate indictments. (Bill Clinton only had two, and Barack Obama saw zero officials indicted.) In his 1991 book, *Sleepwalking Through History: America in the Reagan Years*, journalist Haynes Johnson derived a broader statistic: "By the end of his term, 138 Reagan administration officials had been convicted, had been indicted, or had been the subject of official investigations for official misconduct and/or criminal violations." For a paper delivered to the annual meeting of the American Society of Criminology in 1992, Professor Frank E. Hagan, who wrote a widely used criminology textbook, calculated that "actual crime and wrongdoing during the Reagan administration exceeded that of previous presidents, including Nixon, Harding, Grant, and Buchanan. Between 1980 and 1988, over 200 individuals from the Reagan administration came under either ethical or criminal investigation."

The plunder so pervasive under Reagan—who seemed personally oblivious to the thieving that surrounded him and never profited from corruption himself—reached from the White House all the way down to the regional offices of the federal government, and beyond US borders to Iran, Nicaragua, Israel, and Switzerland. The scandal that came closest to toppling Reagan, and at one point threatened to culminate in his impeachment, was Iran-Contra, a highly complex web of schemes usually boiled down to a pair of illegal transactions. With the approval of top National Security Council and CIA officials, a marine lieutenant colonel named Oliver North and his coconspirators in and out of government sold missiles to the enemy regime of Iran—and then diverted some of the profit from those sales to finance the Contras, a rebel group in Nicaragua seeking to overthrow that country's communist government. (This dubious plan supposedly included a deal to release seven American hostages held by an Islamist terror group in Lebanon, which never came to fruition.)

While the attempt by top officials to subvert congressional authority with covert operations and funding was baldly unconstitutional and autocratic, Ollie North and his cohorts insisted that their motives were purely "patriotic" after their activities were exposed. An ideologue who became popular on the Far Right as a militaristic icon, North could not quite conceal the greed and grifting that pervaded the entire affair.

The first of North's circle to plead guilty to federal crimes was Carl "Spitz" Channell—in his case, charges of charitable fraud and money laundering. Unsurprisingly, Channell had once served as the chief fundraiser for NCPAC. He registered a couple of conservative nonprofit groups that collected millions for the Contra cause from elderly and mostly female right-wingers and then illegally used the tax-deductible proceeds. With North's assistance, the dapper Channell arranged visits to the White House and presidential thank-you notes for the "blue rinse lady donors," as he derisively dubbed them. He even bestowed nicknames on several of his favorite marks, dubbing them "Hamhocks," "Mrs. Malleable," and "Dogface," among other affectionate sobriquets, while lying to them about the tax deductions they supposedly could claim for funding his endeavors.

Like his former boss Terry Dolan, Channell was a closeted gay man—and he found a way to finance his dalliances with donations from conservatives who might not have appreciated how he used their money. Back then, NPR reported that his organization, known grandly as the National Endowment for the Preservation of Liberty, had diverted some of the money it had raised to "male companions of the group's gay executives, including Channell, for unspecified consulting services." Channell's rip-offs amounted to small change, however, when the full scope of the Iran-Contra scam came to light. The network of former military and intelligence officers who had facilitated North's plans, along with various international operatives and rogues, siphoned off millions from their covert sales of US weapons into secret Swiss bank accounts and other "investments." In coded communications, North's associates—former air force major general Richard Secord, shady business executive Albert Hakim, ex–intelligence officer Thomas Clines, and several other confederates—referred to their operations as "the Enterprise."

At every turn, in public testimony and in court, the Iran-Contra gang wrapped themselves in the flag. They portrayed themselves as secret warriors against Soviet imperialism who had defied a feckless Congress to safeguard national security. In reality, they had acted as lawless brigands, scandalously violating constitutional norms to pursue a bloody and unpopular policy—and they had done so in pursuit of personal gain. Lawrence Walsh, the independent counsel who prosecuted North and his cronies on behalf of the United States, had no illusions about their motives. In his final report on the case, Walsh noted: "In 1986, the Enterprise received $30.3 million from the sale of US Government property [missiles and other weaponry] to Iran . . . Only $12.2 million was returned to the United States. Direct expenses of the Enterprise were approximately $2.1 million. Thus, the amount of US Government funds illegally held by the Enterprise as its own was approximately $16 million."

A significant portion of those funds went to the Contras, whose leadership included drug smugglers and other criminals, while another chunk ended up in Swiss accounts controlled by Secord, Hakim, and Clines, not all of which could be accurately traced. Records and testimony showed that Secord alone skimmed as much as $2 million in 1985 and 1986. At least $16,000 went to purchase a security system for North's private home, and as much as $200,000 reportedly financed a fund for the lieutenant colonel's children.

Secord, Hakim, and their associates employed a variety of subterfuges to hide the money and conceal their operations. They created various shell companies and accounts, partly to evade tax authorities but also to hide their enormous profits on weapon sales from the Contra leadership. They also insisted that outside donors, including Saudi royals, send funding to the Enterprise's Swiss accounts, rather than to the Contra leaders, so they could continue to skim big profits. Ultimately, all the conspirators, including North, were caught in brazen lies about the money to Congress and Walsh, not to mention the IRS.

Federal courts overturned North's conviction on three felony charges because the prosecution had used testimony he had given to Congress while under a grant of immunity. Secord pleaded guilty to perjury, agreed to cooperate with Walsh, and received two years' probation. Hakim also cooperated and got two years' probation and a small fine. Clines was convicted of four felony counts and sentenced to four years in prison. Reagan escaped any consequences for this misadventure, as did Vice President George H. W. Bush and CIA director William Casey, all of whom had prior knowledge of North's illegal acts.

As scandals go, the Iran-Contra affair was among the most colorful and consequential, but far from the costliest. Around the same time that a Lebanese newspaper first exposed the secret US arms sales to Iran, Americans began to learn of an entirely different Reagan scandal involving a Bronx manufacturing firm called Wedtech. As a small and supposedly minority-owned maker of defense equipment and parts, Wedtech had received fat military contracts and special deals. But as an investigation by then US attorney Rudolph Giuliani revealed, the firm's success was greased by bribery of local and federal officials, including National Guard officers, as well as members of Congress; its corrupting reach snaked into the Reagan White House, where political director Lyn Nofziger and public liaison chief Elizabeth Dole helped arrange up to $250 million in no-bid contracts for Wedtech. Two members of Congress, two state legislators, a National Guard general, and several others went to prison for Wedtech-related crimes.

Before Wedtech filed for bankruptcy in late 1986, it had started double billing the Pentagon and forged an estimated $6 billion worth of government invoices. But for Reagan, the most embarrassing aspect of Wedtech's fall concerned Ed Meese, one of the president's closest advisers and a conservative icon in his own right. The Wedtech scheme began to come apart shortly after Reagan elevated Meese from presidential counselor in the White House to head the Justice Department as attorney general.

Investigators uncovered a series of transactions connecting Meese to the scandal, through his personal financial adviser, his former White House deputy, and a personal friend, E. Bob Wallach, who had lobbied Meese to obtain special treatment for Wedtech. Responding to the firm's lobbyists, including Nofziger and Wallach, Meese had pressured the Pentagon on behalf of Wedtech. Around the same time, he had earned a quick $40,000 from investments with W. Franklyn Chinn, a personal financial adviser who happened to be a consultant and later director of Wedtech. Meese failed to follow federal ethics rules in reporting these transactions—and was referred for investigation, along with Nofziger, by an independent counsel.

Although independent counsel James McKay never brought any charges against Meese, due to "insufficient evidence" of illegal activity, his report was nonetheless damning. Wallach and Chinn had provided various financial benefits to Meese, and Meese had assisted Wedtech in obtaining at least $32 million in federal contracts. Finding Meese habitually indifferent to the appearance of ethical impropriety and lacking judgment in dealing with friends and colleagues on official matters, McKay referred the attorney general to the Justice Department's Office of Professional Responsibility for further investigation. By then, Meese's ethically dubious conduct had provoked deputy attorney general Arnold Burns and associate attorney general William Weld, who headed the department's criminal division, to resign in protest, along with four of their aides. They had quit because the White House refused to force Meese to resign. In July 1987, Burns and Weld told a congressional committee that Meese's unethical conduct had permanently stained the Justice Department. Meese resigned in disgrace a few days later, still insisting he had done nothing wrong.

In the same investigation, former White House political director Lyn Nofziger was found guilty on three counts of illegally lobbying Meese and other Reagan officials. But an appeals court dominated by

Reagan-appointed judges overturned his conviction because prosecutors had not proved that he knew his actions were illegal.

Implicating Meese, Nofziger, two members of Congress, and other officials highlighted Wedtech's criminality, but that scandal was only one facet of far broader corruption that infected the Pentagon during Reagan's massive defense buildup. After a small defense contractor complained that a consultant had tried to sell him confidential Defense Department information, the FBI opened an investigation dubbed Operation Ill Wind that continued for nearly eight years. Using wiretaps and other methods often employed against organized crime suspects, the case resulted in convictions of a long roster of government officials, defense consultants, and corporate executives, as well as the brother of New York senator Alfonse D'Amato, a prominent GOP lobbyist. Such major corporations as United Technologies, LTV Aerospace, and Grumman Corporation were also swept into its net, paying hundreds of millions in fines.

Sleaze also infected the Environmental Protection Agency, whose very mission was despised by the right-wing ideologues Reagan appointed to run it. Dozens of EPA officials resigned during his first term because they had violated federal law, often by favoring industrial polluters they had formerly served as lobbyists or consultants. When the Reaganites weren't blocking cleaner air or water, they were misusing massive sums to favor Republican officials seeking reelection. Ignoring science, they directed Superfund money, intended to restore the most toxic sites in the country, on a partisan basis.

The House Energy Committee's subcommittee on oversight found that assistant EPA administrator Rita Lavelle, a former employee of chemical and aerospace companies, "was obsessed with orchestrating activities in the Superfund program for partisan political purposes. . . . In her efforts to influence election campaigns, Ms. Lavelle circumvented established agency procedures and placed sensitive negotiations on an 'election track' without regard for the [environmental] consequences." Notwithstanding Reagan's attempt to protect agency officials with dubious claims of executive privilege, Lavelle was eventually convicted on four counts of perjury. The agency's illegal stonewalling of

Congress also led to the resignation of EPA administrator Anne Gorsuch Burford (the mother of Trump-appointed Supreme Court justice Neil Gorsuch).

Egregious as the EPA's mismanagement proved to be, the looting of the Department of Housing and Urban Development by crooked officials and lobbyists showed that the Republican devotion to "small government" evaporated whenever big money could be grabbed. Once upon a time, NCPAC's Terry Dolan had boldly described the New Right's ideal federal budget, which would include nothing for housing or any other domestic needs: "99 percent for defense—keep America strong—and 1 percent on delivering the mail. That's it. Leave us alone." When Republican operatives and lobbyists saw their party gain control of the multibillion-dollar HUD budget, however, their philosophical objection to public spending suddenly vanished—a moment that recalled Ayn Rand cashing her Social Security checks, except that the HUD swindlers were corrupt crooks and not a misguided old crank.

Reagan's HUD secretary, Samuel Pierce—a Black New York Republican whose name the president never seemed able to remember—spent most of his eight years in office cutting budgets and laying off staff, rather than providing housing, yet there was plenty of money around to feed the Republican grifters. They targeted the department's moderate rehabilitation, or "mod rehab," program, under which local governments selected private developers to renovate buildings for affordable housing. In fact, however, the selection of projects became centralized in the HUD secretary's office under the control of Deborah Gore Dean—a top assistant to Pierce and partisan Republican who happened to be the stepdaughter of former attorney general John Mitchell.

Dean was far more candid than Pierce, who had claimed the selection of projects wasn't political. She regarded mod rehab as a "discretionary program" subject to partisan influence. Subsequent investigations revealed a massive feeding frenzy, as connected Republicans bellied up to the HUD buffet on behalf of developers who paid them fat consulting fees. Near the top of the food chain was a gang of former HUD officials and Pierce associates, who had formed a consulting outfit after leaving the department. They won subsidies for thousands of housing units that amounted to tens of millions of dollars—and then either refused to testify in congressional investigations or took the Fifth Amendment. That included Pierce, the first cabinet secretary to claim protection against self-incrimination since the Teapot Dome scandal in the twenties.

The boodlers who had worked for HUD at least possessed some knowledge and experience with housing—a description that didn't apply to the many higher-profile political hacks who showed up with their palms open.

Frederick Bush, who was deputy finance chairman for George H. W. Bush's 1988 presidential campaign (and not a relative, despite their surnames), was allowed to skim off $268,000 from a grant to Puerto Rico, although he did no work on it. Bill Taylor, a member of the Republican National Committee and former state chairman of the Florida Republican Party, formed a consulting firm that raked in more than $500,000 in cash and shares for a hundred hours of lobbying on projects in Florida, Georgia, and Texas. He used his Republican stationery to push projects to HUD officials and boasted about it when called to testify in the congressional investigation. "I find nothing wrong with letting people know I am on the RNC," he said. "I'm very proud of the fact." Representative Christopher Shays, a Connecticut Republican on the Oversight Committee that probed HUD, told Taylor, "I wish you were a Democrat because I am embarrassed. Instead of representing your party, you cashed in on your party."

So did James Watt, Reagan's former Interior secretary, a man known for his outlandish libertarian views who had nevertheless set up a lobbying shop when he left the cabinet under fire. Watt pulled down more than $400,000 in consulting fees for a few phone calls and a thank-you note to Pierce, but insisted during congressional testimony that his lobbying work had been "legal, moral, ethical, and effective." At the same time, he admitted that "the system is flawed" because wired hacks like himself were gorging on big fees. Watt clearly had a point, because he—and more than a dozen other former officials who had dined on Reagan's HUD buffet—found themselves facing prosecution by an independent counsel after the congressional investigations concluded. It was obvious that many of the well-connected witnesses had lied, while others had conspired to rig grants for themselves or their clients. Although several of Pierce's former aides were convicted of felonies and even did time, the former HUD secretary skated off without any charges. As for Watt, although he was originally indicted on twenty-four counts that included perjury and obstruction of justice, he ultimately pleaded down to a misdemeanor, getting five years' probation and a $5,000 fine.

The most glaring miscarriage of justice in the HUD scandal involved a certain lobbyist who had helped to elect Reagan and boasted connections to the top Republicans in the Senate, the House, and every potential presidential nominee: Paul Manafort. Based solely on his influence over Deborah Gore Dean, Manafort earned $326,000 to win funding for a mod rehab and rent subsidy deal in Seabrook, New Jersey, where town authorities didn't even want the proposed project. They thought its $43 million cost for 325 residential units was a scandalous expenditure, but Manafort succeeded in lobbying them as well. The result was not only that the lobbyist earned about $1,000 an hour—or about $2,500 an hour in current dollars—but then glommed a 20 percent share of the project itself for his own development company.

The mayor of the township where the project was located told Congress, "I think it's a horrible waste of taxpayers' money. People in our community are outraged." But it was an especially sweet deal for Manafort, who got advance notice that HUD would approve financing for the Seabrook project and then purchased his share for $4.4 million, two weeks before the agency's formal announcement.

Testifying before the House Government Oversight subcommittee investigating the scandal, Manafort righteously declared, "We worked the system as it existed. I don't think we did anything illegal or improper." Moments later, he added thoughtfully, "For the sake of debate, you could call this influence peddling." None of the prosecutions touched Manafort, who went on to far more ambitious scams and schemes around the world. Reaping a massive reward for a wasteful project that nobody wanted, a bonanza awarded for little work only because he knew the right Republicans, Manafort was a case study in Reaganism's perversion.

The late conservative wit P. J. O'Rourke captured the desultory end of the Reagan era when he wrote, "Republicans are the party that says government doesn't work—and then they get elected and prove it." What O'Rourke didn't mention then was how the conservatives behind Reaganism had made government into a conduit for personal profit, even as they promised to shrink the leviathan state. Inevitably, that grifting mentality perverted every corner of conservatism—including the bombastic moralists of the religious Right.

7

Profits (and Prophets) Without Honor

Despite the scandals that heralded the end of his presidency, Ronald Reagan would long remain a venerated name among Republicans—not for reasons of policy or principle so much as branding. Beyond the usual plutocratic emphasis on tax cuts for the wealthy and well-connected, few of his administration's achievements seemed to motivate his partisan heirs. What did persist—and indeed metastasize—was the energized and organized religious Right, which rose to prominence in American political culture during the Reagan era.

Yet much of what everyone knows about Reagan and the religious Right is false, beginning with the movement's claimed origin as a spiritual uprising in response to the Supreme Court's *Roe v. Wade* decision legitimizing abortion rights in 1973. The true story of the movement's genesis is considerably less inspirational—and can be traced back to a familiar figure, the direct-mail entrepreneur Richard Viguerie, and the cohort that helped him to establish the New Right as a prelude to Reagan's election.

In spring 1979, Viguerie and his associate Paul Weyrich—who had overseen the creation of the National Conservative Political Action Committee (NCPAC), the Heritage Foundation, and numerous other "movement" organizations—went down to Lynchburg, Virginia, from Washington to meet with Rev. Jerry Falwell, a local pastor with a rapidly developing national profile. Some observers had suggested that

Falwell, whose Thomas Road Baptist Church was among the fastest-growing evangelical congregations in the country, might be "the next Billy Graham," although he lacked the devotional gravitas, stately presence, and splendid baritone voice of the renowned minister.

Despite his Catholic upbringing, Viguerie had deep insight into the evangelical community, which he saw as an enormous potential market for the New Right's divisive political messaging—and fundraising. Christians of varied denominations, but especially the fundamentalist variety, had long proved themselves vulnerable to cons and scams of all kinds, from faith healing to promises of prosperity through prayer. In the hands of a figure like Viguerie, politicized religion could become yet another powerful messaging channel to relieve the gullible of their cash. Over the ensuing decades, the religious Right would engulf the Republican Party and the conservative movement. It would become indistinguishable from the disreputable preachers who exploited the faithful to become fabulously rich and politically cynical, as they eventually proved in their idolatry of that ultimate golden calf, Donald J. Trump.

More than two decades before he met with Falwell, Viguerie had worked with Rev. Billy James Hargis, who possessed only a diploma-mill divinity degree, to rake in copious donations from the Oklahoma preacher's radio ministry. At the same time, Hargis had used his Christian Crusade outfit to promote a toxic combination of extreme anti-communist paranoia and hostility to the civil rights movement, which it denounced as an instrument of leftist subversion. His direct-mail operation and broadcast appeals had hauled in tidy profits that allowed Hargis to enjoy a big lifestyle. But despite his occasional incursions into national politics, his operation never achieved the scale that Viguerie imagined, even as fundamentalist and evangelical churches expanded across the country.

In the wake of the civil rights movement—and in reaction to federal enforcement of school integration across the South—many of those churches had established "Christian academies" as a segregated option for their lily-white congregations. Among the most successful of those white Southern ministers was the portly and ingratiating Falwell. His church's Sunday services furnished the backdrop for *The*

Old-Time Gospel Hour, a lucrative radio and TV broadcast that Falwell had inaugurated in 1956. Equally impressive was Falwell's use of the most advanced methods available to monetize his sermons. Just three years before meeting Viguerie, he had hired a Massachusetts-based marketing firm, Epsilon Data Management, whose executives set up an effective data management and mailing system for Thomas Road that brought in millions and then tens of millions of dollars. While Falwell was the first televangelist to hire Epsilon, other major evangelical pastors, including Pat Robertson, Rex Humbard, and Jim Bakker, soon followed his lead.

Falwell had first drawn national attention as an opponent of civil rights with an infamous sermon titled "Ministers and Marches," in which he directly attacked Dr. Martin Luther King Jr. for exploiting Christianity and associating with alleged communists. (Indeed, Falwell insinuated that King might well be a communist himself.) "Preachers," he intoned, "are not called to be politicians but to be soul winners." At a time when Billy Graham was donating money to bail King out from Southern jails, Falwell had castigated pastors who dared to oppose segregation and support civil rights, which he ever so wittily dubbed "civil wrongs." His segregated Lynchburg Christian Academy, founded in 1967, pulled in plenty of revenue and, like Hargis before him, he regarded the federal government's intervention in civil rights as yet another assault on the faithful by the international communist conspiracy. When the Justice Department finally got around to scrutinizing the tax exemptions of those segregation academies in 1978, under President Jimmy Carter, himself a Southern Baptist, right-wing evangelicals like Falwell were outraged.

Viguerie's associate Paul Weyrich, an extremely conservative Catholic who by then had been trying to draw evangelical ministers into the political Right for years, was slightly sardonic in recalling why that effort finally succeeded. "What galvanized the Christian community was not abortion, school prayer, or the Equal Rights Amendment," he said years later. "What changed their minds was Jimmy Carter's intervention against the Christian schools trying to deny them tax-exempt status on the basis of so-called de facto segregation." As Weyrich surely knew, the very conservative Southern Baptist Convention had by then affirmed women's right to abortion on at least three occasions: in a resolution passed at its 1971 convention, two years before the *Roe* decision; in another resolution at its 1974 convention the year after; and then at its 1976 convention, the year Carter was elected.

By the time Weyrich and Viguerie went to see Falwell, both were also aware that the evangelical community was erupting in fury over a 1978 court decision voiding the tax exemption of Bob Jones University, the nation's most notorious segregated "Christian" educational institution. Rather than seeing their tax exemption as the federal subsidy that it was, evangelical leaders regarded it as an entitlement of their faith—and saw the government's intrusion on their racist practices as a violation of religious freedom. Having expanded and renamed his original "seg academy" as Liberty Baptist College (which he had ambitions to transform into Liberty University), Falwell felt personally implicated in the Bob Jones case.

For decades evangelical leaders had resisted the urge to fully engage with the political sphere, which they saw as worldly, sinful, and unsafe for the faithful. Falwell had gone further than most in expounding his extremely right-wing political views—while pretending to be above politics—as he had done during the civil rights era. In the bicentennial year of 1976, he had launched a national "I Love America" tour with his school's choral group, visiting more than forty cities (including Little Rock, Arkansas, where none other than Bill Clinton, then the state's Democratic governor, joined his rally on the steps of the state capitol). But that tour had been a fundraising gimmick, not a political campaign.

The pitch from Viguerie and Weyrich on that spring afternoon was simple. Using his national television platform and evangelical connections, Falwell would launch a new ecumenical conservative movement, to be dubbed "the Moral Majority," while Viguerie would put together a state-of-the-art fundraising operation and Weyrich would develop a political and legislative program. They aimed to build a powerful religious Right that could elect "Godly men" to Congress—and defeat the hated Carter in 1980. While their ideas surely appealed to the preacher, who shared the same far-right ideology, he didn't initially believe that evangelical congregations would participate in political action.

Viguerie and Weyrich responded by proposing a national survey of fundamentalist Christians about their political interests and concerns, at an estimated cost of $30,000, with Falwell contributing $10,000. The results, unveiled a few months later at the Lynchburg Holiday Inn, revealed an enthusiasm for politics that surprised Falwell and launched him on a new path. Almost immediately, Viguerie turned to promoting the latest manifestation of his direct-mail empire through *Conservative Digest*, a promotional publication he owned and sent to subscribers from his lists. The cover of its August 1979 special issue hailed "Born Again Christians: A New Political Force," and featured a lead story by Weyrich headlined "Building the Moral Majority."

What Falwell's new partners may not have understood right away was how ardently he would embrace their methods—or why he was so desperate to haul in the bonanza of donations that a politicized religious crusade might bring. They may not have known, for instance, that the institutions he oversaw, Thomas Road Baptist Church and Liberty Baptist College, had only recently emerged from severe financial difficulties due to Falwell's mismanagement—and would soon descend even further into unsecured debt. The finger-wagging "fiscal conservative" had run his operations so recklessly and deceptively that he finally had provoked the wrath of the Securities and Exchange Commission.

In the spring of 1973, the SEC had brought a complaint against Thomas Road Baptist Church charging that it had engaged in "fraud and deceit" by selling $6.5 million in bonds to expand the church and school without sufficient collateral. Upon investigation, the federal auditors found that the church was already mired in millions of dollars of debt beyond what its prospectus—replete with false statements—had disclosed to the mostly elderly people who had purchased those bonds. For instance, the prospectus claimed that Liberty Baptist College, a ramshackle operation that had scarcely any proper facilities, was accredited (it wasn't). So sloppy was Falwell's bookkeeping—overseen only by a church volunteer—that SEC investigators couldn't determine how much he had spent or what he had done with the bond proceeds.

At least some of the funding had been spent to market *The Old-Time Gospel Hour* TV show, which brought in hefty proceeds to the church every week. Taking to the pulpit, Falwell accepted no responsibility and instead told his congregation that "the devil is after us. God knows we've done nothing wrong."

A federal judge disagreed, ordering the church to pay off the bonds immediately, ousting Falwell from overseeing the financial affairs of Thomas Road, and entrusting the church's accounts to an appointed committee of five Lynchburg business leaders. Although Falwell himself was cleared of "intentional wrongdoing," he didn't regain full control of Thomas Road's money until the bonds were fully repaid several years later. The "I Love America" tours that Viguerie and Weyrich saw as signs of Falwell's national prominence were among the desperate measures taken by the preacher to pay off those fraud-tainted securities.

With that disgrace finally behind him, however, Falwell saw a prosperous future for Thomas Road, Liberty Baptist College, and his TV productions in tandem with the Moral Majority. According to biographer Dirk Smillie, the would-be Christian political boss "imagined the synergies between this new national political organization and his direct-mail operations back home. The potential to enlarge his fundraising footprint was staggering, he thought. . . . Legally, they would have to be separate organizations. Functionally, they would grow each other. The free media from voter registration and political mobilization rallies necessary to defeat Carter would be staggering. Falwell's donor rolls would explode." Even before the new Moral Majority opened its first official state chapter offices in downtown Lynchburg, Falwell took immediate action to build the kind of nationwide political money machine that he and his partners envisioned. He got started with a cynical trick perpetrated on an old colleague.

Enlisting Elmer Towns, a prolific Christian author and academic who had helped to found Liberty Baptist College, Falwell traveled to Murfreesboro, Tennessee, to visit the celebrated fundamentalist publisher and pastor John R. Rice. A longtime friend of Towns, Rice published the *Sword of the Lord*, a leading fundamentalist newspaper that counted among its subscribers nearly every evangelical pastor in

America. He was the kind of old-fashioned pastor who rejected all things secular, such as embroiling churches in political organizing and fundraising. So at their meeting with Rice, Falwell neglected to mention the big new project he had started with Viguerie and Weyrich and focused instead on the expansion of his college as a means of evangelizing the world. As Smillie tells it, he explained to Rice that he and Towns wanted to "double Liberty's size in the next five years" and create a "Notre Dame for fundamentalists. . . . We could surely use your help."

Falwell wanted to get his hands on the *Sword of the Lord* mailing list, which included two hundred thousand pastors overseeing every church in the Southern Baptist Convention and many more, all of them wielding influence over congregations and wealthy donors who could write checks to the Moral Majority (and Liberty Baptist College, too).

Unaware of Falwell's political agenda, of which he would not have approved, the eighty-four-year-old Rice naively offered to turn over the mailing list that same day. He took them to his bank, where the subscription lists were kept in a vault on big spools of magnetic tape. On the flight back to Virginia, Smillie wrote, Falwell and Towns "felt as if they had just raided Fort Knox." That purloined list, combined with names provided by Falwell and Viguerie, formed the core of a database that would soon encompass millions of evangelical and fundamentalist donors.

ALTHOUGH TAX-EXEMPT AND thus nominally nonpartisan, the Moral Majority reached an early decision to back Ronald Reagan for president in 1980, its first electoral campaign. While far from "perfect," in the eyes of Falwell and his political partners, the former California governor struck them as likely to prevail over the increasingly unpopular incumbent Carter—and willing at least to give lip service to the religious Right's objectives.

In the wake of what proved to be a watershed election, Falwell proclaimed that his organization's multimillion-dollar effort to register and mobilize its supporters had been essential to Reagan's victory. Nobody has ever measured precisely how important those evangelical voters were to the Republican sweep, which unseated several veteran Democratic senators, but analysts of every stripe agreed that the Moral Majority represented an important breakthrough for faith-based conservatism. What mattered more in the long term was the incestuous relationship that developed between predominantly white evangelical and fundamentalist leaders and Republican Party politicians—an alliance that would prove corrupting to both church and party. Their fervent embrace of right-wing ideology would drive many evangelical ministers to defend even the most immoral figures in politics, so long as those politicians were Republicans—and those crooked Republicans reciprocated by elevating vain, demagogic, and greedy televangelists into icons of partisan loyalty.

Amid the celebration on the right that followed Reagan's inauguration, the dour Weyrich offered a prescient warning to Moral Majority supporters. While they might expect the new administration to serve their agenda of ending abortion, reinstating school prayer, curtailing gay rights, and protecting Christian private schools, he urged them to keep such presumptions in check. "We will have to fight for anything we get," he said.

Over the ensuing years, disappointment with Reagan among the religious Right activists extinguished much of their initial enthusiasm. The affable president routinely offered rhetorical endorsement of their ideology, yet his political decisions, such as the nomination of Sandra Day O'Connor to the Supreme Court, often infuriated them. Many of the religious Right leaders who had championed Reagan—and his even more suspect running mate, George H. W. Bush—publicly expressed their chagrin. Pat Robertson, the Virginia-based televangelist whose Christian Broadcasting Network made him Falwell's principal competitor for leadership of the religious Right, became so frustrated with the Republican administration and the Moral Majority that he started an alternative political group. Robertson's Freedom Council served as a nascent campaign front when he declared his own presidential candidacy in 1987 against Bush. Falwell stood out as an inveterate loyalist, even as his partners Viguerie and Weyrich voiced their own sense of alienation from Reagan—and he didn't hesitate to endorse Bush over Robertson in 1988.

Whatever his unspoken concerns over administration policy, Falwell saw enduring profit in his close identification with the White House, quite literally. As an organization, the Moral Majority itself never achieved the kind of financial success that its founders had foreseen—and ultimately proved to be a drain on Falwell's resources. But the Reagan connection still paid "spectacular dividends" to Thomas Road Baptist Church, *The Old-Time Gospel Hour*, and Liberty Baptist College, finally renamed Liberty University in 1984. By 1985, contributions to the Falwell ventures reached $110 million and soared to $135 million the following year. In its best year, during Reagan's 1984 re-election campaign, the Moral Majority only raised $11 million. But as Falwell had predicted, the proceeds from political engagement nevertheless proved enormous. The problem was that no matter how much Falwell's enterprises brought in, the expenses consistently overran revenues by millions. His promiscuous commingling of politics and religion also drew unwanted attention from the Internal Revenue Service, which disapproved of the subsidies flowing from *The Old-Time Gospel Hour* to the Moral Majority. The IRS voided the TV show's tax exemption for 1986 and 1987, while imposing a fine of $50,000 for past offenses—but that was merely an incidental cost of doing business that discouraged him not at all.

As televangelism grew into a multibillion-dollar industry, the flow of huge profits to individual pastors—and their abusive practices—burst into public view when a series of lurid scandals suddenly engulfed several fundamentalist celebrities. These eruptions would begin with revelations of an extramarital affair, an encounter (or two or three) with a prostitute, or even a sexual assault on a church employee. But when the steamy gossip evaporated, what emerged was a tableau of greed and indulgence that no Christian apologetics could justify.

That was how Jim Bakker, impresario of the popular PTL televangelism network and the Heritage USA religious theme parks and resorts, both worth hundreds of millions of dollars, ended up in the clutches of Falwell. Bakker and his wife, Tammy Faye, had started out as the hosts of *The 700 Club* on their fellow televangelist Pat Robertson's Christian Broadcasting Network but had struck out on their own to make a fortune preaching the "prosperity gospel"—a boldly entrepreneurial and utterly preposterous brand of evangelism that promised viewers unlimited health and wealth if they tithed regular donations to the ministry.

The Bakker empire expanded for decades, until rumors of Jim's dalliance with a church secretary began to circulate among his fellow evangelists, including Falwell. Spread by the rival televangelist Jimmy Swaggart, who would soon fall from grace for consorting with prostitutes himself, the rumors about Bakker were true. In March 1987, at a meeting in Palm Springs, Bakker made a startling request to Falwell, whom he hardly knew: "Jerry, I want you to take over PTL." He would later say they had agreed that Falwell's stewardship of PTL would only serve as a temporary respite from a "hostile takeover" by Swaggart or another Bakker antagonist. But while the leader of the Moral Majority couched his takeover of PTL in religious language, as a spiritual rescue, his deeper motives reflected the same avarice that he would later denounce as the Bakkers' principal sin. With Jim and Tammy Faye out of the way and PTL's reputation somehow refurbished, Falwell could see the TV ministry's huge donor base bringing in even more money.

A propaganda war broke out in the media, featuring a flood of leaks about the Bakkers' mad extravagance and larcenous mismanagement—including the purchase of his-and-hers Rolls-Royces, million-dollar salaries, and even an air-conditioned doghouse. The ongoing soap opera of rapacious excess earned PTL an unflattering nickname: "Pass the Loot." And it soon emerged that Bakker and an aide had bribed a buxom church secretary named Jessica Hahn to keep quiet about their sexual encounter, which he called "consensual" and she described as rape.

Convicted by the Justice Department of embezzling millions in church funds, Bakker ended up serving five years in prison while the mascara-streaked Tammy Faye tearfully pleaded his innocence. Despite

Bakker's downfall and exile, however, the windfall anticipated by Falwell didn't materialize. Instead, within less than a year, he resigned as chief executive of the bankrupt PTL, as donations from disillusioned followers dried up.

Rejecting any personal responsibility for PTL's ultimate failure or his own role in it, Falwell told the media that God had ordained the entire fiasco to bring down the Bakkers. "I am convinced that God led me to Heritage in 1987. . . . Heritage had become the Mecca of the 'prosperity theology' movement. God wanted it terminated. I now clearly see that Jehovah God gave me the very unpleasant and painful, but necessary, task of exposing and calling a halt to this modern Sodom and Gomorrah." The less uplifting truth was that Falwell had attempted to appropriate the ill-gotten proceeds of the prosperity gospel from the Bakkers—and that the horde of hucksters who followed in their path would continue the same sad swindle in the decades that followed, their credibility enhanced by their symbiotic relationship with Republican politicians, all the way to 2016 and the advent of Trump, their perfect presidential candidate.

WHILE FALWELL AWAITED the cornucopia of PTL riches that never arrived, the metastasizing televangelism scandals tore into his own organization's finances. The 1987 deficit for Falwell's enterprises soared to nearly $40 million with no relief in sight; donations to *The Old-Time Gospel Hour*, which had been declining already, dipped sharply by 30 percent. At the same time, Falwell continued to spend millions on building Liberty University, even though its revenues from tuition lagged far behind expenses and it had no endowment. He turned again to the same financial scheme that had gotten him into so much trouble with federal regulators a decade earlier: the issuance of Thomas Road Baptist Church bonds, to be hustled on faith to small investors.

The underwriter for Falwell's biggest bond issue was Willard May, a financier who had built AMI Investment Corporation, a Texas-based firm that specialized in ecclesiastical securities. Unlike most such church bonds, which are uninsured by the federal government, May claimed that his were covered by a kind of bond insurance written by another company he owned. Promising big returns, May's bonds were ignored by ratings services and largely unregulated. Charles Keating, the anti-pornography crusader who would later become infamous as a savings and loan swindler, was among AMI's largest investors.

The obvious marketing target for Thomas Road bonds included not only the church's parishioners but Falwell's fans among the *Old-Time Gospel Hour* audience and the Moral Majority mailing lists. He sent a letter touting the bonds to every church member, promising returns as high as 11.5 percent, and then published a story in the *Moral Majority Report* promoting the bonds and praising May as a devout businessman. The promotion swiftly sold $32 million in bonds to more than two thousand small investors. The euphoria following Thomas Road's successful bond issue was short-lived, however. Texas insurance authorities forced May to close his bond insurance outfit because he was "unauthorized" to operate in that business. Not long after, the state's banking regulators charged May with wrongfully investing church money in risky securities and seized control of his investment funds, which they declared insolvent.

Among the assets seized by regulators was Falwell's church property, which had served as collateral for the Thomas Road bonds. The church ended up in the portfolio of Charles Keating's properties taken over by the Resolution Trust Corporation when his savings and loan empire, which held a major share of May's company, went belly-up. Meanwhile, the individual investors who had trusted Falwell learned the hard way that he—and they—had made an extremely costly mistake. Forced to sue when the bonds defaulted, they found themselves with no choice but to settle for pennies on the dollar. It was small comfort when federal prosecutors hit May, himself a former preacher, with a six-count indictment for fraud. The SEC accused May's AMI firm of deceiving thousands of investors, who had bought its bonds for their individual retirement accounts, by promising fat returns and no risk. Its salesmen and promotional literature had told them that the big banks were "falling apart"—and that buying AMI bonds was "doing the work of the Lord."

Douglas Hudman, a lawyer for the bondholders, told a reporter that his clients were "Moms and Pops cashing in their IRA money because their local minister and Falwell's letters said they'd be doing God's work. . . . All it was doing was going to fund Mr. Falwell's continued indebtedness. It's kind of sickening."

As Falwell struggled to save his church and university from ruin—laying off hundreds of employees, withdrawing *The Old-Time Gospel Hour* from all its TV markets outside Virginia, and selling off real estate—he somehow managed to absolve himself from any culpability. It was God's will, it was the fault of regulators, it was anybody's responsibility but his own, though he (and his naive investors) had experienced the same ordeal ten years earlier, when he had issued bonds backed by insufficient revenue. Indeed, he continued to attempt to market bonds to rescue his operations, but when Kemper Insurance finally agreed to sell them, nobody was buying.

Falwell's financial crisis marked the end of the Moral Majority, already on a downward trajectory since the second Reagan midterm election three years earlier, when Republicans fared poorly. He had officially stepped down as the political organization's chief executive in 1987, declaring that he would withdraw from public life and return to religion full-time, while continuing to chair its board of directors. "I'm rededicating my life to preaching the Gospel," he told reporters. "My real platform of influence is my spiritual ministry." He maintained control through an aide he appointed as a figurehead chief executive—and when the time finally arrived for the charade to end, it was Falwell who made the announcement. Rather than acknowledge the Moral Majority's decline and grim fiscal outlook, he drew a big picture of success for the religious Right, which he described as "solidly in place" and "winning," with increased power in Congress and the courts.

From the very beginning, Falwell had exaggerated the Moral Majority's size and impact. He had often claimed to register millions more voters than the organization's small budget could ever have supported, along with grossly inflated figures for its membership and newsletter circulation. Viewed from another perspective, however, his depiction of a reinvigorated and powerful constituency on the religious Right was accurate. The void left by the implosion of the Moral Majority would soon be filled by his sometime rival Pat Robertson, who had already begun to transform the apparatus of his failed 1988 presidential campaign into a new organization that he called the Christian Coalition. Morally compromised as the "nonpartisan" Moral Majority had been in its fealty to Republican politicians, the Christian Coalition and its members would be used far more cynically for profit and power by GOP operatives. And rather than improving the moral tenor of American politics, the result of Falwell's efforts—and of those who followed in his path—was to transform evangelical Christianity into a politicized, tribal, and hostile creed.

The budgetary tribulations of Jerry Falwell Ministries would not fully abate for decades, long after he had gone to his ultimate reward. In the meantime, he came to rely on his ambitious and not particularly devout eldest son, Jerry Jr., then a young lawyer, who saw the ministry primarily as a real estate and educational conglomerate. Jerry Jr. had never been much concerned with faith or values.

Before Jerry Jr. could revive the fortunes of Liberty University, however, his father was required to seek assistance from increasingly dubious sources. Legitimate financial institutions, such as the giant Arkansas investment bank Stephens Inc., had loaned millions to Falwell on the strength of future bond proceeds and real estate assets. When those bonds couldn't be sold, the firm's bond counsel at the Rose Law Firm in Little Rock advised foreclosure on a Liberty University building known as North Campus. Along with hundreds of students and classrooms, both Falwell and Jerry Jr. had to vacate space they occupied there. They had been evicted in humiliation from their own offices, with no more money to be gotten from banks, investment bankers, or bond salesmen. Still floundering three years after the Moral Majority's demise and the repeated bond failures, Falwell was saved again by a pair of Lynchburg direct-mail entrepreneurs named Daniel Reber and Jimmy Thomas, who had raised money for Liberty University and a host of conservative causes. Their rescue plan involved the formation of a nonprofit corporation called Christian Heritage Foundation, which would purchase all of Falwell's bad debt at a steep discount and wipe it from his ledgers. They paid $2.5 million for $12.5 million worth of Willard May bonds—which provided the bondholders about fifteen cents for every dollar they had invested.

When Falwell announced this providential rescue on *The Old-Time Gospel Hour*, he described Thomas and Reber as "good Samaritans" who had made huge personal sacrifices to help Liberty and Thomas Road. "Thank God for friends like Dan Reber and Jimmy Thomas," he cried. Their bailout of Liberty was "the greatest day of financial advantage" in its history. The only flaw in this inspirational sermon? The entire story was a lie. Behind Reber and Thomas, straw investors who had sacrificed nothing, stood the Reverend Sun Myung Moon's immensely wealthy and controversial Unification Church. Falwell had been saved from ruin by an infamous foreign cult. Moon had swindled and virtually enslaved thousands of young cult devotees to promote a toxic "religious" doctrine that fundamentalists like Falwell regarded as heretical at best and satanic at worst.

Falwell was hardly alone in consorting with the "Moonies," as the Unification Church and its followers were derisively known. Bedazzled by Moon's money and his professed hostility to communism, American conservatives had quietly embraced the Korean evangelist, who had insisted that he spoke for God and "Godism," ever since the late far-right Senator Strom Thurmond helped him to enter the United States in 1971. Revelations about his cult's abuse of its disciples, his smuggling of enormous amounts of cash, and even his conviction and imprisonment for tax evasion had done little to damage his connections with right-wing and Republican leaders. Like many other figures on the religious Right, who had collectively taken tens of millions of dollars from Moon, the Lynchburg preacher felt he had no choice but to lie. The relationships that Falwell and other white evangelicals had forged with Moon were theologically and ethically indefensible. When those faith leaders accepted Moon's money—and then concealed it—they entered a moral frontier from which they could not return.

WITH THE ADVENT of Bill Clinton's presidency, Falwell crossed another bright ethical line. The election of a Democratic president, after twelve years of rule by Republicans whom Falwell had endorsed and befriended, marked the beginning of a "culture war" that has only intensified in the decades since. For Falwell, the Clinton administration presented an opportunity to return to politics, scarcely half a decade after he'd pretended to quit. Clinton's election, as one religious Right organization thundered, was "a repudiation of our forefathers' covenant with God." It provided an opportunity to make money, too.

By 1994, Falwell had reactivated the Liberty Alliance, a political committee that he had started several years earlier as an umbrella for Moral Majority operations. It provided a convenient way for him to join the "Clinton crazies," fanatical volunteers in the culture war whose principal weapons were conspiracy theories about the Democratic president (and his feminist wife, Hillary) encompassing almost every imaginable variation of crime, from cocaine smuggling to treason to murder. In that era before streaming video, Falwell undertook to popularize those vicious myths by producing and distributing a series of VHS tapes that presented them as "investigative journalism."

The first video Falwell distributed through his church and political networks was titled *Circle of Power*, which opened with a soliloquy by a Clinton adversary named Larry Nichols, who told of "countless people who mysteriously died" after somehow thwarting the former Arkansas governor's ambitions. Taking the disputed suicide of White House counsel Vince Foster as its starting point, the video tied Clinton to a series of suicides, accidental deaths, and unsolved homicides in his home state—all appropriated from a website run by a militia-linked lawyer in Indianapolis.

The list included thirty-four names of Clinton-connected individuals who had supposedly died under suspicious circumstances, including four army crewmen killed in a helicopter crash in Germany, a Democratic campaign strategist felled by a heart attack, an elderly Little Rock attorney who crashed a single-engine plane on a fogbound airstrip, and dozens of similar instances. There was no actual evidence to link any of those unfortunate events to Bill or Hillary Clinton—nor was there a shred of proof to support the film's insinuations that the Clintons had been involved in a massive financial fraud and cocaine smuggling from a rural airport.

That didn't discourage Falwell from bearing false witness against them, knowing that he had an audience whose hunger for defamatory attacks on the Clintons was insatiable. He had provided financing for the film, produced by a fundamentalist filmmaker named Pat Matrisciana, and it was promoted on national television as *Jerry Falwell Presents Bill Clinton's Circle of Power*. Far from a legitimate exercise in reporting, the film featured interviews with Clinton adversaries who had all been paid to appear and tell their tales; some were paid royalties from videotape sales. The next version, dubbed *The Clinton Chronicles*, reached a much wider audience after Falwell and Matrisciana released it in the spring of 1994. Although Falwell later denied subsidizing the scurrilous video, which was denounced as perverse fiction even by Republican-leaning newspapers like the *Arkansas Democrat-Gazette* and *The Wall Street Journal*, the financial records of Matrisciana's front group, Citizens for Honest Government, showed that he was lying. The Liberty Alliance had underwritten all the video's production costs.

As cinema, the *Clinton Chronicles* video resembled the primitive anti-communist films of the 1950s, with a pseudo-documentary format, a narrator who warned of impending doom in a rich baritone, and a moody score reminiscent of *The Bride of Frankenstein*. And like those old movies about the communist conspiracy, the video depicted the "Clinton machine" in paranoid terms as wielding "absolute control" over Arkansas and abusing that power for sinister and selfish purposes. As a reporter for the *Democrat-Gazette* established in an exhaustive analysis, there was scarcely a single accurate statement in the entire script, including laughable errors about the simplest and most straightforward facts.

Awful as it was, *The Clinton Chronicles* in its various versions became a semi-underground sensation—the precursor of a conspiracy industry that would plague every Democratic candidate and president in the decades that followed. It was also highly profitable, selling hundreds of thousands of copies and reaching millions of Americans via bootleg copies and broadcasts. If Falwell didn't profit personally, his organizations certainly did. But one day in October 1994, Falwell learned what the Gospel of Mark meant when the saint asked, "What shall it profit a man if he shall gain the whole world and lose his soul?" Invited to address a preachers' conference in Little Rock at Immanuel Baptist Church, his appearance had to be relocated when the church's pastor, Rex Horne, refused to let Falwell speak there. The outraged Horne had seen a televised excerpt from *The Clinton Chronicles* on *The Old-Time Gospel Hour*—and felt that his colleague from Lynchburg had brazenly violated the Ninth Commandment's injunction against bearing false witness.

"I happened to tune in on a Sunday morning," Horne said. "I saw Falwell promoting the tapes that have proven to be scurrilous and full of innuendo and falsehoods directed against not just Clinton but other Arkansans. I could not, with good conscience, go along with it any longer."

For Jerry Falwell, the ends had come to justify the means, even if that meant inventing and broadcasting the vilest falsehoods against his fellow citizens. He could get away with that, at the cost of a dented reputation, and even turn a buck in the process. He had created a religious Right that was politically strong and ostensibly high-minded, but hollow at its moral core. In the years and decades ahead, its fall from spiritual grace and conservative ideals would only accelerate. Among the most notorious betrayers of those ideals, in the pursuit of money and power, would be his own eldest son, Jerry Falwell Jr.—who rushed to endorse an immoral, unscrupulous, and blasphemous leader named Donald J. Trump—and then brought exposure and disgrace upon the Falwell empire.

8

Let Us Prey

Of all the rhetorical strategies deployed by Republican politicians in recent decades, none has proved more durable than their insistence that God wants them to rule America—and that their opponents are impious, atheistic, materialistic, or even worse, inspired by Satan. Defying the customs of normal political debate and conflating religious faith with ideological conviction, it is an assertion impervious to factual contradiction or logical argument. It can be persuasive to the unwary and unsophisticated, as generations of faith-based con artists have demonstrated on these shores since long before the founding of the American republic. The intense attraction between purportedly Christian swindlers and right-wing demagogues is not accidental. They are often working the same kind of grift. And they both resent any government interference in their dubious operations.

While politicians of both parties historically courted the blessing of faith leaders like the legendary evangelist Billy Graham, those routine benedictions gave way in recent decades to much bolder claims of divine sanction. Declaring his candidacy for president in 2000, George W. Bush spoke frankly and often about his own salvation. He had discarded the arid Episcopalian creed of his forefathers to find salvation as an evangelical Christian. He offered various versions of his conversion, always suggesting that Jesus had rescued him from alcoholism and placed him on a path toward the fulfillment of his destiny. Sincere or otherwise, that inspirational narrative also served as the foundation for "compassionate conservatism"—a phrase Bush used to describe his own outlook and the philosophy guiding his presidency.

Then governor of Texas, he strived to avoid the political obstacles encountered by George Herbert Walker Bush, whose service as Reagan's vice president had done little to quell the suspicions of him among religious conservatives. Not only had Pat Robertson run against him in the 1988 Republican presidential primaries, but, in a conspiracy-heavy book, the televangelist had insulted the elder Bush as "an unwitting agent of Lucifer." (He nevertheless endorsed Bush in the general election, presumably on the principle that even the devil's dupe is better than any Democrat.) Soon thereafter, Robertson founded the Christian Coalition, a new national organization that took over where Falwell's Moral Majority had faltered.

"I am a fiscal conservative and a family conservative. And I am a compassionate conservative, because I know my philosophy is optimistic and full of hope for every American." With those words, Bush aimed to finesse the political paradox he faced. To win the Republican nomination, he had to be acceptable to every right-wing faction, from disgruntled libertarians to zealous fundamentalists; to win the presidency itself, he had to avoid the angry conservatism that had repelled Americans during the Clinton era. Newt Gingrich's Capitol Hill "revolutionaries" had alienated suburban moderates with their ultra-partisanship, self-righteous hypocrisy, and anti-government extremism. Although the House Speaker's colleagues had defenestrated him, his brief tenure and impeachment fiasco had left behind a cloud of acrid smoke.

Bush and his chief political handler, Karl Rove, knew they couldn't afford to alienate the Far Right, yet somehow had to attract voters in the center. "Compassionate conservatism" became their solution, a gambit that left political observers puzzled and gawking, as if they had witnessed the candidate literally running in two directions at once.

The intellectual basis for compassionate conservatism could be found in the policy prescriptions of Marvin Olasky, a professor of journalism at the University of Texas who also published *World*, an ultraconservative, fundamentalist newsweekly. With the assistance of the Heritage Foundation and other right-wing think tanks, Olasky wrote three books promoting religious charity as a moral alternative to the sinful welfare state. Among those who extolled Olasky's ideas was Gingrich himself, who clearly understood that "compassion" could serve as a convenient scrim for the dismantling of Social Security, Medicare, Medicaid, and other popular social programs. Less savvy Republicans, including Dan Quayle, George H. W. Bush's former vice president, perceived the slogan as an insult. It was "an attack and a criticism on conservatives," Quayle told *The New York Times*.

Despite such reactions, or perhaps because of them, compassionate conservatism proved to be a brilliant stroke of public relations that lasted just long enough to pull suburban votes. It was really nothing more than a series of images of a smiling Bush with Black and Hispanic children. Its yawning emptiness was soon revealed after he reached the White House where, as speechwriter David Frum would later explain, the staff understood it as "less like a philosophy than a marketing slogan." Or to be more specific, a political scam.

Even before Bush took office, ominous glimpses of his right-wing religious cabal appeared in Washington. At an enormous "prayer luncheon" held in a hotel ballroom on the day before his first inauguration, the keynote speech was delivered by John Ashcroft, then in the thick of difficult Senate hearings over his nomination as attorney general. Notorious for theocratic extremism, Ashcroft had insisted on being blasphemously "anointed" with oil by Supreme Court Justice Clarence Thomas, in the manner of the ancient Hebrew kings. The prayer luncheon's principal sponsor was the Washington Times Foundation, a tentacle of the Unification Church led by Sun Myung Moon, the self-proclaimed messiah who had done federal prison time for tax evasion and illegally combining his business and religious entities. At the luncheon, Moon received an award for his "work in support of traditional family values" (which presumably didn't include his cult's kidnapping of thousands of young people whom he forbade to contact their parents). Before returning to his palatial home on a Hudson Valley estate,

Moon sternly reminded his fellow religious leaders that scripture enjoins them "to fast, to serve others, to be sacrificial."

Moon operated ostensibly charitable organizations along with his huge media, educational, and industrial holdings. In that way, he resembled his fellow luncheon guest Jerry Falwell, who by then had become a faithful sentinel and financial beneficiary of the Moon empire. Like his Korean benefactor, who had since bestowed a scandalous million-dollar speaking fee on the first President Bush, Falwell was a loyal promoter of the Bush family's political enterprises. Another religious celebrity on hand was Pat Robertson, a former Bush critic who had become a dependable ally. The wealthy televangelist and Christian Coalition leader also controlled Operation Blessing, a far-flung charitable organization that would eventually glom a share of the new president's faith-based federal boodle.

Robertson, too, had encountered problems with government authorities, partly due to partisan violations of the Christian Coalition's tax-exempt status—and partly due to Operation Blessing's misuse of certain assets to serve his commercial enterprises. Specifically, the charity's airplanes were found to have secretly transported personnel and equipment for a diamond-mining enterprise in Zaire, undertaken with the blessing of the late and unlamented dictator Mobutu Sese Seko. That operation had followed a plea from Robertson on *The 700 Club* for donations to support an airlift of refugees from war-torn regions in the Congo. In 1999, a series of articles about that episode by the *Virginian-Pilot* newspaper had resulted in a state investigation of Operation Blessing. That probe's outcome was deeply embarrassing. Virginia's Office of Consumer Affairs charged that Robertson "willfully induced contributions from the public through the use of misleading statements" and called for legal action against the televangelist. But the Republican governor and attorney general, both supported by the Christian Coalition and subsidized by large contributions from Robertson, saw no reason to seek indictments or fines.

The centerpieces of George W. Bush's compassionate conservatism were his education plan, titled No Child Left Behind, and his "faith-based initiative" directing federal funds to private charities, including religious institutions. But due to the deficits caused by the recession and his giant tax cuts, the education bill he ultimately fashioned with the late Democratic senator Edward Kennedy fell far short of the originally proposed funding. One statistic summed up the Bush administration's priorities: his tax cuts for the rich amounted to more than fifty times the total amount he requested for new education spending.

The vaunted "faith-based initiative" met an equally dismal fate. David Kuo, the former deputy director of the White House Office on Faith-Based and Community Initiatives, recalled in his 2006 memoir how Senate finance chair Chuck Grassley had set aside a budget line of $6 billion per year in tax credits aimed at encouraging charitable giving to organizations fighting poverty. But the president's legislative team told the stunned Iowa Republican to "get rid of" the charity tax credits, because the money was needed instead for a higher political priority: the $100 billion cut in the estate tax that then affected less than 1 percent of American families at the very top of the income scale.

With compassionate conservatism effectively gutted, Bush found a lump of coal in his 2002 Christmas stocking from John DiIulio, a senior presidential adviser who had overseen the White House Office of Faith-Based and Community Initiatives. If Marvin Olasky struck some observers as an oddball and others as a grifter, DiIulio looked more like a true believer. A moderate Democrat, the University of Pennsylvania professor had become one of the nation's leading academic exponents of compassionate conservatism. Devoutly Catholic, he didn't necessarily share all of Bush's religious or social views but had joined the administration because he believed it would foster innovative programs to assist the poor.

After several months of utter frustration, however, DiIulio became the first senior Bush adviser to quit. The disillusioned professor then sent an emotional seven-page letter to journalist Ron Suskind, who used it to anchor a devastating *Esquire* exposé. In his letter, DiIulio depicted a White House steeped in partisan cynicism and devoid of competent policymakers. According to him, political boss Karl Rove and his aides subordinated every aspiration to their media and political strategy, which resulted in a "virtually empty record on compassionate conservatism."

"There is no precedent in any modern White House for what is going on in this one: a complete lack of a policy apparatus," DiIulio wrote. "What you've got is everything—and I mean everything—being run by the political arm. It's the reign of the Mayberry Machiavellis." That was DiIulio's snippy nickname for Rove and his aides, "who consistently talked and acted as if the height of political sophistication consisted in reducing every issue to its simplest black-and-white terms for public consumption, then steering legislative initiatives or policy proposals as far to the right as possible." By then, DiIulio knew that Rove had gleefully corrupted the president's "faith-based initiative" into a self-serving patronage operation. During the 2002 midterm campaign, administration officials suddenly showed up at inner-city churches, with federal funding to entice support from African American ministers. A half-million-dollar grant was quickly slated for Robertson's quasi-charitable Operation Blessing, a timely election-year gift to the leader of the Christian Coalition.

"There is a virtual absence as yet of any policy accomplishments that might, to a fair-minded nonpartisan, count as the flesh on the bones of so-called compassionate conservatism," concluded DiIulio.

So-called compassionate conservatism. That phrase, written by a man who said he still loved and admired George W. Bush, resounded with disillusion. Yet DiIulio still held out hope that in the years to come, his ideal of a conservative program to uplift the poor might be realized. It never happened. The implosion of compassionate conservatism in no way discouraged Republicans and their allies on the religious Right from insisting that God was on their side—and that the Almighty had chosen Bush to lead the nation. This overbearing approach, contrary to their rote professions of humility, had been planted by Bush himself during the months before he declared his candidacy—and emphasized even more strongly after the 9/11 attacks.

"I think that God picked the right man at the right time for the right purpose," intoned popular Christian broadcaster Janet Parshall. General William Boykin, frequently in trouble for mixing his private religious beliefs with his military duties, argued that it must have been God who selected Bush, since a plurality of voters hadn't. "Why is this man in the White House? The majority of America did not vote for him. He's in the White House because God put him there for a time such as this."

"I've heard a lot of 'God knew something we didn't,'" concurred Ralph Reed, who had moved on from the Christian Coalition to the Georgia Republican Party. "In the evangelical mind, the notion of an omniscient God is central to their theology. He had a knowledge nobody else had: He knew George Bush had the ability to lead in this compelling way."

According to *Time* magazine, Bush himself spoke privately of "being chosen by the grace of God to lead at that moment." Olasky's *World* magazine quoted a Rove deputy named Tim Goeglein: "I think President Bush is God's man at this hour, and I say this with a great sense of humility." Even Bush's usually reserved father hyped the spooky theory, speculating that his defeat by Clinton had set up his son's divinely ordained presidency. "If I'd won that election in 1992, my oldest son would not be president of the United States of America. . . . I think the Lord works in mysterious ways."

WITH THE TWIN disasters of the Iraq War and the financial crisis staining his legacy, Bush lost the celestial aura that had once illuminated his regime. The right-wing consensus that God had selected him didn't outlast his presidency. Over the years that followed his departure from Washington, Dubya and his family—including his father and his brother Jeb, a 2016 presidential aspirant and former Florida governor—became objects of casual disdain within their own party.

Evangelical leaders who had once revered Bush eventually would drape the mantle of divine providence over his nemesis, Donald J. Trump—a twice-divorced philanderer, former gambling magnate, and infrequent churchgoer who boasted of molesting women and paid off a porn star to silence her about a sexual encounter. Trump was an unlikely successor to the mandate of heaven. Never burdened by intellectual consistency, however, the evangelical leaders who had endorsed Bush because he was so earnestly and ostentatiously religious found a way to argue the opposite case for Trump. The unexpected rise to power of this irreligious reprobate demonstrated, they said, that God indeed works in mysterious ways.

The same kind of profane speculation—suggesting that Bush had been ordained by the Almighty—would be echoed decades later by the religious sycophants surrounding Donald J. Trump, a man whom Bush undoubtedly scorned and who berated him in turn. The irony of hearing such profane nonsense, spouted by many of the same religious leaders who had once endorsed him, could hardly have been lost on Dubya. His party had discarded him but doubled down on the parody of Christian piety that transformed a politician into a religious icon. Whether Bush understood or not, those dubious claims of divine sanction for him had set the stage for Trump's unholy consecration.

On another level, Trump's overthrow of the Bush dynasty and his capture of the white evangelical leadership were both rooted in his undeniable appeal to a growing megachurch constituency: the right-wing preachers who identify with Word of Faith or the prosperity gospel.

Word of Faith is a uniquely American and nondenominational movement with no ordination procedures or hierarchy; its teachings emphasize the absolute prophetic authority of pastors and the imperative to make offerings of money to them as the only way to acquire heavenly blessings of wealth, health, and status. As might be expected, it has long attracted more slick salesmen than reverent ministers, especially those who can perform on television. For Trump, a biblically illiterate but talented demagogue, the prosperity gospel was a perfect fit.

Yet long before Trump decided to run for president, it was Bush who first elevated the prosperity gospel preachers—a disreputable crew, routinely rejected by most evangelical Christians as heretical con artists rather than legitimate spiritual leaders. Obsessed with material wealth as a sign of God's grace and despising government action on behalf of the poor, the blatantly greedy proponents of the prosperity gospel hardly could have been more hostile to the ideals of compassionate conservatism. Before his first term ended, Bush had dropped compassionate conservatism from his agenda and his speeches. What mattered much more to him was the political power wielded by a certain Word of Faith preacher based in the key swing state of Ohio.

UNTIL 2004, THE televangelist Rod Parsley had not been well-known outside his hometown of Columbus, although he had established a twelve-thousand-member megachurch and appeared daily on Trinity Broadcasting Network. His ascent to political stardom began that year with a ballot initiative banning same-sex marriage in Ohio—a local issue that happened to mesh perfectly with the gay-baiting national campaign strategy conceived by Karl Rove to reelect Bush in 2004.

Eleven states had antigay marriage referenda on their ballots that year, and Democrats suspected the White House of coordinating the crusade. Rove and his deputy Ken Mehlman had coordinated closely with state-based campaigns against gay rights (and clearly felt no compunction in encouraging antigay bigotry, despite the fact that Mehlman himself was a closeted homosexual and Rove's own adoptive father was also gay).

Known as Issue One, the Ohio initiative passed with 63 percent of the vote—and veteran analysts believed the antigay crusade drove a narrow Republican victory in what was otherwise an extremely close election. At least one poll showed that the issue of gay marriage had boosted Bush by as much as six points. And the organizing effort behind Issue One had depended heavily on Parsley, who had spent nearly a year leading evangelical preachers across the state to register and organize hundreds of thousands of voters.

Ranking Republican leaders and right-wing pundits embraced Parsley as an avatar of "moral values," from Bill Frist, then the Senate majority leader, to then Texas governor Rick Perry, columnist Ann Coulter, and Bush himself, who invited him to the White House and brought him on conference calls with other religious leaders. He would have had little use for compassionate conservatism or any other government effort to aid the poor, as he once told an interviewer. "I'm convinced the best thing government can do to help the poor is to get out of the way," he said. "If government reduced taxes, removed industrial restraints, eliminated wage controls, and abolished subsidies, tariffs, and other constraints on free enterprise, the poor would be helped in a way that [Aid to Families with Dependent Children], Social Security, and unemployment insurance could never match."

What made Parsley's sudden stardom most notable, however, wasn't his standard-issue right-wing ideology, which he shared with most Southern Baptists, white evangelicals, and many other conservative Christians. In his conspicuous alliance with Republican politicians, including the president of the United States, Parsley represented acceptance for the prosperity gospel—an outgrowth of Christianity traditionally rejected by both mainstream Christians and fundamentalists like Jerry Falwell as ungodly and heretical.

When Falwell publicly denounced purveyors of the prosperity gospel, he was talking about Jim and Tammy Faye Bakker—but Parsley, in exploiting his followers and misusing their donations, bore a distinct resemblance to the infamous couple. His World Harvest conglomeration of church, school, and broadcasting operations raked in upward of $40 million annually. He lived in a 7,500-square-foot mansion, owned several cars, and kept more than one private jet (which he used to visit Las Vegas from time to time). The deceptive techniques employed by Parsley to fleece his flock were familiar to anyone who has studied the prosperity preachers. Congregants could free themselves from debt if they burned their bills and tithed their meager savings to him. He promised they could escape financial stress—as well as any health problems, no matter how grave—if only they purchased the miraculous objects he hawked on his website and TV broadcasts, such cheap kitsch items as "prayer cloths" and "covenant swords." He pressured congregants to tithe 10 percent of their income to World Harvest, with the constant reminder that "the Bible says to withhold the tithe is to rob God."

Assuring his followers that he was a divinely inspired prophet and thus anointed by God, he constantly emphasized that obedience to him was not really a choice but a heavenly commandment. Like other Word of Faith preachers, Parsley would quote a favorite passage from Psalms whenever anyone dared to question his dictatorial methods and illicit accumulation of wealth: "Touch not my anointed and do my prophets no harm."

The late Ole Anthony, a Texas minister who made a vocation of exposing Word of Faith scammers, sending at least one of them to prison, took a dim view of Parsley's machinations. To investigative reporter Sarah Posner, Anthony described Parsley as a "power-hungry" figure with "an extravagant lifestyle that has become the hallmark of televangelists these days." (So flagrant were the abuses of the Word of Faith ministries that a conservative Republican, Senator Chuck Grassley of Iowa, opened a Senate Finance Committee investigation into six of them—Paula White, Joyce Meyer, Creflo Dollar, Kenneth Copeland, Eddie Long, and Benny Hinn—based on Anthony's findings. Pressure from religious Right organizations swiftly brought that inquiry to a whimpering conclusion, with no prosecutions or fines and a recommendation for a toothless oversight commission. The bitterly disappointed Anthony said that while the Senate dithered, "the most desperate and the weakest in our society are being raped by these guys.")

Feeling no shame over his ostentatious displays of wealth, Parsley bluntly rejected any notion of accountability or transparency. How much money he raised and how he spent the proceeds remained hidden from his parishioners and donors. In response to written questions from Posner, he admitted that World Harvest had never tried to join the Evangelical Council for Financial Accountability, a voluntary religious ethics group that requires public disclosure of audited financial statements and report. Instead, he told Posner, World Harvest conducted an annual independent audit "through the scrutiny of the board of directors"—which consisted of himself and his parents. He never disclosed those "audits" or any evidence of how his outfit spent money ostensibly raised for charity. The conservative Christians at Ministry Watch, a nonprofit that monitors the financial probity of churches, gave World Harvest its lowest rating of F for transparency.

Rod Parsley wasn't the only prosperity gospel hustler who could brandish a fulsome endorsement by President Bush and other top Republicans. Urged by his adviser Doug Wead, Bush had reached out early in his first campaign to John Hagee, an older Word of Faith televangelist based in San Antonio. Besides preaching at his Cornerstone Church and on Trinity Broadcasting Network, Hagee was a prolific author, whose book *Jerusalem Countdown*, demanding a preemptive US military strike against Iran, sold nearly five hundred thousand copies and reached the pinnacle of the Walmart inspirational bestseller list. In his book *Mastering Your Money*, Hagee revealed how to obtain financial abundance through faith and tithing. The secret was "revelation thinking," which rejects reason, logic, and independent thought as demonic and relies entirely on inspired knowledge received directly from God (and His anointed prophets such as Hagee):

"Reason givers are controlled by their minds," according to Hagee. "They do not ask God how much they should give; they ask their [certified public accountant]. Revelation givers are controlled by the Holy Spirit. They see God as their supplier. Revelation givers do not give according to what they have, but according to what God can supply." Therefore the path to riches was to give to God—meaning to Hagee himself, of course.

"God Almighty controls the economy of America, and God controls your income! Your source is God, not the United States government. . . . When you give to God, He controls your income," he went on. Whether to become rich, Hagee told his followers, was a simple personal decision. "The difference between living a life of prosperity and a life of poverty is a matter of choice. . . . Tithing is a choice. If you choose not to tithe, you will be living under a financial curse." And when praying and tithing didn't bring wealth, that wasn't due to fraudulent preaching but to insufficient faith (and not giving enough).

While Hagee's former congregants told Posner that the onerous tithing had caused them to miss mortgage payments and skip Christmas gifts, the pastor himself did very well. Before he converted his nonprofit Global Evangelism Television into a church, exempt from IRS reporting requirements, he was known to make over a million dollars a year. Since then, his salary has been a closely held secret. A trust set up in his name owns a ranch valued at over $5 million in Brackettville, Texas, with its own private airstrip, where Hagee's fellow televangelist and friend Kenneth Copeland once flew in to join the pastor on a weekend hunting expedition.

Hagee had not only signed up with the Bush campaign in 2000 but published an election-year book promoting the Texas governor, *God's Candidate for America*. "If you are concerned about the sort of America your children and grandchildren will grow up within," Hagee declared, "then you need to cast your vote for George W. Bush and the Republican Party." According to *The New York Times*, Hagee's early endorsement—along with those of Falwell and Robertson—helped Bush "win over skeptical evangelical conservatives."

Nearly two decades later, when Donald Trump burst into national politics, he struck a chord with the prosperity gospel preachers, who recognized a kindred grifting spirit. Just like them, he had risen from local notoriety to national prominence, as a TV star on *The Apprentice*. Just like them, he focused on image and brand rather than substance and believed that his wealth conferred wisdom. Just like them, he was suspicious of intellectuals and scientists, while highly confident in his own swaggering, baseless assertions. The Bush Republicans who despised Trump probably never realized how their affirmation of the prosperity gospel's fraudsters had paved the way for someone just like him to take over.

LONG BEFORE GEORGE W. Bush left office, the contrast between his party's moralistic stance and the moral emptiness of its leadership had become impossible to ignore. Mimicking Bush and the political preachers who supported him, many of Washington's most corrupt elected officials would insist that they stood for God's will. Such a figure was Representative Tom DeLay of Texas, a former exterminator who rose to the highest ranks of power in Congress and the right-wing Republican elite. He painted over his sleazy fundraising and corrupt lawmaking with a brush of piety, insisting that he would "stand up for a biblical worldview in everything I do and everywhere I am."

In practice, that meant empowering extremely crooked lobbyists while shaking them down for money and favors. The top dog in that predatory pack was a close friend and golfing partner of DeLay named Jack Abramoff, nicknamed "Casino Jack." Abramoff earned that moniker for his role in a scheme that swindled Native American tribes out of tens of millions of dollars as their reservation casinos fought over gambling permits and market share. Representing the Indian casinos proved to be a lucrative racket that mostly involved closing down competitors through government action, or expanding their own operations, or both. It became even more profitable when Abramoff and his partner Michael Scanlon hosed their naive Native clients—whom they privately ridiculed as "fucking morons," "monkeys," and "the stupidest idiots in the land for sure"—with grossly inflated invoices. Estimates of their total haul ranged from $65 million to $80 million.

Chief among the consultants recruited by Abramoff to assist in the Indian casino operation was Ralph Reed, the evangelical Christian political operative who founded the Christian Coalition with Pat Robertson. For a sweet fee of $4 million, Reed's assignment was to fabricate "grass-roots anti-gambling" groups that Abramoff could then deploy to stifle the tribal competitors of his clients. Here it is worth recalling Reed's pivotal role in mainstreaming the religious Right as the slick and personable public face of the Christian Coalition. Telegenic, articulate, and well educated, the thirtyish Reed emanated sincere faith; all too often, reporters marveled at his "choirboy" appearance, and they were onto something. He appeared on the cover of *Time* magazine as an icon, his carefully lit portrait framed by a dramatic headline: "The Right Hand of God."

Even skeptics were startled to discover the deep fakery of this cherubic character when the Abramoff scandal broke. After the Christian Coalition began to falter financially—partly because its small donors believed George W. Bush had at last established a godly government—Reed parted ways with Robertson to start a new career as a politician and lobbyist. In a pleading email to Abramoff, an old friend from their years together in the College Republicans, he asked for gigs: "Hey, now that I'm done with the electoral politics, I need to start humping in corporate accounts! I'm counting on you to help me with some contacts."

Abramoff obliged, instinctively understanding how the former Christian Coalition honcho could exploit the evangelical community in advancing their clients' goals. For a skillful hypocrite like Reed, it was a simple mission to "get our pastors riled up" against yet another sinful gaming establishment—as he boasted in an email to Abramoff—because they worried about gambling's destructive impact on families. At one point, Reed even persuaded James Dobson, then the most powerful evangelical leader in the country, to rouse opposition to a proposed Texas casino. As a lobbyist, Reed made millions, often by discarding positions he had taken as a Christian evangelical leader and adopting the views of his corporate clients. Evangelical Ralph had been a fierce critic of China's government for suppressing Christian churches; lobbyist Ralph smoothed the way for China's most-favored-nation trade status by organizing a phony Alliance of Christian Ministries in China that sponsored ads claiming expanded trade would benefit missionary work.

Abramoff found still other uses for Reed's sway over truly pious people, such as his effort to preserve exemption from US labor laws for the Northern Mariana Islands, an American territory where manufacturers could operate sweatshops that produced items marked MADE IN USA under horrendous conditions. Their mostly female migrant workers, many from China and Thailand, endured sexual slavery and forced abortions as well as low wages and dangerous factories. Nearly every big name in the American rag trade contracted with factories there. Sporting the logo of something called the Traditional Values Coalition, the mailer charged that "Big Labor Union Bosses . . . want to pass a law preventing Chinese from coming to work on the Marianas islands"—supposedly in order to "silence the gospel." On the islands, according to Reed's mendacious pamphlet, the sweatshop workers (and sex workers, too) would be "exposed to the teachings of Jesus Christ . . . and return to China with Bibles in hand, ready to spread the gospel and start home churches."

The actual conditions endured by female laborers on the islands would have outraged any authentic Christian. Overworked and underpaid, many ended up as prostitutes who, if they got pregnant, were forced to undergo abortions. Young women who showed up expecting to get restaurant jobs found themselves hustled into bars where they were coerced into drinking and having sex with male tourists. Behind this plot to protect the territory's sweatshops and brothels from reform was none other than House majority leader Tom DeLay, who had visited the Mariana Islands on lavish junkets sponsored by Abramoff and his local clients that hosted dozens of Republican politicians and commentators. Abramoff spread around plenty of campaign money and easily recruited DeLay to defend the Marianas' factories from modern labor standards. Along with Reed and a crew of hired right-wing "journalists," they portrayed the Marianas as a libertarian utopia when in fact the islands were a sinkhole of indentured servitude and sex tourism.

Under Abramoff's direction, Reed sent messages to conservative Christians on his direct-mail lists, urging them to contact their Republican representatives about opposing the imposition of federal regulation on the islands. Aware that Reed would lose credibility with Christian groups if he were seen taking money from gambling lobbyists, Abramoff routed his payments and those to other subcontractors through right-wing nonprofit groups, including Americans for Tax Reform and the National Center for Public Policy Research, which took a cut for themselves for laundering the dirty money. The Senate Indian Affairs Committee's report on the scandal showed that Reed had received a total of $5.3 million from Abramoff's law firm through those cutouts.

When Reed and Abramoff called on Americans for Tax Reform to conceal their financial maneuvers, they knew that their old crony Grover Norquist, the founder and boss of ATR, would help out—for a price. Together they had been known as the College Republicans' "triumvirate," running the national organization together for years as they rose in conservative ranks. (For some reason, the College Republicans spewed forth a generation of powerful Republicans that included such upstanding figures as Roger Stone, Paul Manafort, and Karl Rove as well as Norquist, Reed, and Abramoff.) Best known for his strict antitax pledge—which he has demanded that all Republican candidates endorse, with considerable success—Norquist has long been a premier right-wing power broker in Washington. Republican legislators and even presidents had long since learned to fear his wrath if they dared to support a tax increase. For decades, he has also served as a de facto manager of the conservative coalition, convening a broad strategy and discussion session in his offices every Wednesday that attracts top leaders from right-wing organizations, congressional offices, and the White House (when a Republican is president).

But Norquist—perhaps reflecting his "free-market" zeal—also maintained a quiet and richly rewarding side hustle as a lobbyist. The lobbying firm he founded, Janus-Merritt Strategies, represented such major "swamp" clients as the federally backed home loan giant Fannie Mae (the Federal National Mortgage Association), the drug manufacturing behemoth PhRMA, Rupert Murdoch's News Corp, and a variety of gambling corporations and associations.

Norquist displayed a flexible attitude toward market principles when necessary to accommodate his big-money clients. After PhRMA paid $140,000 in fees to his lobbying firm, Americans for Tax Reform announced its opposition to legislation that would have allowed US citizens to purchase pharmaceutical drugs manufactured in Canada at far lower prices than those made in the United States. The lower Canadian prices resulted from government regulation and therefore shouldn't be available here, according to Norquist—a position deemed absurd by other free-market advocates such as the Cato Institute.

Selling the imprimatur of Americans for Tax Reform helped Norquist to raise nonprofit funding, too. When he first began to work with Abramoff during the Clinton administration, he agreed to oppose a beverage tax opposed by one of Casino Jack's clients, for a price. According to an email from Abramoff to one of his law firm colleagues, Norquist would work to kill the tax if their law firm became "a major player with ATR." He helpfully suggested a donation of $50,000. "What is most important however is that this matter is kept discreet," noted Abramoff. "We do not want the opponents to think that we are trying to buy the taxpayer movement." Attracting that kind of suspicion would be truly inconvenient.

The Abramoff scandal didn't end well, at least not for the smirking lobbyist and several of his associates. Norquist's former lobbying partner David Safavian, another College Republicans alumnus, eventually went to prison for lying to the FBI and obstructing its investigation. Abramoff himself drew a four-year sentence and more than $23 million in fines following his 2008 guilty pleas to fraud and tax evasion charges. Abramoff's partner Scanlon, former Ohio representative Bob Ney, and a host of lesser hustlers and aides, nearly a dozen in all, pleaded guilty to federal charges and either did time or received probation for testifying as government witnesses.

The Justice Department never issued any indictment of Reed or Norquist, despite their deep immersion in Abramoff's corrupt schemes. Both claimed ignorance of their friend and benefactor's illegal conduct, insisting that they simply didn't know what he was doing, even when documentary evidence refuted their alibis. Almost nobody believed them, as Reed discovered when he mounted an unsuccessful campaign for lieutenant governor in his home state of Georgia in 2006. Even when fellow Republicans called on him to withdraw from the race because he was dragging down other Republican candidates, he refused—and lost in a landslide. Aside from a spate of bad publicity, however, neither Norquist nor Reed saw any lasting consequences for their collusion with Abramoff or the character defects that their exposure revealed. The ethical standards that might once have barred them from leadership on the Republican right had been lowered drastically, and kept shrinking until they evaporated altogether.

Nobody ever challenged Norquist's primacy in Washington's conservative circles; his Wednesday meetings continued as usual and his unsavory lobbying activities were consigned to the newspaper archives. Reed lay low for a few years, but by 2009, he had founded a new organization, the Faith and Freedom Coalition, to take up the mission of the Christian Coalition and the Moral Majority with sophisticated voter-targeting technology and millions of dollars from wealthy Republican donors.

In 2012, Reed played a major role in Mitt Romney's presidential campaign, persuading white evangelical voters that they could support a conservative Mormon even if their pastors had occasionally denounced the Church of Latter-day Saints as a satanic cult. Less than four years later, his keen political instincts sensed that Donald J. Trump would win the Republican presidential nomination, and he signed onto the campaign. When Trump assumed office, he named Reed to his White House "faith advisory group," affirming the prodigal activist's return to national prominence.

Scandals would erupt and then fade away, while the nimblest opportunists, boodlers, and operators would remain untouchable, their sins mostly forgotten and always forgiven.

9

Spilling the Tea Party

The transformation of the Republican Party into a fetid sump of extremism, conspiracy, gaslighting, and outright grifting didn't occur in a single election cycle. That malignant change occurred gradually, over the course of decades, eroding the intellectual and moral foundations of what had once been a truly grand political formation with roots in American traditions of liberty, enterprise, patriotism, and religious faith. But there were certain moments when the grim metamorphosis sped up, intensified, and began to seem irreversible—such as that fateful day in the summer of 2008 when John McCain selected Sarah Palin as his running mate. The flawed calculations and cascading recriminations that drove Palin's trajectory as a national political phenomenon became a compelling storyline for books, movies, and television. McCain's feckless choice steered conservatism toward the vacuous populism and conspiratorial paranoia of the Tea Party and a dress rehearsal for Trumpism.

It was no accident, as the old communist cliché goes, that the same political operatives who ushered Palin onto the GOP ticket—including McCain aides and advisers such as Steve Schmidt, Nicolle Wallace, and Bill Kristol—became ardent and outspoken leaders of the Never Trump movement among Republicans and ex-Republicans. They understand what they did—and their guilt over that watershed debacle continues to haunt them.

Until the rise of Trump, it was hard to comprehend how a politician as intellectually and temperamentally unsuited to high office as Palin could have reached such proximity to ultimate power. What McCain's campaign team learned in their backward selection process—naming her first and vetting her later—blew their minds. She barely understood the structure of the health care system, the basics of the financial crisis, or any of the other national issues that dominated the 2008 election. Palin's mental cupboard didn't just have a few empty shelves. Her mind was a dark and terrifying vacuum, almost wholly devoid of useful content for a major party candidate. Somehow she had vaulted from small-town mayor to state governor without acquiring even the most basic grasp of history and government. Remarkably, she required emergency tutoring on the two world wars and various other middle-school fundamentals. She had simply never heard of the Federal Reserve System. She didn't know why there are two Koreas. She didn't know which nations (the United States, Mexico, and Canada) belonged to the North American Free Trade Agreement. And she had to be told that Africa was not a nation but a continent.

Attempts to instruct the would-be vice president sent her into "a catatonic stupor," according to frustrated McCain aides. The effort hardly seemed worthwhile anyway since she scorned expertise while placing far higher value on her own overrated "common sense."

As the first woman chosen for a national ticket by the Republican Party, Palin's novelty obscured the glaring fact that she was not their first deeply underqualified nominee. A dismal precedent dating back two decades existed in the person of Dan Quayle, the young Indiana senator whose surprise elevation onto the 1988 GOP ticket with George H. W. Bush discarded any consideration of competence or maturity for the youthful appeal of a clean-cut, blond frat boy. Party strategists whispered that they thought Quayle would attract women voters (which suggests that Palin at least represented a tiny step forward for feminism). Like Palin, Quayle could hardly articulate the policy positions he was supposed to advocate; like her, he too had needed stock phrases stuffed into his brain to simulate cognition. But Quayle's tentative style as a candidate indicated that he knew his own limitations, as Palin plainly did not. While he seemed to deserve pity more than mockery, she projected a bullying assurance that only "elitists" would ever insist on actual command of facts and policy.

That her belligerent approach insulted the same people to whom she was pandering evidently never occurred to Palin or her Republican handlers. When she debated her Democratic counterpart Joe Biden, a title bout that turned into a rout, the then senator from Delaware earnestly described his own modest background—and showed that intellectual coherence, breadth of knowledge, and basic diction need not be tokens of "elitism."

The same conservatives who had depicted themselves for decades as the last line of resistance to the "dumbing down" of American culture, standing up heroically against affirmative action for women and minorities, supposedly preserving standards in schools and workplaces, now rushed to Palin's defense. They brushed aside her lack of experience and intellect, confident that qualifications and merit no longer mattered to the "real Americans" whom Palin claimed to represent. Nor did they worry that Palin was the ultimate in tokenism, representing exactly what conservative Republicans had always claimed to scorn as quota politics and political correctness. She was a right-wing religious ideologue with female gender characteristics, and nothing else mattered to her backers. With overweening arrogance, they hoisted up an entirely vacuous nominee for vice president, thinking they were assured of a general election victory. Epitomizing that hubris was Grover Norquist, the Jack Abramoff crony, who boasted that "the Republicans were looking at decades of dominance in the House and the Senate" and could expect to maintain control of the White House, too.

The presence of Palin on their ticket proved embarrassing for the Republicans and surely contributed to the party's defeat in November 2008. But during that campaign, even as the political press highlighted her shortcomings, the Alaska governor developed a national following of slavish admirers. She exploited their devotion in what became a well-worn path: a book deal, a reality TV show, a Fox News gig, a super PAC, a YouTube channel, and much more. She abruptly quit as governor after less than two years in office, setting off to build her "maverick" brand by delivering speeches in primary states and teasing a presidential run that would never happen. In a pattern that would become typical of Tea Party direct-mail hustles, Palin's SarahPAC would take in one or two million during a political cycle—and then spend well under 10 percent on candidates. The bulk of SarahPAC contributions would be squandered on consultants and other expenses, with a strong emphasis on more fundraising. Even conservative columnists—not to mention comedians—began to refer to Palin as a "grifter."

Her undiscouraged followers nevertheless formed a hard-core cult, in defiance of polls that consistently showed her poor approval ratings. Pundits who dared to question Palin's capacities or motives could expect angry vilification by her masses of fans. The few outspoken skeptics on the right, including Ann Coulter and RedState blogger Erick Erickson, complained that anyone who expressed the slightest doubt about the "hockey mom" would be buried under hate mail from her admirers. The Palin bubble finally deflated only when she had to admit that she didn't plan to enter the 2012 primaries.

Until then, as Conor Friedersdorf explained in *The Atlantic*, Palin profited enormously from the intersection of two noxious modern trends—the commoditization of fame and the monetization of ideology. "Until Palin came along," he wrote, "no one realized that a politician could successfully leverage the celebrity gained in a presidential campaign into a multimillion-dollar fortune, and quickly. Less than a year after Palin resigned the governorship of Alaska, ABC News estimated that she'd earned $12 million . . . Past presidents excepted, did any make as much out of their notoriety?" Palin couldn't sustain the celebrity grift at that level for more than a few years. But her postelection career established a precedent and drew together a durable constituency for the know-nothing, pit-bull politics that she embodied.

WHAT THAT MIGHT portend for American politics began to materialize on February 19, 2009—almost exactly a month after the presidential inauguration of Barack Obama—when Rick Santelli delivered a furious rant on the floor of the Chicago Mercantile Exchange. The CNBC correspondent angrily denounced the Troubled Asset Relief Program (TARP), a proposed stimulus bill, and other efforts to stabilize the economy following the 2008 financial crisis. He baited the traders swarming around him with the idea of tax money subsidizing "losers" who could no longer support their mortgages. Then he said, "We're thinking of having a Chicago Tea Party in July. All you capitalists that want to show up to Lake Michigan, I'm gonna start organizing."

The reason behind the irritation of the traders and their spokesman on cable television was plain enough: the government had restricted their usual obscene bonuses in recognition of the fact that they had been saved by taxpayer funds from their industry's gross misconduct—and should not be rewarded for surviving on the public teat. After his viral moment passed, Santelli didn't organize anything. Within hours, others seized the opportunity, however, including a social media grouplet that called itself Top Conservatives on Twitter (TCOT), which hosted a conference call the next day inspired by Santelli's rant. A blogger and author named Michael Patrick Leahy brought together approximately fifty TCOT members from around the country.

Deciding to "strike while the iron was hot," they announced the first National Chicago Tea Party Day to be held a week later, on February 27. With a suitably vague platform of "limited government as authorized by the Constitution, fiscal responsibility, and free markets," they officially launched the National Tea Party Coalition, which soon had its own website. The founders included a handful of personalities—Jenny Beth Martin, Dana Loesch, Judson Phillips, and Amy Kremer—who would advance to leadership roles. Several of them would eventually gain prominence in the entourage of Donald Trump, Palin's political heir.

Whatever motivated its founders, the Tea Party movement instantly attracted unsavory would-be allies from under the rocks, including figures from the militia movement, the John Birch Society, the racist Council of Conservative Citizens, and nearly every other far-right formation in the country. Just as quickly, the new movement showed signs of the nativism and racism that had confronted Obama during the 2008 campaign, which only grew more pronounced when he entered the White House. Most Tea Party activists lived in the states of Confederacy, where white voters often felt free to express racial animus against the first Black president, and toward Black Americans more generally. Their unrestrained bigotry provided space for the rapid growth of "birtherism," the conspiracy theory asserting that Obama himself had been born not in Hawaii but in Kenya, the homeland of his father, and that he was therefore ineligible to serve as president. Trump signaled his own interest in national politics by intervening in the birther controversy, questioning Obama's legitimacy, and even hiring private detectives to "investigate" the president's origins.

In its earliest incarnation, the Tea Party had a grassroots aura that attracted larger, lavishly financed right-wing outfits in need of authenticity. By coincidence or not, the well-established network of political pressure and policy organizations run by far-right billionaires Charles and David Koch had established a dormant US Tea Party in 2002—and their seasoned operatives immediately leaped to assist the new movement. Americans for Prosperity (AFP), the principal organizing arm of the Koch network, immediately offered a list of five hundred thousand supporters gathered on petitions it had circulated to the National Tea Party Coalition, which mounted more than fifty protest events across the country on February 27, a week after the first conference call.

The other political outfit elbowing its way into the Tea Party parade was FreedomWorks, a "grassroots" construct headed by former Republican House majority leader Dick Armey. FreedomWorks had emerged several years earlier, along with AFP, from a previous Koch front called Citizens for a Sound Economy. (That entity had gone dormant in 2004.) Armey was a well-known Texas Republican who had come to power as majority leader after his party took over the House in 1994. He and his cronies—Speaker Newt Gingrich and House majority whip Tom DeLay—proceeded to rack up excesses in spending and sheer boodling that made their predecessors look stingy. Asked back then why the Republicans suddenly were devouring so much more federal pork than the Democrats, Armey replied bluntly: "To the victors go the spoils." When he left Congress in January 2003, Armey joined up with Citizens for a Sound Economy, which became FreedomWorks a year later. Though not an attorney, he also signed on as an adviser to DLA Piper, one of the capital's biggest bipartisan law and lobbying firms, which boasted of Armey's influence-peddling prowess on its website.

As for AFP, its Koch-appointed chief executive was Tim Phillips, a longtime GOP operative. He had cofounded the lobbying and consulting firm Century Strategies with Ralph Reed—the former Christian Coalition director who had fallen from grace in the Jack Abramoff scandal. In short, lurking behind the Tea Party's pitchfork-wielding, anti-Washington posturing was a pair of veteran Beltway lobbyists who would control the movement's money and messaging.

Any political differences between AFP and FreedomWorks were minor. Both operated "astroturfing" projects to mimic grassroots support for right-wing ideology, both were heavily and covertly funded by corporate interests, including the fossil fuel, health care, and tobacco industries, and both quickly swung into action to boost the visibility of the Tea Party movement. As early as the February 27 Tea Party demonstrations, both organizations joined in sponsoring local rallies, donating leaflets and other communications material to Tea Party chapters, and leading sessions to train organizers.

The influence of AFP and FreedomWorks escalated quickly as the Tea Party organizers mounted a major nationwide tax protest on April 15, 2009. The original Tea Party movement's grassroots character was swiftly subsumed into the corporate right-wing apparatus. Not surprisingly, the Tea Party formations around the country soon began to reflect the policy preferences of their corporate sponsors by mounting protests against smoke-free laws and tobacco taxes as well as "cap and trade" tax measures seeking to mitigate climate change. (The Koch brothers had by then funneled an estimated $50 million to groups that either denied climate change or opposed efforts to reduce carbon emissions.)

Over the years, a small clique of lobbyists and consultants sidled through a series of revolving doors connecting AFP and FreedomWorks with major tobacco companies, energy conglomerates, and trade associations. Shielded by tax laws that allowed their donors to remain concealed, the funding for these organizations was opaque if not entirely hidden. The ordinary Tea Party activist would have no way of knowing that their movement's expenses had been subsidized by the likes of R. J. Reynolds, Verizon, and ExxonMobil along with well-established right-wing foundations. For decades, the Koch brothers and their allies had spent millions to build "the underpinnings for a movement not quite ready to be born. The absent ingredient was rage," wrote reporter Adele Stan in a 2010 profile titled "Tea Party, Inc." But by 2009, Stan noted, "with the collapse of the economy and the election of the nation's first African-American president, the supply chain of rage was complete, and the Tea Party came roaring to life."

The rise of the Tea Party dovetailed with Republican propaganda targeting Obama, amplified by Fox News and a thousand lesser outlets in traditional and new media. Ignoring the role of President George W. Bush in the economic rescue program adopted and extended by his successor, the Tea Party began with angry populist rants against the TARP, that notorious "bailout" of drowning banks and insurance companies. Obama's economic stimulus program, officially known as the American Recovery and Reinvestment Act, only made them more furious, as did the new president's decision to subsidize the failing auto industry.

Yet while the recovery was slow, most economists believed that the nation had just barely escaped a horrific rerun of the Great Depression. The rampant inflation predicted by the Tea Party's ideological gurus never appeared. Denouncing "socialism" and warning that American freedoms were in danger, those same "populists" never mentioned that both the TARP and auto investments would prove to be not only essential to preserving economic stability but ultimately profitable to the Treasury (as they eventually did)—without any federal bureaucratic takeover. And despite their roars of outrage over the banking abuses that sparked the 2008 financial crisis, the Tea Party's overseers saw no reason to demand the prosecution of any of the culpable bankers and brokers. Accountability for the true authors of the 2008 financial crisis would have required action by the Justice Department, the Treasury, and other federal agencies—action that the elites behind the Tea Party opposed for reasons of both ideology and corporate policy.

Rather than hold bankers accountable for their crimes, the Tea

Party propaganda apparatus overseen by the Koch brothers and their like-minded cohorts stoked anger at the Right's usual targets—not only federal "bureaucrats" and Democratic politicians but immigrants and anyone else who might be depicted as a "taker" of government assistance. (Exempted from those despised categories were the elderly white Americans receiving Social Security and Medicare, who were deemed to "deserve" their benefits.) Surveys of Tea Party supporters consistently detected a powerful hostility toward Black Americans and other minorities. With the nation's first Black president as their principal target, it was almost too easy for the Tea Party Republicans to stir the same fear and paranoia that had fueled right-wing propaganda since the fifties. Not only was Obama secretly a Muslim and a socialist, but he was planning to institute Islamic law, confiscate firearms, surrender American sovereignty to the United Nations, and install himself as president for life.

Only the "real Americans" could stop him. Television and radio ads for the Tea Party candidates often featured guns and broadly hinted at violence, even civil war. As Palin told them: "Don't retreat. Reload!"

If the boiling fury of the Tea Party was misdirected, however, the power of its activist base could not be denied, as the rest of the country discovered in the wake of the 2010 midterm elections, when Republicans regained control of the House in a wave election that saw seventy congressional districts turned red. Although Democrats just barely retained control of the Senate, that same election saw several "establishment" Republican senators replaced by figures associated with the Tea Party, including Mike Lee of Utah, Rand Paul of Kentucky, and Ted Cruz of Texas. Unsure whether to confront or cajole the spreading insurgency, Republican leaders mostly did neither. Even before the 2010 midterm, Palin chose to align herself with the insurgents by announcing that she would address the fledgling National Tea Party Convention in Nashville, Tennessee, rather than the far larger and somewhat more respectable Conservative Political Action Conference in Washington, DC. Right-wing pundits saw her choice as a claim staked on the movement for her own political future.

"I get why she did it," RedState blogger Erick Erickson told *Politico*. "It is a purposeful decision on her part to try to claim a segment of the conservative movement as her own." Other observers pointed to the Tea Party convention sponsor's agreement to cover Palin's lucrative speaking fee, then estimated at more than $100,000.

When Sarah Palin rushed to cash in on the Tea Party, she found herself in a surging swarm of grifters—some veterans and some neophytes, but all eager to milk the new movement's supporters. Behind the National Tea Party Convention that had paid her exorbitant fee was a Tennessee attorney named Judson Phillips, who specialized in defending drunk drivers. Phillips had been one of the conservative activists on the original February 2009 conference call immediately after Rick Santelli's cable rant—and he soon saw a way to monetize the movement in his own backyard.

When Phillips took the lead in organizing Tea Party chapters in his home state, the activists who joined had urged him to establish a nonprofit umbrella group, with a PayPal account to channel donations into its bank account. But according to Kevin Smith, a local web designer who stepped forward to help the Tennessee group, the lawyer "kept dragging his feet" rather than set up a nonprofit political committee.

Then, as Smith told Talking Points Memo, Phillips suddenly announced on a radio show that he intended to charter Tea Party Nation as a for-profit corporation and the associated PayPal account channeled all funds into his wife's bank account. Confronted by the volunteers whose efforts he had exploited, the DUI lawyer told them that he had been forced to set up a for-profit Tea Party because the Obama administration was planning to "ban nonprofits." He assured them that the use of his wife's bank account would be "temporary." When he failed to keep that promise, Smith and other activists quit—and Phillips threatened to sue them for fraud.

"I can't even describe to you the anger we had with him, using our volunteer labor and our passion for the movement to build his start-up," Smith told Talking Points Memo reporter Zachary Roth. When Phillips disclosed his plans for the National Tea Party Convention, he confirmed their suspicions. Slated for the swanky Gaylord Opryland hotel in Nashville, with ticket prices starting at $549, the convention plainly aimed to attract high rollers, not the middle Americans who had flocked to the Tea Party banner.

As the odor of profiteering arose around the National Tea Party Convention, Erickson sniffed that the event "smells scammy." Several conservative organizations subsequently withdrew their endorsements; a United States senator and a member of Congress canceled their scheduled appearances; and Palin herself declared that she would "donate her fee" to "the cause" (although she never specified which cause). Local Tea Party activists even threatened to picket the Gaylord in protest.

"We never did this to make us rich or famous," wrote Sherry Phillips, Judson's wife and cofounder of Tea Party Nation, in a message to its members. "Quite the contrary, we are patriots who love our country, our members and the people who are coming to Nashville to attend this great event."

The convention's opening speech, delivered by a former Colorado Republican congressman named Tom Tancredo, highlighted the movement's unvarnished nativism and bigotry. In Nashville, he said Obama had been elected by "people who could not even spell the word 'vote' or say it in English," and suggested a "civic literacy test" for voters, like those used in the segregationist South.

Palin's keynote remarks, delivered to about six hundred people in the hotel ballroom, were devoid of any memorable or substantive content—and yet the crowd repeatedly interrupted her with standing ovations and chants of "Run, Sarah, run!" When an interlocutor referred to "President Palin," she responded with a smile and nothing more.

A year later, in July 2011, Tea Party Nation tried to hold a second national convention at a Las Vegas resort hotel. But by then, the group's poor reputation had caught up with Phillips. He was forced to postpone and then abandon the event, resulting in judgments against him for unpaid hotel bills and interest totaling $748,000.

When Tea Party Nation fizzled, Phillips remained active in politics, forming a political action committee that supported Roy Moore, the former Alabama judge and US Senate nominee accused of dating underage women. Phillips eventually took up a different legal racket, but that, too, ended badly. In 2018, the Tennessee Supreme Court suspended him from the practice of law, upon determining that he posed "a threat of substantial harm to the public." Specifically, he had ripped off dozens of legal clients seeking to cancel vacation timeshares, some of whom charged that he had accepted retainers and then ignored their messages and phone calls.

According to the *Orlando Sentinel*, he was "disbarred for trying to swindle timeshare owners into thinking they canceled their timeshares—and taking off with the money he earned from the fraudulent transactions." The paper reported that "more than 90 consumer fraud complaints" were brought against Phillips, along with lawsuits filed by several resorts in Orlando, Las Vegas, and Fort Lauderdale. He was disbarred a second and final time in 2019, "unable to defend himself against 41 pending disciplinary complaints."

While Phillips proved to be a small-time crook who soon stumbled over his own greed, the Tea Party had room for a variety of self-serving "activists" and outright con artists—which sparked ongoing and sometimes vicious conflicts over the potential swag.

AMONG THE HARSHEST Tea Party critics of Judson Phillips and his National Tea Party Convention was a fellow movement honcho who had, like him, participated on the initial February 2009 conference call. Jenny Beth Martin, a longtime Georgia Republican activist, told anyone who would listen that her organization—the Tea Party Patriots—would certainly not participate in the convention. "When I've talked to our members, they've said this is entirely too expensive" to represent a grassroots rebellion.

When she heard Santelli's rant, Martin was toiling as a house cleaner and angrily mulling the federal government's assistance to the undeserving. After her husband's labor contracting business failed in 2007, they had been forced into bankruptcy, losing their home and selling off their twin Lincoln Navigators, with more than a million dollars still owed in back taxes. She had thrown herself into the Tea Party movement, joining up with two others from the February call—Mark Meckler and Amy Kremer—to found the Tea Party Patriots.

Meckler was a Sacramento-based lawyer and online marketing executive who had once been among the most successful salesmen for Herbalife, the multilevel marketing and pyramid scheme that was eventually sanctioned and fined more than $200 million by the Federal Trade Commission. Kremer was a former Delta Air Lines stewardess, single mother, and political blogger—a Sarah Palin superfan, still brooding over the election of Barack Obama, whom she fervently believed to be a native of Kenya and "not eligible to be President of this great country."

Before long, the Tea Party Patriots had gathered enough local chapters under its social media umbrella to boast of a large national membership. In June 2009, the Patriots incorporated as a 501(c)(4) nonprofit, which allowed its directors to raise and spend limitless amounts of "dark money" from unnamed donors. Within a year, Martin had achieved a measure of fame and plaudits from *Time* magazine as one of its 100 Most Influential People, while Meckler nabbed a commentating gig on Fox News.

But Kremer felt overshadowed and, by the fall of 2009, she had defected to a competing group in California, the Tea Party Express, after joining its barnstorming summer bus tour. Her friendship with Martin swiftly disintegrated, leading the Tea Party Patriots to officially sever ties with Kremer. When she retaliated by claiming ownership of the group's name, website, and email lists, Martin and the board of directors got a court injunction forbidding her to use any Tea Party Patriots lists or trademarks. The litigious breakup didn't end there, however.

Toward the end of 2010, a year that would see the Tea Party reach its zenith in the Republican midterm sweep, someone using the name "Dale Butterworth" posted a brutal accusation against Kremer on the Tea Party Patriots' Facebook page. It said she had allowed her boyfriend (and later husband) James Lyle to sexually abuse her daughter, Kylie, a minor, and then kicked her daughter out after the girl reported Lyle to the police.

None of the accusations were true, and Butterworth turned out to be Jenny Beth Martin's husband, Lee Martin, who had occasionally used the same pseudonym to post false charges of adultery targeting other critics of Tea Party Patriots.

After three years of litigation, the group settled with Kylie Kremer for an undisclosed amount. But as Stephanie Mencimer reported in *Mother Jones*, the legal battle between Amy Kremer and the Martins continued. Forced to give a sworn deposition, Lee Martin eventually admitted that he had written the false Facebook posting to discredit Kremer and Tea Party Express—because he and the Tea Party Patriots saw them as "competitors for the same pool of donor money." Although Lee Martin lost the lawsuit, resulting in a million-dollar-plus judgment against him in a Georgia court, he managed to avoid paying up. So did the Tea Party Patriots, with the help of Republican attorneys and a scheme that diverted donor funds to a newly incorporated Tea Party Patriots Citizens Fund, also controlled by Martin.

The bitter enmities among the Tea Party groups didn't hinder any of them from running their hustles over the ensuing years, as they brought in millions of dollars from the unsuspecting rubes who believed their paranoid attacks on Obama and their soaring rhetoric about the Constitution and limited government. It was essentially the same direct-mail racket pioneered by Richard Viguerie decades earlier, except under different names and employing online technology. The contracts arranged by Martin with outside fundraising firms resembled those Viguerie deals, too. For instance, MDS Communications—an Arizona outfit that also raised money for the Republican National Committee, Martin's supposed "establishment" nemesis—got as much as seventy cents on each dollar that donors thought would go to "patriotic" campaigns. Capitol Resources, another GOP fundraising firm in Iowa, kept 75 percent of the receipts.

Jenny Beth Martin retained control of the net proceeds in her role as the "national coordinator" of the Tea Party Patriots and dictated her own compensation. That meant as much as $300,000 in the 2012 presidential election year, plus first-class travel and other perks. She had come a long way in a short time from personal bankruptcy and cleaning other people's houses. Over the ensuing years, her $15,000 monthly fee for "strategic consulting" and additional payments from other Tea Party Patriots entities eventually added up to as much as $450,000 annually. Those self-dealing maneuvers infuriated the local Tea Party activists who learned about them, as did the massive payments to GOP insider consultants. According to a report in *Mother Jones*, the Tea Party Patriots New Mexico state coordinator vented her disenchantment as early as January 2011 in an email to fellow members:

> The Tea Party Patriots national website clearly states that 100% of the funds raised go to furthering OUR efforts. Well, I guess that's true AFTER paying out salaries, consultants, telemarketers, attorneys, etc. . . .
>
> And yes, Jenny Beth and Mark Meckler hired a consultant without most of us even knowing about it and now that consultant has encouraged and those two have decided to start soliciting donations from our own local tea party participants so that they can pay themselves, their consultant, their telemarketers, and their attorneys.

Another disappointed local leader in California told *Mother Jones* that Martin and Meckler were diverting money from the grassroots to enrich themselves and their new cronies, while pretending to assist local Tea Party organizations. "They make it seem like they help local groups," she said. "None of that money ever goes back to local groups."

Kremer didn't appear to be pulling down as much money as her old rivals. In 2011, she told a *Roll Call* reporter that her monthly salary as national chairwoman of Tea Party Express amounted to $4,000. Whatever Kremer was earning, a heavy stream of revenue flowed through the organization to its actual bosses at Russo Marsh, the longtime Republican consulting outfit in Sacramento that had created it to revive the firm's own moribund political action committee, an anti-Obama entity known as Our Country Deserves Better.

In the weeks following Santelli's rant, a Russo Marsh associate named Joe Wierzbicki had sent the firm's principal, Sal Russo, an ambitious proposal to "position us as a growing force" within the Tea Party movement. He suggested a national tour, with "an awesome looking bus," to target "big spending Democrats" for defeat in the upcoming midterm. That plan succeeded well beyond Russo's expectations, vaulting the Tea Party Express into a top spot among the scuffling Tea Party groups and bringing in millions of dollars annually. Much of the money from that haul went from the nonprofit Express into the accounts of Russo Marsh and King Media Group, a firm led by Russo's wife, and their subcontractors. During the first year of the Express organization's existence, it raised slightly more than $5 million—of which $3 million went to the firms owned by Russo and his spouse.

The same unrestrained looting continued into the 2012 election cycle, when Tea Party Express brought in $10 million from its naive donors but spent less than $700,000—or 7 percent—on right-wing candidates and campaigns. The largest chunk went to Republican presidential candidate Mitt Romney—not a Tea Party type at all. (Sarah Palin didn't endorse Romney until twenty-four hours before Election Day, when she gave him a lukewarm send-off; her PAC sent him a token $5,000 donation.) That $10 million didn't include another $1.2 million raised by Russo Marsh's other PAC, the Committee to Defeat Barack Obama (CDBO), which also tapped the Tea Party Express lists. Of the money raised by CDBO, 73 percent went to its executive director—the prescient Tea Party enthusiast Joe Wierzbicki—along with his employers and colleagues at Russo Marsh.

Unsuspecting right-wing rubes still coughed up another $12 million for Tea Party Express in the 2014 midterm. During that cycle, a Republican critic writing for The Daily Beast assessed the fundraising practices, financial transparency, and election track records of five major Tea Party organizations, finding that Tea Party Express was "the worst of the worst." Having raised a little more than $9.5 million, the group spent an eye-rolling 96 percent on consultants and expenses, with only 4 percent devoted to candidates, campaigns, and organizing. All along, they never hesitated to spend additional thousands on lavish steak house dinners and luxury casino hotel rooms.

Back when *The New York Times* asked Russo about the sweetheart deals between his Tea Party organization and his consulting firms (and those steak house and casino charges), he bristled. "This has not been a profitable activity for us. We have plowed every penny back into this thing." By that, he may have meant they plowed the money raised—after salaries and commissions and three bus tours—back into raising more money. Which they kept doing every year until those donor lists were exhausted.

EVERYTHING CHANGED FOR the Tea Party grifters in 2015, when Donald J. Trump elbowed his way into the Republican primaries and won. Trump ingested the movement whole, scarcely pausing to burp, in full confidence that its mercenary leadership would rush to support him despite his disdainful attitude toward the principles the movement supposedly upheld. He knew instinctively, as they did, that his popularity among their followers as a race-baiting "birther" would dispel any qualms over his personal morality, business practices, or murky ideology.

Unlike most of the Tea Party leadership—such as her enemy Amy Kremer—Jenny Beth Martin at first resisted Trump fiercely. A supporter of Senator Ted Cruz, who had enjoyed backing from Palin and Tea Party groups in his 2012 Senate primary, she denounced the wealthy New Yorker as a fake. "Donald Trump loves himself first, last, and everywhere in between. He loves himself more than our country, he loves himself more than the Constitution. He doesn't love you, me, and he doesn't love the Tea Party," she ranted at the March 2016 Conservative Political Action Conference. "Donald Trump has no business thinking he's Tea Party, and every Tea Party person who truly loves the Constitution should take that into account when casting their vote." But like her pal Cruz, who endured a brutal public humiliation by Trump, including wild insults to his wife and father, she soon surrendered to the new boss. The Tea Party Patriots Citizens Fund, which she had set up to avoid the Lyle libel judgment, spent over a million dollars on robocalls and other media to support Trump in November 2016.

Kremer went hard for Trump from the beginning, having departed from the Tea Party Express. She registered TrumPAC, a new political action committee, in January 2016, which was later forced to change its name for hijacking his name and brand in a violation of federal election rules. A tweet of recognition from Trump himself established her credibility in his MAGA movement—and eventually led to a measure of notoriety for her and her daughter, Kylie, as instigators of the January 6, 2021, insurrection. On that day, she would deliver a telling speech at the Ellipse, just south of the White House.

"I come from the Tea Party movement, and I'm asked all the time: What happened to the Tea Party?" she would tell the inflamed and restive crowd. "Well, we're still here. We just grew and morphed into something bigger and better—the MAGA movement."

But that infamous January day would have to wait. In the meantime, Trump's ascent swiftly reduced the once vibrant Tea Party to the dismal condition of a used tea bag. Fittingly, its obituary in *Politico* magazine was authored by Beltway campaign finance lawyer Paul Jossey, a former employee of one of the Tea Party scam outfits. "The Tea Party movement is pretty much dead now, but it didn't die a natural death," Jossey wrote. "It was murdered—and it was an inside job. In a half decade, the spontaneous uprising that shook official Washington degenerated into a form of pyramid scheme that transferred tens of millions of dollars from rural, poorer Southerners and Midwesterners to bicoastal political operatives." With unsparing and detailed examples showing how that scheme operated, including the names of individual operatives and the amounts of money raised, Jossey angrily indicted the Republican Right for swindling its own benighted supporters. "Today," he wrote, "the Tea Party movement is dead, and Trump has co-opted the remnants." The remnants assuredly did not include the movement's vaunted commitment to balanced budgets, as Trump ran up the deficit by trillions of dollars; limited government, which Trump mocked with his attempts to intimidate the press and expand presidential power; and the Constitution, which Trump would violate wantonly and openly seek to suspend.

10

How Not to Get Rich Quick (or Cure Cancer, Ever)

When modern con artists launch a scam, they know that the most easily and profitably swindled marks are quite likely to identify themselves as "very conservative." Cocooned within the hermetic media system that validates their prejudices and insulates them from inconvenient truths, right-wing Republicans are a vulnerable cohort—often elderly, isolated, and insecure, with at least some disposable income. After decades of conditioning by propaganda outlets that have only become more powerful and pervasive since the advent of social media, they are more likely than their fellow Americans to believe the most outlandish conspiracy theories, the most alarming economic predictions, and the most paranoid interpretations of everyday news stories, from incidents of gun violence to unwelcome election outcomes.

In recent years, the explosive growth of the QAnon cult—premised on the notion that dozens of prominent Democrats and Hollywood stars consume the blood of infants to remain young—has demonstrated that many of them will believe quite literally anything. And the QAnon phenomenon has shown too that the unbelievable can be sustained indefinitely even amid increasingly ludicrous claims—"JFK Jr. is still alive!"—and countless disappointments. As social psychologists have long observed, the inevitable failure of those prophecies—warning of a communist takeover, an economic crash worse than the Great Depression, and many alternative catastrophes—almost never dissuade the gullible. There is always an explanation and a new implausible prediction.

The forecasts of national doom that began as small-time direct-mail appeals from Red-baiting "experts" on the communist menace during the fifties have metastasized into enormously profitable online scams of seemingly infinite variation. These entrepreneurs have developed and refined a marketing formula that can be applied to widely diverse offerings, from overpriced gold coins and worthless penny stocks to crooked financial advice and fake cancer "cures."

The same paranoid mindset that leaves people open to conspiracy theories—about the economy, the federal government, the medical "establishment," and the very future of the country—also makes them receptive to a sales pitch for those dubious products. If you convince an audience of rubes that the despised Democratic president is going to plunge the nation into a depression, then you can probably persuade them that the only sound investment for their savings is an overpriced gold coin. Or that their family's security requires buying preserved foods in enormous quantity. Or even that the always worsening crisis can be turned into a financial bonanza—if only they are made privy to your secret (and usually self-serving) investment tips.

Political prognostications and overheated rhetoric were coupled with exhortations to buy costly private newsletters touting tainted financial advice and other scam products, all of which would supposedly shield them and their loved ones from American society's impending cataclysm.

THE EXISTENCE OF an affluent middle-class cohort that would believe preposterous scare stories dated back to the McCarthy era, when Red-baiting charlatans could terrify a gullible audience with rumors of armed African communists just across the southern border, lurking until the command came to enforce a takeover by the United Nations. But that kind of hysteria came and went, persisting only among a remnant of boobish believers. It was not until the nineties, during the era of the "Clinton scandals," that the right-wing operatives, media celebrities, and entrepreneurs who profited from such narratives realized there was a furious mass audience, incessantly demanding more and more. And the same folks who would believe anything might also be induced to buy almost anything their trusted leaders were selling.

From that insight arose new business models that made grifting a reliable source of income for any "conservative" commentator, celebrity, or pundit able to attract an exploitable fan base—and the dominant feature of right-wing politics in the United States. Grifting fit neatly into the political outlook of the Right, with its hostility to government regulation—because regulation inherently hinders and might even punish any perpetrator of unlawful scams.

True freedom, for these self-styled "libertarians," meant the absence of laws and regulations that protect the public from all kinds of rip-offs, along with the bureaucrats and prosecutors who enforce them. For them, ideology meshed seamlessly with self-interest. Indeed, many of these extreme ideologues yearned for a final reckoning—usually a financial cataclysm triggered by overweening Democrats—that would destroy what they described with disgust as "the administrative state" (also known as *liberal democracy*). While engineering that twilight upheaval, they would continue to pursue politics for profit, mostly at the expense of their fellow "conservatives."

Among the notable pioneers of such apocalypse marketing was James Dale Davidson, an author and self-proclaimed economic "expert" with no academic background in that discipline. While he first earned real notoriety during the Clinton years, Davidson had been active on the right since the late sixties, when he founded the National Taxpayers Union (and eventually named young Grover Norquist, fresh out of Harvard, as its executive director). They shared a mission that Norquist would describe years later as reducing government to "a size where I can drag it into the bathroom and drown it in the bathtub."

The advent of a Democratic presidency, after more than a decade of Republican rule, provoked many on the right to foretell disaster of every variety, especially financial. In his 1993 book, *The Plague of the*

Black Debt: How to Survive the Coming Depression, the author flatly predicted a "deep depression" that would end Bill Clinton's presidency after one term while boosting the national debt by a trillion dollars.

"I am as sure of this as I am that the sun will rise tomorrow," he wrote. The sun came up, but when none of his other prognostications materialized, Davidson wasn't discouraged. Instead, he spent the next few years drawing attention to himself—and, not incidentally, his expensive financial newsletter, *Strategic Investment*—by promoting conspiracy theories surrounding the tragic suicide of Vince Foster, a forty-eight-year-old White House deputy counsel who had been Bill's boyhood chum and Hillary's law partner.

Despite exhaustive investigations that led not one but two independent counsels—Robert Fiske and Kenneth Starr—to conclude that a depressed Foster had killed himself, Davidson used his newsletter to trumpet claims of foul play, insinuating that the Clintons had murdered their friend. If Clinton refused to wreck his presidency, then Davidson would do it. When he hired three handwriting "experts" to claim that Foster's suicide note had been forged—and promoted the charge across right-wing talk radio—subscriptions to his newsletter skyrocketed.

Davidson's warnings fit perfectly with the official response to Clinton from Republicans on Capitol Hill. In his first budget, the new president, fearing the impact of big deficits left by his GOP predecessors, had imposed a hefty new marginal rate on the wealthiest taxpayers—according to Republican lore, the "biggest tax hike in history." A furious Newt Gingrich and his right-wing caucus told Americans that Clinton's tax increases would cause an immediate recession and lead to even larger deficits; in fact, the economy soon boomed, and Clinton became the first president in decades to balance the budget and begin to pay down the national debt.

Davidson, too, had felt certain about looming economic ruin and his accusations of a White House murder plot. Soon enough, he assured *The Washington Post*, there would emerge "overwhelming evidence that Foster was murdered." The title of his next book, published on the eve of the 1996 election, connected the plots: *Who Murdered Vince Foster? And Why the Biggest Political Scandal in History Is Also the Biggest Financial Story of Our Lifetimes*. This 116-page jeremiad bluntly envisioned "Watergate-style hearings" and prosecutions that would ruin the Clintons, crash an overleveraged stock market, and ultimately tear down the entire edifice of the liberal state.

Still smarting over those erroneous conjectures a decade later, Davidson insisted the Clinton boom was "a hoax" that had been "faked by the government."

Contrary to his conspiracy theory, Foster's death was neither the biggest political scandal nor the biggest financial story—not even close—but by attaching himself to a burgeoning right-wing conspiracy, Davidson contrived to promote his newsletter, his crank theories, and his dubious investment expertise to a rapidly growing cohort. With that creative stroke, he fashioned a model that would be replicated again and again, until it became a fully integrated and often dominant mode of grifting enterprise in the Republican Party.

He and his coauthor, the British Tory peer and former newspaper publisher Lord William Rees-Mogg, continued to produce books that combined far-right ideology with financial speculation. The most notable, titled *The Sovereign Individual* and published in 1997, foretold a world in which governments, nation-states, and social order would collapse, digital currencies would replace all other forms of money, taxation and regulation would become impossible—and the Clintons would be exposed as the Mafia-style ringleaders of a narcotics empire. It denigrated democracy as the twin of communism and welcomed the advent of a dystopian world dominated by a tiny minority of the super-rich.

Although *The Sovereign Individual* was marred by obvious errors about the direction of the world economy and the advent of "digital gold," among others, it nonetheless attracted powerful fans, in particular among the most rightward-leaning mandarins of Silicon Valley. The PayPal billionaire and Trump backer Peter Thiel wrote an admiring introduction to a new edition in 2020 that emphasized its influence on his own political outlook and urged it on readers as "an opportunity not to be wasted."

Davidson's newsletter and books were the products of a much larger Baltimore-based publishing enterprise, Agora Inc., which seized upon his method of combining a direct-mail (and later email) sales pitch with a right-wing political message.

Appealing to paranoia and prejudice in a vein similar to the campaigns pioneered by Richard Viguerie decades earlier, the Agora promotions came to feature endorsements from a panoply of right-wing political figures, including former Texas representative Ron Paul, former Speaker Newt Gingrich, and former Arkansas governor Mike Huckabee, as well as ideologically aligned media outlets such as RedState and *National Review*. Emphasizing the nightmare vision of an America on the edge of social disintegration and economic chaos, their messages were always calculated to spook recipients and promised answers in an Agora newsletter—available right away to anyone who pulled out a credit card to subscribe for $1,000, a bargain if you believed Newt.

Other newsletter pitches were more specific and targeted—and sometimes ran up against the law.

In the most notorious example, an Agora newsletter called *Pirate Investor*, published by one Frank Porter Stansberry, claimed to have "super-insider" details on a nuclear-weapons disposal agreement between the United States and Russia that could provide a 100 percent return on investment almost instantly—to anyone who subscribed, that is (also for that nice round $1,000). That venture drew the scrutiny of the Securities and Exchange Commission, which lodged a complaint against Agora, *Pirate Investor*, and Stansberry in November 2003, alleging in federal court that they had "engaged in an ongoing scheme to defraud public investors by disseminating false information in several Internet newsletters published by Agora or its wholly owned subsidiaries."

The complaint noted that even after Agora learned the SEC was investigating its business, the company's newsletters "continued to publish emails promoting numerous securities"—often penny stocks—"accompanied by fantastic claims of quick profits or inside information . . . [and] touted stocks that it claims will double or triple in value over the next year. . . . The money-making investments featured in the reports are typically microcap issuers with cures for cancer or AIDS or a technological breakthrough."

The SEC accused Stansberry—who moonlighted as a columnist for the ultra-right political outlet WorldNetDaily—of simply fabricating his claims of inside sources and proprietary information on the nuclear deal, a charge he persistently denied. A federal judge eventually upheld a $1.5 million fine against Stansberry, although the judge found that Agora specifically wasn't responsible for its subsidiary's rip-off. "Stansberry's conduct undoubtedly involved deliberate fraud, making statements [about a stock] that he knew to be false; Pirate acted in reckless disregard for regulations when it published Stansberry's unbelievable claims without a shred of confirmation," the forty-nine-page decision declared.

Stansberry spent years contesting the SEC case while continuing to combine far-right political messaging with sales of investment newsletters by independent writers on his firm's website. In 2010, he produced an apocalyptic, anti-Obama video titled "End of America" that foretold the impending crash of the US financial system.

Stansberry moved in February 2020 to vacate the SEC's permanent injunction against his firm in federal court, which the agency didn't oppose. The injunction was lifted, and Stansberry has continued to do business while proclaiming its commitment to "compliance" with high standards and transparency. Its rating on the Trustpilot business review website in 2023 was "Poor," with angry consumers venting about incessant email spamming, automatic newsletter renewals, and other shoddy practices.

Over the interceding years since his SEC misadventure, Stansberry became embroiled in a much more tragic scandal that has left reverberating suspicions that may never fully recede. In 2006, a young Stansberry & Associates financial writer named Rey Rivera went missing, until his body was found a week later in a room under a hole in the roof of the Belvedere Hotel in Baltimore, not far from the company's office. Although police determined that Rivera had committed suicide, perhaps jumping from the hotel roof or a parking structure next door where his car was found, he left no note.

A longtime personal friend of Stansberry, Rivera had reportedly rushed out of his house on the day he disappeared after receiving a call from the Stansberry firm's switchboard. But nobody at the firm acknowledged making the call. The bizarre and anomalous circumstances of his demise—and the fact that he had quit his job at Stansberry six months earlier to return to California with his wife—aroused questions that inspired a book, an episode of Netflix's *Unsolved Mysteries* series that aired in 2020, and an ongoing controversy. Stansberry says that he fully cooperated with the police investigation and offered a reward of $1,000 for information about his friend's death.

EVEN AS AGORA, Stansberry, and similar outfits churned out high-priced, low-value investment counseling, they faced increasing competition on other media—notably including personalities connected with Fox News Channel and Fox Business Channel, where analysts who were sufficiently telegenic could build trust with an enormous audience of potential marks. And in at least one glaring case, the abuse of that trust was so egregious that even the Fox News hierarchy, which has tolerated and even encouraged ethical breaches of every kind, felt obliged to boot the offender off the air. But not until Tobin Smith had appeared on Fox business programming for over twelve years.

Smith was a star on Fox business programming, appearing as a market analyst and host on both Fox News and Fox Business shows such as the top-rated *Bulls and Bears*. The network connection bolstered his own credibility and that of his NBT Group website and newsletter business.

What eventually caught up with Smith was a habit of promoting dubious penny stocks—usually through right-wing email newsletters or lists from the likes of Dick Morris, the late Herman Cain, and *National Review*, among others—while receiving substantial compensation from the companies whose shares he pitched. For instance, Smith's NBT Group took $50,000 from a small tech firm called IceWeb, which he then pushed on investors with unrestrained enthusiasm. "NOW that you understand just a little about what's happening in the world of

Cloud Storage and Big Data Analytics," he wrote on May 24, 2012, "you understand ALL you need to know to make a damn FORTUNE from this under 25 cents stock." Within a few weeks, the value of the IceWeb shares had fallen to two cents.

Around the same time, Smith became equally excited about Boldface Group, a celebrity cosmetic licensing firm associated with the Kardashian sisters, whose shares were then selling for under fifty cents. "Buying shares of Boldface Group (BLBK) now, while you can still get them at less than 50-cents is the chance of a lifetime to cash in on the NEXT celebrity money machine! Owning shares of Boldface Group stock (BLBK) opens the door for you to participate in the kind of celebrity profits that are usually available only to groupies, agents and rich friends," and so on.

Boldface Group had paid $50,000 in compensation to Smith's company as an "editorial fee." Within six months, the share price had dropped to six cents—and the following year, the value of BLBK had plummeted so far that the company was forced to execute a reverse stock split of one new share for every one hundred outstanding shares, in order to remain listed as an over-the-counter stock by OTC Markets Group.

The deal that led to Smith's ouster from Fox involved Petrosonic Energy, exposed by a reporter for MarketWatch, a Dow Jones financial news website owned, ironically enough, by Rupert Murdoch's News Corp. As noted below, Murdoch seems untroubled by financial conflicts of interest so long as his media conglomerate reaps the benefits of those arrangements and not just individual employees (as in Glenn Beck's infamously lucrative partnership with Goldline, a precious metals and numismatic marketing outfit that was a major advertiser on his Fox show).

After MarketWatch reported that Smith's NBT Group took a $50,000 "sponsored investment research" fee from Petrosonic, Fox bounced him for violating network policy forbidding any Fox Business employee from accepting "financial consideration of any kind whatsoever to issue research, advertisements, or to otherwise promote individual stocks or securities."

The case of Charles Payne, another Fox personality with dubious ethics, raised questions about the network's commitment to enforcing its ethics rules—and demonstrated yet again how right-wing ideologues could financially ensnare unsuspecting rubes. A New York stock analyst with his own firm, Wall Street Strategies, Payne started out as a Fox regular in 2007. He had special cachet on the network as a Black right-winger with a blustery disdain for the poor and a willingness to twist economic facts to fit his own political narrative. He was also perfectly willing to use his credentials to boost companies that paid him on the side.

Not long after Fox bounced Tobin Smith, Media Matters for America's Eric Hananoki published a lengthy investigation proving that Payne had accepted thousands of dollars from companies whose shares he promoted—and which later turned out to be virtually worthless. A prime example was an early-childhood education outfit known as Brainy Brands, which produced video discs, books, and learning games. After taking $40,000 from a marketing firm on behalf of Brainy Brands, Payne claimed that it would "become a market leader" and "turn $10,000 into $33,000." He repeatedly forecast a potential rise in its stock price from $1.35 to $4.50 per share, or 233 percent, "within 36 months." Within two years, however, the company had almost disappeared, its stock essentially worthless at a price under a half of a cent per share.

Payne played similar games with the stocks of other microcap companies, including a "nutritional" outfit selling an artificial sweetener that he touted as potentially rising 400 percent in value—before its shares crashed to six-hundredths of a penny.

If Fox had vetted Payne before hiring him—as perhaps it did—the network's executives would have known that the SEC already had sanctioned him for precisely the same dishonest behavior exposed years later by Media Matters. In 1999, Payne and his company agreed to pay $35,000 in fines for unlawfully promoting the stock of Members Service Corporation, a holding company with interests at various times in hotel, casino, telecommunications, and energy businesses. Payne never revealed to his clients that Members had paid him to push its shares. By then, the company had long since gone out of business, and the NASDAQ exchange delisted it.

Payne's star nevertheless rose and rose at Fox, which gave him his own show on the network—*Making Money with Charles Payne*—not long after the exposure of his shady exploits. He can be seen regularly on such marquee shows as *Fox & Friends*, usually echoing Republican Party talking points against the minimum wage and clean energy rather than hawking penny stocks.

The right-wing marketplace was never monolithic, of course, which has meant that discrete segments respond to a plethora of religious, ideological, regional, and thinly disguised racial appeals. Mike Huckabee, the former Arkansas governor, Republican presidential hopeful, and Fox News talking head, could reliably attract the most credulous marks, by the tens of thousands, on the religious right. For more than a decade, Huckabee had been an ordained Southern Baptist pastor and the head of the Arkansas Baptist State Convention, which inspired his entry into politics. Besides his credibility among white evangelicals, "Huck" had also built a mammoth email list of responsive and exceptionally naive fans who had followed him ever since his strong showing during the 2008 Republican primaries.

Reflecting his spiritual credentials, Agora used the affable preacher's endorsement to push a phony health product with a scriptural spin. Introducing an email message from an officiously named Agora subsidiary, Huckabee assured his hundreds of thousands of followers that the Health Sciences Institute had "important information to share with you." Specifically, a message touting a "Biblical cure for cancer" attributed to a secret interpretation of passages from the Book of Matthew. For the incredible bargain price of only seventy-four dollars, Agora would forward the vital facts about this lifesaving nostrum—which, on closer examination, turned out to be nothing more than advice to consume fewer carbohydrates. It wasn't a cure, nor had the prophets described it as such.

Not surprisingly, as recounted by Tim Murphy in *Mother Jones*, Huckabee disclaimed any responsibility for the messages sent out under his name. When questioned on CNN about the "hucksterism" he had endorsed, Huckabee breezily compared the scam emails to the cable network's product advertising and added, "I didn't actually run that part of my company."

Meanwhile, the Health Sciences Institute kept churning out its fearful political messages, always linked to a bogus cure. There was nobody scarier than Barack Obama, at least during his presidency, which was why the "institute" sent yet another email promoting a miraculous treatment that "vaporizes cancer in six weeks"—and supposedly withheld from suffering Americans by the villainous Obama administration.

THE OBAMA YEARS saw the metastasizing of the conspiracy culture that had taken root as a permanent feature of American politics during the presidency of Bill Clinton—and the rise of media celebrities on the right whose entire persona depended on the promotion of that culture in its most toxic forms. Not surprisingly, those same figures eagerly exploited the anxieties of their audience for profit in the most shameless fashion.

Among the disreputable figures who came to prominence during that period is Glenn Beck, who climbed from beginnings as a manic "morning zoo" AM radio jock in the Pacific Northwest, driven by alcohol and cocaine, through radio syndication to mass television audiences on Headline News and Fox News Channel. Beck built his audience with nightly diet of conspiratorial rants that reached back to the John Birch Society, specifically author and public speaker W. Cleon Skousen. So extreme was Skousen—and so discredited—that he drew the disapproving glare of FBI director J. Edgar Hoover as a "professional anti-communist" and fraud. (Notably, Skousen had worked for the Christian Anti-Communism Crusade, run by Fred Schwarz, another profiteer despised by Hoover.)

On a whiteboard, Beck would draw arcane diagrams that outlined imaginary plots involving dozens of alleged secret radicals, from Obama and billionaire George Soros to the Goldman Sachs investment bank and the ISIS terror network—all working to undermine American sovereignty in service of a New World Order. Owing to their machinations, Beck regularly emphasized on both his radio and TV programs, the US economy was doomed to collapse, with "100 percent guaranteed hyperinflation like Zimbabwe" on the horizon.

The only truly secure store of value, as he told viewers again and again, was gold—and the best way to acquire gold was to buy it from Goldline International, a California-based firm that was one of the nation's largest precious metals dealers. Not only was gold the safest investment, but according to Beck, those New World Order conspirators, aided by dastardly big-government liberals, would soon confiscate privately held gold bullion to corner the commodity for themselves.

Driving that false narrative into the skulls of their fans with metronomic insistence, Beck and other right-wing endorsers—including his Fox News colleagues Mark Levin, Mike Huckabee, and Laura Ingraham—sent thousands of customers fervently in search of gold. Sales were estimated in the hundreds of millions of dollars.

Whether Goldline paid Beck as a spokesman, which appeared to be confirmed on its own website and in videos he made for the company, or whether the firm was merely his most faithful advertiser on radio and television, there was no doubt of his devotion. Following investigations by ABC News and a congressional subcommittee, and later by California prosecutors, as well as other state and federal agencies, there was also no doubt that Goldline's sales methods were permeated with deception and fraud.

Testimony and documents showed that Goldline sales personnel, pretending to be "investment advisers," subjected customers to high-pressure boiler-room techniques. At first promising to deliver gold bullion, they would later cajole their customers into buying gold coins at an enormous markup, lying to them about the potential seizure of bullion by the government. Rather than protecting their savings, the Goldline customers thus courted financial ruin, because the coins they bought were priced at least twice as high as their value if melted down. In short, the price of gold would have had to double before Beck's dupes could break even.

After the ABC investigation and a parallel congressional probe, the city attorney of Santa Monica filed a nineteen-count criminal complaint against Goldline and its top executives that included misdemeanor charges of grand theft, fraud, and conspiracy as well as false advertising. A year later, those charges were settled with Goldline agreeing to $4.5 million in customer refunds, an $800,000 fund to compensate future claims, and strict rules governing disclosure of markups, in exchange for withdrawal of the criminal indictment. Goldline hailed this humbling compromise as "a victory," and Beck never stepped away from the company for an instant. He brushed off the criminal charges as merely further evidence of a government plot to control gold.

More than a decade after his involuntary departure from Fox News, Beck has started a series of enterprises, including BlazeTV, a "conservative" website and digital television service, his radio program and podcast. He continues to hawk Goldline, which features a one-minute endorsement video from Beck on its corporate website.

The demographic reached by Goldline through Beck and his fellow Fox hosts is still the primary target for scammers marketing gold—as the Commodity Futures Trading Commission (CFTC) revealed in early 2020, when it unveiled a major investigation pursued in cooperation with law enforcement authorities in thirty states. The federal and state agencies accused Lucas Asher and Simon Batashvili, both Los Angeles residents associated with Metals.com and Barrick Capital Inc., of defrauding at least 1,600 "conservative and religious investors" of as much as $180 million in sales of grossly overpriced precious metals since 2017. Pitching the potential marks on telephone calls and through social media, salesmen told them that the federal government might seize their assets in the event of a market crash—unless those holdings were converted into precious metals, *The Wall Street Journal* reported.

The salesmen convinced their dupes to liquidate their retirement accounts and spend the proceeds to purchase gold or silver at markups ranging as high as 300 percent, the government's complaint alleged, which caused instantaneous losses. They "swindled tens of millions from the victims, who were targeted for their politically conservative and Christian leanings," according to Heath Tarbert, then the CFTC chairman. The government complaint also alleged that those Metals.com sales personnel "misled investors into believing that . . . Asher and Batashvili were friends with a conservative television and radio personality who recommended buying precious metals."

A year before government regulators took down Metals.com, Quartz news website published an investigative profile of Asher that traced his parallel career as a social media influencer who wears black outfits and red leather jackets while posing on flashy sports cars, flaunting his lifestyle on Instagram. It drew a comparison between Metals.com sales methods and the boiler-room atmosphere of the 2013 film *The Wolf of Wall Street*. Asher evidently aspired to emulate the start-up kings of Silicon Valley, often expressing admiration for Elon Musk and Peter Thiel and billing himself as a private equity investor in their companies.

The Quartz investigation found that Metals.com had amplified the same ideological appeal pioneered by Goldline, directing sales associates to gain the trust of their elderly marks with "a political narrative," using scripts that began with such friendly assurances as, "I'm part of a conservative team. . . . We help Fox News/Hannity/Limbaugh/Levin" or "I don't know what your religious beliefs are, but I'm Christian. Did you know that there are 700 references to gold and silver in the Bible?" Asher sought only customers who were conservative with little faith in government or the economy. If anyone identified themselves as "liberal" or said they didn't like Hannity, "you just hang up," recalled a former salesperson.

Evidently, the elderly right-wing consumers, their savings targeted by young Lucas Asher, needed only to hear mention of a trusted "conservative" to invest their trust in the con.

11

In Very Bad Faith

Even the most ostentatiously moralistic strands of American conservatism on the religious right have been grossly corrupted over the past half century or so by the accelerating drift toward grift.

With their penchant for the perquisites of wealth—from glitzy beachfront estates and flashy jewelry to Rolls-Royce limousines and private jets—both the old televangelists and the newer "prosperity gospel" scammers have normalized the pursuit of money as the highest value undergirding their spiritual authority. No scrim of charitable giving can conceal their brazen greed. Yet somehow these professional Christians have long felt secure in ignoring the injunction set down by their proclaimed Savior in Matthew 6, where Jesus addresses the problem of worldly avarice bluntly and directly: "You cannot serve two masters. Either you will hate the one and love the other, or you will be devoted to the one and despise the other. You cannot serve both God and money."

Until very recently, however, right-wing evangelical leaders such as the late Jerry Falwell Sr. still saw themselves as maintaining biblical standards of integrity—and felt the need to distinguish their own creed and practices from the sinful fraud inherent in the Word of Faith or prosperity gospel movement epitomized by such openly avaricious preachers as Jim Bakker, Rod Parsley, and John Hagee.

When Falwell attempted to take over Bakker's commercialized Christian empire in 1987, he explained his aggressive action by insisting that God had condemned his rival's exploitative conduct. He demanded that the Bakkers "return millions of dollars taken from the coffers of this ministry at the cost of widows" and other innocents who had sacrificed personal savings to support them. "I think this prosperity theology is the most damnable heresy being preached in the world today," the Moral Majority founder warned—and among both evangelical and mainline church leaders, he was hardly alone in that condemnation.

Yet in the decades following Falwell's denunciation, evangelical resistance to the venality and narcissism of the prosperity preachers began to crumble rapidly. Erecting their own business operations and acquiring substantial wealth, the pastors who headed megachurches and cable TV congregations were in no position to criticize the apostasy of Parsley, Hagee, and others of that ilk. Evangelical Christianity had grown increasingly politicized since the days, forty years gone, when prominent fundamentalists had endorsed a saved Southern Baptist and Democrat named Jimmy Carter.

The pressures of an intense and often furious partisanship seemed to blur doctrinal boundaries that had once separated the truly faithful from the faithless. But as the new century unfolded, the most self-serving and even sinister forces within evangelical Christianity were gaining the upper hand. Nowhere were these unwholesome changes more glaring, ironically, than in the fabled institutions created by Falwell himself.

When Rev. Jerry Falwell went to his reward in May 2007, there was no succession struggle between his two sons, Jerry Jr. and Jonathan, because the founding father had long since decreed the stewardship of his legacy. Younger son Jonathan, who had served as minister and executive at Thomas Road Baptist Church, was elevated to senior pastor there after his father's death. First son Jerry Jr., an attorney and real estate developer, took over the presidency of rapidly expanding Liberty University, where he had served as a trustee for several years.

It was a role for which Jerry Jr. had prepared his entire life, not because of his educational values, which were minimal, or his spiritual vocation, which was nonexistent, but because Liberty University was always primarily a business enterprise. As he recalled in a *Vanity Fair* interview, he had learned to regard religion as a field of commerce at an early age, while accompanying his famous father to speaking engagements across the country.

"I'd be the kid in the back of the auditorium selling my dad's books and records to people while he preached. I would have all this money stuffed into every pocket. That was my life." At one of his father's events, little Jerry Jr. sold $2,500 worth of books and records, stuffing cash into his pants and shirt, according to his mother's memoir.

INDULGED BY HIS father, who rarely disciplined him, Jerry Jr. didn't attend church much and cultivated a taste for such forbidden pleasures as rock music and alcohol. Nobody who knew the Moral Majority founder's eldest son well could have mistaken him for a devout Christian. "Religious leader" was a mask to put on for public occasions and political posturing. What mattered more than piety to his father was Jerry Jr.'s demonstrated business acumen, specifically in real estate development and the creation of a profitable "higher education" enterprise.

His official succession to the Liberty presidency simply ratified the authority his father had bestowed decades earlier, at a point in the eighties when loose and dishonest financial practices had pushed the Falwell fundamentalist conglomerate to the brink of bankruptcy. Jerry Jr. succeeded in stabilizing Falwell Inc.—partly by discarding unprofitable elements such as *The Old-Time Gospel Hour* broadcast—and benefited from a timely infusion of millions from an even more outrageous charlatan, the Reverend Sun Myung Moon. Soon enough, he found a way to inflate his father's legacy into a billion-dollar-plus cash machine. What he discovered was a vast new opportunity for personal profit at the expense of the rubes.

REV. JERRY FALWELL'S original vision for Liberty University—the ideal that he sold to its earliest supporters among the wealthy Southern Baptist elite—was to build his little Bible college into a world-class academic and athletic center. In his pitch to donors, the enterprising Virginia pastor conjured up a "Protestant Notre Dame" that would graduate thousands of young men and women and stand up not only to the Catholic intellectuals from South Bend but all the secular smart alecks of the Ivy League.

According to certain carefully selected metrics, those aspirations are nearing fulfillment. Liberty has a nationally accredited law school, a debate team that consistently tops the national rankings—often besting Harvard University and other forensic champs—and a whole host of Division I athletic teams, all housed on a sprawling modern campus with more than fifteen thousand residential students, nestled amid central Virginia's Blue Ridge mountains. At more than $3 billion, the university's endowment is only a fraction of what Harvard and Yale can boast, but roughly equivalent to those of such venerable schools as Amherst, Georgetown, and Williams.

Beneath the surface of those glittering comparisons, however, is a dimmer reality: Liberty is primarily an online business that operates on the same "educational" model as the for-profit colleges whose rip-offs have provoked federal and state crackdowns. In fact, according to *The Chronicle of Higher Education*, Liberty is the second-largest provider of online college courses in the United States, outpaced only by the enormous, profit-making University of Phoenix. Every student who matriculates on the Lynchburg campus is subsidized by six online students—totaling more than 120,000—who buy online courses and may never set foot in Virginia.

Online education is the principal source of the huge fortune accumulated to build the university and its endowment, with the great bulk coming from federal student loans and grants—an ironic form of educational welfare that doesn't trouble the government-bashing Falwell or the school's "libertarian" professors. More than three-fourths of its billion-dollar-plus annual budget is funded by taxpayers, including student loans, Pell Grants, and veterans' benefits. Whatever Liberty lacks in endowment funding is compensated by its successful procurement of federal funds: in 2017, according to *The New York Times Magazine*, only five universities nationwide received more total US Treasury financing.

What all that federal money buys, at least for the online students, is a decidedly substandard diploma (if they ever graduate). Although Liberty is officially a nonprofit institution, it isn't run for the benefit of its students, the Christian community, or the broader society. As Falwell Jr. himself has often boasted, it is run *as a business*, except that of course it doesn't pay any federal or state taxes. While Liberty students and staff have been known to say that the university is "blessed" in its wealth and surroundings, Falwell Jr. is loath to acknowledge heavenly intervention and credits his own financial instincts for the university's prosperity.

"What I will say is that we've always operated from a business perspective," he told *New York Times* reporter Alec MacGillis. "We've treated it like a business."

In practice, treating an educational institution "like a business" means skimping on everything students require in order to learn anything, including decently compensated professors and assistants with enough time to teach, adequate texts and other materials, and remedial resources for those who need them. Given the university's recruitment methods—a boiler-room approach more appropriate to penny-stock swindlers than college educators—there are bound to be many students who need extra help that they never get. While the university's call-center recruiters try to make Liberty sound selective, its credentialing is quite relaxed—apparently anything above a D+ average is accepted.

From a commercial rather than collegiate perspective, however, Falwell Jr.'s success in paring down expenses was undeniable. The average annual instructional cost for each full-time student, across Liberty's online and on-campus populations, was well under $3,000, as MacGillis reported. That amount wouldn't cover even a month of instruction at Notre Dame, which reports spending closer to $30,000 annually per student. Even the University of Phoenix, a corporation frankly devoid of spiritual or intellectual pretension, spends roughly 50 percent more than Liberty on each customer. Falwell Jr. told MacGillis that Liberty's faculty members had warned the online focus would diminish academic standards that were none too elevated in the first place. "The big victory was finding a way to tame the faculty," he boasted. It really didn't matter, he added, because whatever their qualifications, the online teachers "adhere to the fundamentals of the Christian faith, our doctrinal statement." Which Falwell Jr. himself did not, a fact that soon became embarrassingly obvious.

SELF-SERVING, DECEPTIVE, AND profligate as the senior Falwell had been, his namesake eldest son brought a degree of humiliation to the family name that nobody could have anticipated. Junior's eventual downfall, leading to his expulsion from the institution he built and led, resulted from an explosive tabloid sex scandal involving his wife, Becki, and Giancarlo Granda, a twenty-one-year-old pool boy they had met on vacation at the Fontainebleau hotel in Miami. Granda claimed that Becki had seduced him on multiple occasions—while Jerry Jr. played the voyeur. Perhaps contemplating blackmail, Granda had maintained copious files of photos, text messages, recorded conversations, and video that confirmed the relationship, some of which he eventually provided to a Reuters reporter. (Hulu released *God Forbid*, a documentary film featuring interviews with Granda, in 2022.)

Even before the "pool boy" revealed the full scope of his bizarre entanglement with the Falwells, Liberty trustees saw that Jerry Jr. had gone off the moral rails. In August 2020, the drunk and disorderly evangelical leader posted a photo on Instagram of himself posing on a yacht with a young woman employed by Liberty. Both had their pants unzipped. The university swiftly placed him on "indefinite leave," from which he never returned.

Devoted evangelical followers of the Falwells were understandably disappointed to learn the details of this lurid saga when Granda finally told all. Behind the narrative of their consensual trysts, however, lay a series of less titillating but far more costly scams. Just as Jerry Jr. had built an "educational" enterprise that vacuumed up billions in student loans and grants while delivering little academic value, he had continuously siphoned off university funds to enrich himself, his family, and his cronies. The preacher's son became a master grifter, creatively abusing his executive power in ways that would never be tolerated in any honest business, let alone a supposed nonprofit devoted to Christian education.

Once the Falwell grifts began to unravel, they seemed almost endless. The founder's son had run the university as a hub of crony capitalism, much like the Philippines under dictator Ferdinand Marcos. He seemed to skim a personal benefit from everything the university touched. Even that mortifying unzipped-pants photo was snapped aboard a yacht belonging to Rick Hendrick, the NASCAR mogul, who had loaned his six-bedroom, ultra-luxurious vessel to Falwell Jr. on several occasions for Caribbean cruising. He made that generous gesture after Liberty spent untold millions on a NASCAR sponsorship with Hendrick that did nothing to advance the university's proclaimed mission.

Falwell Jr.'s annual salary as president of Liberty University—not including such perks as his automotive allowance, frequent use of the university's private aircraft for personal travel, as well as retirement and other benefits—reached $1.25 million before his dismissal, well above what the presidents of much larger and more prestigious colleges earned at the time. In January 2016, he also put his son Jerry Falwell III, known as "Trey," on the Liberty payroll. Initially described as "administrative assistant to the president," Trey started off with $95,000 in salary plus retirement and other benefits, a mandatory increase of 5 percent annually regardless of performance, and a fifteen-year contract. But at barely thirty years old, Trey seemed to have grown dissatisfied with that nepotistic arrangement. The following year, his father promoted him to "vice president of university services" with a new salary of $195,000, a car allowance valued at over $20,000 a year, plus benefits. Trey's wife, Sarah, also worked for Liberty as "executive director of career partnerships" for a salary of $72,211. The university sold a house and twenty-one acres of university land to Trey and Sarah in a deal that his father unsuccessfully sought to conceal.

Press reports alluded to Falwell's younger son, Wesley, and his wife, Laura, holding positions on the university payroll as well—with annual payments totaling over $100,000—but Liberty has refused to disclose exactly what those jobs were or how much they paid. Like his brother and father, Wesley Falwell also apparently owned outside firms that were paid by the university for services in other murky deals. The atmosphere that permitted this extensive self-dealing extended to many other officials and trustees at the university, which has employed at least twenty relatives of such Liberty "stakeholders." The Falwells piled one grift onto another over more than a decade while Jerry Jr. ran the university. Even as Trey drew an inflated salary to manage university services, for example, he simultaneously owned and ran an outside real estate firm—which held a contract, presumably approved by him or his father, to operate a shopping center owned by Liberty.

The eldest son clearly emulated his dad, who had executed a similar series of petty scams involving university property even before he took over the presidency. A Reuters investigation found that Jerry Jr. had set up a company in 2001 to acquire a parcel of undeveloped land from Liberty, where he then built a strip mall. He contrived this scheme while serving as the university's general counsel, potentially violating his fiduciary duties as well as federal tax law prohibiting the abuse of nonprofits for personal gain. Having paid about $400,000 for the university property, he eventually sold the mall for nearly $3 million.

Four years later, he engineered an even more complex series of transactions to benefit himself. This time, he managed the sale of university land and an adjacent property to a firm controlled by Chris Doyle, who also worked as a property broker for Liberty under Falwell Jr.'s supervision. In his capacity as Liberty's lawyer, Falwell Jr. both wrote and signed the deed of sale. It was a contract involving so many related (and conflicted) parties that it resembled an octopus doing deals with itself.

After the shopping centers were complete, Falwell Jr. spent another

$2 million in university funds to build a tunnel connecting the campus to his property, so students and faculty could safely and quickly walk there beneath the strands of railroad tracks that separated the campus from the mall. Not far from that shopping center is a La Quinta Inn owned by a firm registered to Doyle, whom Falwell Jr. once identified in a deposition as his partner in Virginia real estate ventures. University employees told Reuters that Trey Falwell is a "silent partner" with Doyle in that hospitality firm—and that the university routinely directs parents and other university guests to their hotel.

In an even more notable instance, Falwell Jr. sold off an eighteen-acre racquet sports and fitness facility owned by the university to Benjamin Crosswhite, a twenty-three-year-old former Liberty student who had served as a personal trainer for both him and Becki. Under the president's direction, the university loaned Crosswhite the money to buy its property, then partially leased the facility back from him to help cover his costs. In fact, Crosswhite put down none of his own money toward the purchase. When *Politico* exposed this sweetheart deal, both Liberty and Crosswhite insisted that the transaction was somehow beneficial to the university.

The university's billion-dollar construction program offered still further opportunities for self-dealing and greasing of friends. Another longtime Falwell Jr. pal named Robert Moon received a $750,000 loan in 2013 from Liberty to start Construction Management Associates, which the university subsequently hired to oversee building contracts that brought the company tens of millions of dollars. Moon insisted to NBC News that he had helped the university to save millions in construction costs.

After the revelations about the Falwells' sexual escapades forced him out of the presidency, Falwell Jr. and the university wound up filing lawsuits against each other that were still pending years later. In the aftermath of his dismissal, the university's trustees also hired a leading forensics firm to examine Liberty's major financial and business transactions under his leadership. The trustees opened that probe, which has yet to be completed more than three years later, on the reasonable assumption that the chronic self-dealing, endless interested-party transactions, and relentless scamming had brought the university into possible conflict with federal law, endangering its tax-exempt status.

If Jerry Falwell Jr. never evinced much interest in his father's religious or spiritual pursuits, he displayed a powerful inclination to follow Jerry Sr.'s right-wing politics—with more than a hint of authoritarianism and corruption. Sooner or later, he and Donald Trump were bound to find each other, and in fact, that fated alliance began long before the advent of Trump's first presidential campaign. During the summer of 2012, when Trump first began to explore his political options, he invited Falwell Jr. and other evangelical leaders to a meeting at Trump Tower in New York. The Liberty president took immediately to the developer's blustering style, which so closely resembled his own, and invited Trump to deliver a convocation address at the university in September. In New York, he also met Trump lawyer and fixer Michael Cohen, who struck up a friendship with Falwell and joined Trump on his fall visit to the Lynchburg campus.

At that event, Falwell Jr. described Trump as "one of the most influential political leaders in the United States" and the man who "single-handedly forced President Obama to release his birth certificate." (So much for his father's supposed rejection of racism.) He encouraged Trump to run for president and awarded him an honorary Liberty business degree. The friendship continued into 2014 as Trump began to seriously consider a presidential run.

By then, Liberty University's chief information officer, a close associate of Falwell Jr. named John Gauger, had begun to work with Cohen on some very special projects. As his boss prepared for a possible 2016 campaign, Cohen reached out to Gauger—who augmented his Liberty income with a private internet consulting business called RedFinch—for help in rigging online polls that might boost Trump's national image. He offered Gauger a fee of $50,000.

The first of those schemes involved a January 2014 CNBC online poll to name the country's top business executives. Gauger wrote a computer script designed to vote for Trump over and over but nevertheless failed to elevate him into the top one hundred honorees. On the orders of Falwell Jr. himself, Liberty University's official Twitter account also promoted "our friend @RealDonaldTrump" in the CNBC poll, urging followers to "vote 4 him" with a link.

The following year, Cohen asked Gauger to try again, this time with an attempt to spoof a Drudge Report poll measuring the appeal of possible Republican presidential primary hopefuls. The tech expert managed to provide Trump with enough automated votes in the Drudge poll to reach twenty-four thousand total, which amounted to 5 percent and placed him among the top five contenders.

When Gauger came to New York in January 2015 to collect payment from Cohen—who was reimbursed by the Trump Organization and says he told Trump about the rigged polls—the lawyer surprised him by handing over a blue Walmart bag filled with cash. Back in his hotel room, Gauger spread the bills out on a bed as he counted the take. Cohen later denied the cash payment and claimed to have paid by check, but Gauger had brought Trey Falwell along with him on the New York trip. And the younger Falwell not only snapped photos of the cash but then posted the image on Instagram. Though he later deleted the incriminating photo, its obvious implication lingered: his father had known and approved of the tawdry plot to rig polls for Trump. Or as a "senior Liberty official" said to *Politico*, "The idiot posted a picture of money on a bed? Why do that if you're not involved with it?"

•

WELL BEFORE THE rest of the world glimpsed that telltale "picture of money on a bed," the involvement of Jerry Falwell Jr. in the rise of Donald Trump—and especially in Trump's surprising grip on white evangelical support—had been fully exposed. Falwell's endorsement of Trump in January 2016 shocked many of his followers because several months earlier, he had welcomed Senator Ted Cruz to Liberty University—where the Texan, whose father, Rafael, is an evangelical pastor, had announced his presidential candidacy. At that event, the university helped to contrive an aura of massive support for the senator by requiring every student on campus to attend, whether they liked Cruz or not.

Coming a year after the rigged Drudge poll, the Falwell imprimatur had started to turn the tide for Trump against Cruz, his main rival for the nomination. Falwell had jumped to back Trump shortly after the developer had welcomed support from Sarah Palin, another favorite of the religious Right, with a notorious penchant for grift that coexisted with her fervent Pentecostal faith.

While seasoned political observers were initially puzzled by the evangelical backing that helped Trump clinch the Republican nomination and win the presidency by a whisker in November 2016, their alliance makes a twisted kind of sense in retrospect. It's easier to understand now why Trump gained that crucial support—and why a certain group of evangelical and Pentecostal leaders so swiftly lined up behind him. To put it bluntly, the religious leaders most inclined toward grift and greed (not unlike Trump himself) were also the most eager to join his campaign—and to invent a variety of excuses for an irreligious, profane, and brazenly immoral politician. That cohort was led not only by Falwell Jr. but by the same shifty Word of Faith anglers whose prosperity gospel had been denounced thunderously as heretical by Falwell's own father.

What drew the prosperity preachers and their congregations to Trump, eventually joined by millions of white evangelicals, was how much he resembled the televangelists who were the most successful among them. As the journalist Sarah Posner explained, that was why such a blatant and unrepentant sinner was "able to break the politician mold for evangelical voters who had come to believe that other presidential candidates, for all their faith talk, had ultimately failed to deliver government guided by 'Christian' or 'biblical' values."

"Previous Republican candidates," Posner wrote in *Unholy: How White Christian Nationalists Powered the Trump Presidency, and the Devastating Legacy They Left Behind*,

> cultivated relationships with televangelists in a quest for the votes of their considerable audiences. But more than any other Republican

> candidate, Trump's politics were defined by televangelism itself. Although televangelists operate out of tax-exempt churches, at their core their ministries are businesses, bringing in millions of unaccountable cash, used for enriching the pastor with extravagances like mansions portrayed as parsonages, or private jets held to be essential tools for spreading the gospel.
>
> Televangelism has created an audience, for both church and politics, that is enthralled with showmanship and captivated by powerful personalities and flamboyant tales of miracles and supernatural successes, from cancer healed by prayer to bank accounts suddenly flush with heaven-sent cash.

For Trump, that cultural affinity may have sprung in part from his own religious upbringing. As a boy, he attended Marble Collegiate Church in Manhattan, whose renowned pastor Norman Vincent Peale preached a genteel and comparatively benign precursor of the prosperity gospel. (Although Marble Collegiate is affiliated with the Reformed Church in America and the United Church of Christ, Trump later claimed to be a Presbyterian.) In his 1952 worldwide bestseller *The Power of Positive Thinking*, Peale assured Christians they could achieve health and wealth if they followed his advice in banishing negativity and seeking God's help to achieve happiness. At the time, serious Christian theologians scorned his teachings as heretical and misleading, and some even compared him to a "con man." Young Donald would learn neither critical thinking nor the value of self-knowledge when Fred and Mary Anne Trump brought him and his siblings to hear Peale on Sundays. But at least Peale didn't routinely bilk his parishioners into sending him their paltry earnings.

The same cannot be said for the televangelists who showed up to lay their unclean hands on Trump and offer prayers for his success—even as mainstream religious conservatives expressed revulsion and horror.

It is easy to forget that Donald Trump once faced serious resistance within the Republican Party and the conservative movement. He had been divorced twice and had flaunted his predatory attitude toward women in the press for years. He was a former casino owner and a longtime Democratic donor in his home state of New York, who boasted of his friendship with Bill and Hillary Clinton. His religious beliefs were largely unknown and seemingly unimportant to him. For those reasons and many more, some of the most powerful figures in the evangelical leadership showed not just skepticism but open hostility toward Trump's candidacy.

That hostility erupted in September 2015 at the Values Voter Summit, sponsored annually by the Family Research Council, where all the Republican candidates for president spoke before the nation's most powerful gathering of religious Right activists. Going into that meeting, the factional favorites appeared to be Texas senator Ted Cruz and Mike Huckabee, the former Arkansas governor and Southern Baptist minister. If not in the bottom tier, Trump was nowhere near the top.

In the midst of an anti-immigrant tirade, Trump snarled, "You have this clown Marco Rubio"—and a roar of booing nearly silenced him. To be jeered by that crowd portended trouble in upcoming early primaries in Iowa and South Carolina dominated by evangelical voters. Worse yet, Trump was nearly shut out in the summit's 2016 straw poll, which Cruz won with 408 votes, followed by neurosurgeon Ben Carson, who got 204 votes, while Huckabee and Rubio each pulled around 150 votes. Trump got only 56 votes, or 5 percent. Something had to be done.

Only days later, in a conference room on the twenty-fifth floor of Trump Tower, the prophets of the prosperity gospel rode to the prodigal candidate's rescue. Nearly forty ministers, including such famed televangelists as Kenneth Copeland and Jan Crouch, gathered around Trump, laid their hands on him, and beseeched God in their theatrical style to protect and guide him in his mission to save America. "Any man that wavers is like the blowing wind on the water—let not that man think he shall receive anything," Copeland intoned as he placed his hand on Trump's shoulder. "And so we ask you today to give this man your wisdom, boldly. Make sure and certain that he hears, manifest yourself to him, and we thank you and praise you for a bold man, a strong man, and an obedient man."

Copeland, it should be recalled, was one of six televangelists investigated in 2011 by Iowa Republican senator Chuck Grassley, who suspected them of abusing their tax-exempt, ostensibly nonprofit ministries to siphon off millions of dollars in loot. The evidence of Copeland's greed wasn't hard to find. In a television interview that went viral, he boasted of owning three planes and of investing $25 million in a single year. He lives with his wife, Gloria, in a $6 million house, owned on paper by his Eagle Mountain International Church, and he is said to be worth nearly a billion dollars. He waved off Grassley's probe and said he expected that Huckabee and other Republican politicians would protect him.

Whatever those ministers really thought of Trump, and whatever he really thought about them—he is known to privately mock Christianity as a religion for "fools"—they had much in common. His unbridled pursuit of wealth, his showmanship, his disdain for government, and his propensity to make extravagant promises with no means or intention of fulfilling them all echoed the lifestyle of a top-tier prosperity preacher. Among those present in the Trump Tower conference room on that September afternoon was the popular televangelist who claimed to have led Trump to Jesus Christ—an exuberant and attractive blond millionaire named Paula White, who was the only woman present.

As Mark Pinsky wrote in *Orlando Weekly*, White had positioned herself next to the candidate "with one hand on his stomach and the other on his arm." He patted her hand as he closed his eyes and extended his lower lip in his best imitation of prayer. She closed the meeting with a fervent invocation:

> "Father, we just secure him right now by the blood of Jesus," she prayed. "We thank you that no weapon formed against him would prosper, and any tongue that rises against him would be condemned, according to the word of God. . . . Even as we lay hands on him right now, let your hand be laid upon him. Let him have a greater encounter with you, a greater encounter with the spirit of God. I secure him, I secure his children, I secure his calling and his mantle, in Jesus's name."

When she concluded, Trump embraced her with a kiss on the cheek.

THE BOND BETWEEN Trump and his favorite pastor is overdetermined, as the philosophers might say. If Trump resembled a prosperity preacher in style and character, he might almost be White's twin. Like him, White has been divorced twice and married three times, with a promiscuous past behind her. Like him, she has endured withering press scrutiny of her financial chicanery and shameless hucksterism. Like him, she has weathered damaging scandals—in her case, an alleged illicit affair with another celebrity televangelist, Benny Hinn, with whom she was photographed emerging from a hotel in Rome. And like Trump, White has surmounted the scorn of her betters to win wealth, fame, and a huge cult following.

White was also among the six televangelists called upon by Grassley to justify her church's tax exemption and disprove allegations of swindling her followers. (So was Benny Hinn, her alleged partner in adultery.) She joined Copeland in stonewalling the Senate investigators, and yet there is ample evidence in the public domain to indicate what the probers might have discovered if White had opened her books.

During her marriage to Randy White, a preacher who began an illicit relationship with Paula while he was married and she was a teenager, she helped to establish a Tampa, Florida, congregation called Without Walls International Church in 1991. Endowed with charisma and stage talent, the pair drew thousands of parishioners who, in accordance with prosperity gospel dictates, tithed much of their income to the church. She also commenced a booming career in televangelism, branding herself simply as "Paula" with highly rated programming on Christian TV networks and even on Black Entertainment Television, where she enjoyed a peculiar affinity with Black female audiences.

In all her preaching, whether on the altar or on the screen, White emphasized the prosperity gospel's insistence on tithing, absolute pastoral authority, and the notion that those who gave would be rewarded with robust health and lavish riches. By the time Donald Trump encountered her on television ten years later, she had acquired private jets, luxury limousines, a $2 million estate overlooking Tampa Bay, and would soon own apartments in two of Trump's Manhattan properties—including a $3.5 million flat in Trump Tower. She had enough cash on hand to give her favorite mentor, Bishop T. D. Jakes of Dallas, a $200,000 black Bentley convertible as a present for his fiftieth birthday.

White's questionable finances had come under scrutiny by the Internal Revenue Service in 2004 without any consequence—another similarity to Trump—and in 2007 were the subject of an investigative series published by the *Tampa Tribune*. The newspaper unveiled an independent audit that showed the Whites' operations had grossed almost $40 million during the prior year. During some years, the paper found that their combined compensation had reached $1.5 million, with other family members filling out a church payroll of $5 million annually. At the same time, however, the church that those tithes were intended to support fell into crippling debt—so deeply that a Christian credit union reportedly threatened to foreclose on its two buildings in Tampa and Lakeland. (The latter site shut down a few years later.)

The *Tampa Tribune* exposé brought down the Whites' megachurch as parishioners fled its corrupted pews. Paula White filed for divorce and moved on to found Paula White Ministries, while her husband more or less retired from preaching after an arrest for drunk driving. She took over another, mostly Black megachurch near Orlando and got married again to Jonathan Cain, a musician in the rock band Journey.

Following the Trump Tower conclave, White became the most prominent evangelical endorser of its owner's candidacy, at least until Jerry Falwell Jr.'s abrupt decision to endorse him in January 2016. She told anyone who would listen that Trump was a man of God, that he had found Jesus Christ and was born again, that he had "more integrity than most people I have encountered." She believed he had been chosen by divine intervention, much as various preachers had once suggested about a former president whom Trump despised, George W. Bush.

"I believe that God will raise up a man for such a time as this," said Paula White.

Whether anyone should have believed White, or any of the prosperity preachers so strongly drawn to Trump, was a matter of dispute within the church. More than a few pastors and theologians agreed with the dim assessment of Russell Moore, the chairman of the Ethics and Religious Liberty Commission of the Southern Baptist Convention, who tartly tweeted: "Paula White is a charlatan and recognized as a heretic by every orthodox Christian, of whatever tribe." The corruption that she represented, embodied by Trump, would spread throughout evangelical Christianity until every dissenter fell isolated or silenced.

12

The King of the Con Men

When Donald Trump finally decided to run for president in 2015, after a series of false starts that dated back almost two decades, he fulfilled the hopes of his longtime adviser Roger Stone, the rancid lobbyist and consultant who had first promoted the idea of a Trump presidential candidacy. Stone didn't want Trump to run because he admired his client's aptitude for policy, great patriotic fervor, or deep ideological commitment. For many years he had privately mocked Trump, whom he didn't consider very bright, and often had felt unappreciated by him.

No, Stone only wanted Trump to run because he believed that "Trump" could sell and be sold. Stone understood why American culture was a perfect environment for a political figure whose persona had been fabricated on *The Apprentice*—a reality-TV show cunningly scripted to transform the bankrupted real estate heir into a brilliant billionaire tycoon. What Stone imagined was a recapitulation of *A Face in the Crowd* or *It Can't Happen Here*, ominous narratives of celebrity hucksters ascending to power.

Gullible viewers across the country who tended to ignore most news programming faithfully followed the Trump epic, agog at his brusque and commanding style. The same audience that bought supermarket tabloids filled with alien sightings and conspiracies of all kinds became his most avid fans, thrilled by the fantasy of a president who was "not a politician."

From the beginning, Stone foresaw a Trump presidential campaign built upon spectacle, deception, and malice—the building blocks of "Trump" as a public figure, all elements that the onetime Watergate dirty trickster had long regarded as indispensable to political victory for the Right. Having observed Trump closely for more than three decades, Stone possessed an intimate understanding of how his employer and sometime friend had become a hot commodity.

What alone made Trump's candidacy plausible was "Trump," the media brand that had been marketed and massaged for decades, which bore so little resemblance to the very flawed and possibly even sociopathic human being. The publicity debut of "Trump" had occurred back in the early seventies, when developer Fred Trump insisted that his favored son, heir to a drab outer-borough network of apartment complexes, win recognition as the developer of the Grand Hyatt, a flashy hotel redevelopment on Manhattan's legendary Forty-Second Street, next door to Grand Central Station.

In fact, the Grand Hyatt had been Fred's deal—backed with hundreds of millions of dollars in tax-subsidized financing courtesy of local Democratic machine politicians who owed him favors—but he was eager for spoiled Donald to take the credit. Emerging into the Manhattan media maelstrom, Donald launched himself on a meteor of hype, achieved with the assistance of Roy Cohn, a master manipulator of the New York tabloids.

Cohn schooled his brash young client in the Zen of lying without hesitation or compunction. The narcissistic, perennially insecure Trump wanted so badly to become an icon of success (and sex) that he contrived a phony identity, "John Barron," which he used when promoting himself to the city's gossip columnists. Nobody who had observed the outpouring of "fake news" coverage about Trump in Rupert Murdoch's *New York Post* during the seventies and eighties was surprised to see how the media mogul's Fox News treated him decades later. Susan Mulcahy, who had edited the *Post*'s Page Six gossip spread, apologized in 2016 for helping to forge Trump's iconic status despite his incessant and "pathological" lying.

If tabloid readers believed the myth, New York's actual real estate elite still viewed Trump as a puerile clown, at least until the 1987 publication of *The Art of the Deal*, his first book. Cohn was indirectly responsible for the book, which sprang from a cover profile of Trump in *GQ* magazine. After that issue sold well, the magazine's owner S. I. "Si" Newhouse—who happened to be Cohn's closest friend since childhood—persuaded Trump to produce a memoir for Random House, the publishing giant that Newhouse's company also owned.

The book sold astonishingly well, staying on the *New York Times* bestseller list for a year and becoming one of the most popular books on business ever published. Its success was owed to the fact that Trump didn't write a single word of it, as both coauthor Tony Schwartz and publisher Howard Kaminsky eventually confirmed. ("Trump didn't write us a postcard!" chortled the Random House boss years later.) And the book also succeeded because, despite its label as "nonfiction," so little of its heroic portrait of Trump bore any resemblance to him or his life story.

In a 2016 interview with *The New Yorker*, Schwartz described his authorship of Trump's book, an exercise in mendacity that had earned him millions of dollars, as "the definition of selling out." Undoubtedly, he confessed, abandoning his career as a legitimate journalist was the greatest regret of his life. Having created the spurious "Trump," he foresaw terrible consequences almost thirty years on from that seemingly harmless hoax. The guilt-ridden and apprehensive Schwartz blurted out his recollections of the real Trump as a remorseless liar, a "black hole" of egomaniacal compulsion—and an imposter who in no way resembled the "self-made man" that Random House had foisted on a gullible public.

Starting with the Grand Hyatt deal, Trump always sought to conceal how crucial his father's fortune and connections were to whatever he had achieved in business. (Which wasn't much, in sheer dollar terms, since many financial analysts believe that Trump's personal wealth would be greater today if he had simply invested the hundreds of millions he inherited from his father in a stock market index fund, rather than squandering so much on the casinos, airlines, football teams, and other shiny boondoggles that led to his multiple bankruptcies.)

Instead, he pretended to be the masterful businessman of Schwartz's imagination, always inflating his image with wild exaggerations of the obstacles he had thrust aside and the profits he had seized. Authors who produced factual biographies of Trump in later years, including Gwenda Blair, Wayne Barrett, and Tim O'Brien, came to agree that the "Trump" created by Schwartz—what Blair once called "the founding myth"—had never existed. (Schwartz himself has confessed that the book "should be recategorized as fiction" and retitled *The Sociopath*.)

What Trump contributed to the book's success was a relentless publicity tour. With a presidential campaign looming only months away, Roger Stone came up with a sales campaign inspired by his intuition about Trump's political potential. Fronted by Dan Klores, a frenetic Manhattan publicity agent well-connected to the political press corps, the veteran dirty trickster set up a spurious "Draft Trump" movement. Two months before publication day, he sent Trump to a Rotary Club in New Hampshire to deliver a speech and bought full-page ads blaring the pseudo-candidate's "populist" ideas about national security and trade.

At the time, Trump had no interest whatsoever in running for president. But he didn't mind pretending to be a candidate because his life was an ongoing and ever-expanding theater of make-believe. Klores later declared that the presidential mummery in New Hampshire qualified as "the greatest book promotion of all time," a boast that could easily have been uttered by Trump himself. Unlike the stories recounted in *The Art of the Deal*, at least that remark had some basis in truth.

Indeed, thanks to America's reliably credulous mainstream media, the book's promotional artifice succeeded wildly. It sold millions of copies, establishing "Trump" in the public mind as a figure of prodigious enterprise and immense wealth. Precisely the opposite was true, as the real-life Trump demonstrated during the next several years. Not only was he about to embark on a series of reckless and ill-fated business ventures, but he would be forced to seek chapter 11 bankruptcy protection for six of his companies and would destroy his business relationships with every major American bank.

YET ANOTHER ENDURING fraud sprang from *The Art of the Deal*, when Trump announced that he would be donating his share of the book's royalties to charity. In 1988, he set up the Donald J. Trump Foundation, supposedly to carry out that vow, specifically mentioning that he would direct funding "to the homeless, to Vietnam veterans, for AIDS, multiple sclerosis . . . Originally I figured they'd get a couple of hundred thousand [dollars] but because of [the book's] success . . . they'll get four or five million."

Subsequent investigations proved that those philanthropic promises were as hollow as Trump's claims to be a genius executive or, for that matter, a bona fide billionaire. Not only did he mostly fail to make good on his pledged donations, but for a period of nearly thirty years, he routinely misused his foundation's tax exemption to advance his own personal, political, and financial interests. He paid Trump Organization debts and judgments from the foundation's accounts and gave more to Ivanka's ballet school than all the causes he had vowed to champion combined. He even used foundation funds, secretly, to make sure that a painting of him brought the highest price at a Hamptons society event—and then jumped on Twitter with this boast: "Just found out that at a charity auction of celebrity portraits in E. Hampton, my portrait by artist William Quigley topped list at $60K."

To ensure his total control of the foundation, Trump created a Potemkin governance structure, with his three adult children, Don Jr., Eric, and Ivanka, seated on a powerless "board of directors" alongside Allen Weisselberg, his company's chief financial officer (who was convicted of a similar tax fraud in 2022). The fake board never selected any recipients of foundation money and never even met after 1999. Rather than a legitimate charitable organization, Trump operated the foundation as a tax-exempt subsidiary of his profit-making corporation, directing its millions of dollars—mostly provided by outside individuals and organizations doing business with him—toward almost any purpose other than charity. Compared with his purported billions or the scale of donations made by others with similar fortunes, the amount that Trump donated toward charitable causes was miniscule.

By 2008, he had basically stopped making any charitable donations from his own personal funds and merely used the foundation to make himself appear generous while redirecting funds donated by business partners and associates. When *The Washington Post* examined all his claimed donations between 2008 and 2016, its reporter found "one gift from Donald Trump's own pocket . . . for less than $10,000." During the 2016 campaign, he released a list of his charitable contributions. Not a single one represented a donation of his own funds.

Trump would enjoy decades of posturing as a philanthropist, however, while he exploited the Trump Foundation for his own profit and self-aggrandizement. Its exposure as a massive, ongoing violation of tax laws and a moral disgrace would only occur as a consequence of his presidential campaign—and only after he and his political minions had defamed the Clinton Foundation, an honest and highly effective public charity, with a vicious campaign of unfounded attacks, led by Steve Bannon (who would himself be indicted a few years later for ripping off a nonprofit organization that he founded).

EVEN AS TONY Schwartz set down page after page of overweening claims in *The Art of the Deal*, Trump was disproving its thesis in real life—as he did in 1986, when he tried to salvage his failed Harrah's at Trump Plaza casino in Atlantic City by paying the Holiday Corporation a fee of $70 million to take it over. The ensuing cascade of bad deals that brought Trump to the verge of personal bankruptcy was epitomized by his 1987 purchase of New York City's legendary Plaza Hotel, a vanity acquisition that he could ill afford even at a reasonable price. In hindsight, he appears to have been played for a fool by Robert Bass, a Texas investor, who had bought the nineteen-story landmark only four months earlier before selling it to Trump for a record-breaking $407.5 million, the highest price ever paid for a hotel in the United States.

Nobody, including Trump himself, believed that the Plaza's value justified that expense, which didn't include any necessary repairs or "contingencies" as would be normally included in any purchase agreement. At the time, its annual revenues remained stagnant at around $12 million—nothing like the amount needed to finance renovations and interest.

But the business genius plunged onward, assigning his then wife Ivana to oversee a remodeling of the Plaza while he turned his attention to making other pretentious deals, including his $365 million buyout of the Eastern Air Lines shuttle, which he renamed the Trump Shuttle and attempted to transform into a "luxury" service, complete with steak dinners, gold-tinted lavatory hardware, and a series of trendy gimmicks such as laptop rental. None of these schemes sufficed to overcome soaring fuel prices and competition from Pan Am Airways, which operated its own shuttle services.

Already overextended, Trump simultaneously gambled on a big expansion into the Atlantic City casino industry, borrowing a billion dollars to build the Trump Taj Mahal. By March 1990, less than three years after the publication of *The Art of the Deal*, its putative author was forced into negotiations with more than seventy financial institutions, led by Citibank, that had concluded he would soon be wiped out—and that they would lose up to $4 billion when he went down.

Rather than foreclose and put him on the street, the banks decided to use Trump as their pitchman in disposing of his properties—including almost everything he owned—and put the "billionaire" on a strict allowance of $450,000 a month to operate the Trump Organization while they tried to recoup his losses. He even had to wangle a promotional deal with Harry Winston, the diamond merchant, to get a loaned engagement ring for Marla Maples, the actress-model he wed after dumping his first wife, Ivana. Among the items divested were his superyacht, his personal jet, the Trump Shuttle (sold to Delta Air Lines), and the Plaza Hotel, which went for $100 million less than Trump had paid three years earlier. Interviewed about that humiliating outcome by *The New York Times* decades later, he spun it as a "fantastic deal" and added a gratuitous lie by claiming that he owned "100 percent" of the hotel when it was sold.

While the history of Trump's terrible business record has been thoroughly and widely reported in the financial media (except on Fox Business, of course, where he is still lionized), he maintained a sterling reputation in the marketplace of gullible marks.

THE REFURBISHING OF Trump's reputation—and the renewal of his capacity to profit from the stupidity of his admirers—could only be achieved through the miracle of reality TV, the mythologizing superpower of the most powerful American medium. Only those who fully understood how that superpower worked—and how it had transformed the tarnished "Trump" into one of the nation's most admired celebrities—were able to anticipate the success of his presidential campaign.

Among those who came to believe that his television career had been crucial to Trump's rise was biographer Maggie Haberman, who reported on him extensively for both *The New York Times* and CNN before writing *Confidence Man: The Making of Donald Trump and the Breaking of America*, her aptly titled 2022 biography. She once described him with pithy condescension as "a former real estate executive who ran a relatively small firm, who constantly was trying to make himself look much bigger so people didn't see, in various ways, how small he was." In her estimation, and she was far from alone, Trump's starring role in *The Apprentice* for more than a dozen years on national television had been indispensable to inflating his personality to presidential stature.

"There could not have been a President Trump" without *The Apprentice*, in Haberman's view. She recalled a revelatory moment when Roger Stone explained to her that the TV show had elevated Trump among its huge audience of viewers because "the line between news and entertainment is much thinner for people watching it than [for] people working in the news industry." Reality TV invented an alternative world in which Trump was the titanic character portrayed in *The Art of the Deal*, bamboozling millions of viewers into believing that was him in real life. According to show business lore, the seed for *The*

Apprentice had been planted when a stranger gave a copy of the book to Mark Burnett, the show's creator, long before he became one of Hollywood's most prolific producers.

Except for Burnett, who—despite some ambivalence about Trump's poisonous politics—has remained close to him, the former producers of *The Apprentice* have admitted forthrightly that the show's depiction of its protagonist and his business was laughable. It was an elaborately staged video rendition of the urban myth popularized in *The Art of the Deal*. Featuring a weekly plot constructed around a "business challenge," every episode concluded with Trump barking, "You're fired," at one hapless contestant. The producers often faced the challenge of building an episode backward from Trump's erratic decisions about whom to dismiss, since he had a poor sense of actual merit or performance. In short, every script was utter hogwash, contrived to make Trump look smart, decisive, and successful.

Both Trump and Burnett claimed he had been reluctant to commit to the show because he was too busy with his "flourishing real estate empire," as *The New Yorker*'s Patrick Radden Keefe wrote in a sardonic profile. The show's line producers frankly ridiculed that notion. "Most of us knew he was a fake," said Jonathon Braun, who oversaw the show's first six seasons. "He had just gone through I don't know how many bankruptcies. But we made him out to be the most important person in the world."

The camerawork elevated Trump, too, often shooting him from below to create an imposing effect, showing him as he emerged from limousines and helicopters, or as he presided over an elaborate "boardroom" set constructed in Trump Tower, carefully choreographed and underscored by the sound of drums and cymbals. The Trump Organization's dismal reality, as encountered by producer Bill Pruitt, was "chipped furniture . . . a crumbling empire at every turn. Our job was to make it seem otherwise."

Like Tony Schwartz, Pruitt confessed that he felt responsible for "putting forth a manufactured story about a billionaire whose empire was, in actuality, crumbling. . . . *The Apprentice* was a scam put forth to the public in exchange for ratings." He expressed shock at "how quickly and decisively the world bought" the Trump fantasy. "Did we think this clown, this buffoon with the funny hair, would ever become a world leader? Not once. Ever," he told *People* magazine.

The inescapable irony is that by projecting a fake image of Trump triumphant, the producers constructed a real one—namely, the show itself. Running for fourteen seasons, with spin-offs including *Celebrity Apprentice*, while earning hundreds of millions of dollars for Trump and Burnett, this TV flimflam rebuilt Trump's fortune and made him into a cultural icon. It was the inflated stature bestowed by the phenomenon of *The Apprentice* that transformed Trump into a viable candidate for public office. Long before he acted on those aspirations, however, he began to take full advantage of the trust and admiration the show had inspired in millions of celebrity-worshipping rubes. And then he took advantage of that faith again, and again, and again.

From its first season onward, *The Apprentice* promoted Trump enterprises of all kinds, from hotels and golf clubs to casinos and branded items like Trump Ice bottled water, while collecting big promotional fees from other businesses mentioned on the show. To its deluded audience, the "Trump" brand meant wealth and luxury—everything tacky, phony, and gold-plated that he had so loudly proclaimed "the best."

By then, Trump had been blacklisted by almost every bank in North America. The touted developer could no longer develop any real estate—not as an actual builder, as he had once done with projects like Trump Tower and the Grand Hyatt that had made his reputation. What he lacked in credit, however, he compensated with celebrity, which turned out to be an exploitable commodity not only in the United States but around the world. His post-bankruptcy line of business involved licensing the use of his name on luxury buildings as a symbol of success and opulence. In major cities across the globe, he would find credulous chumps, many quite wealthy, who were susceptible to the Trump Organization's hyperbolic sales pitch. And in those same cities, Trump would also find unscrupulous (or sometimes unwitting) partners prepared to smooth and promote his deals.

The millennial Trump real estate ventures relied heavily on flimflam, fakery, and outright fraud. According to an exhaustive investigation by

ProPublica and WNYC Radio, the same pattern of malfeasance and duplicity showed up in these projects repeatedly. In places as near as lower Manhattan, Fort Lauderdale, and Tampa, and as distant as Panama City, Baja California, and the Republic of Georgia, the Trump Organization (including Ivanka, Eric, and Donald Trump Jr.) got into the business of licensing their surname to construction firms that guaranteed profits to the Trumps up front.

The principal role of the Trumps in these deals was to lure potential investors and buyers, working with a local developer who paid them for the use of their name—and agreed to pay a slice of every sale as well, not only of apartment units but of incidental items such as minibar bottles and snacks.

To begin construction, at least two-thirds of the projected units would have to be sold in advance (or so investors were led to believe). In these projects, with Trump's increasing reliance on laundered money, many units were sold to concealed buyers using shell companies—while Donald or Ivanka Trump would assure investors that the Trumps had invested money themselves and provide deceptive figures about how many units were already sold. Even if enough funds came in to commence building, the projects often failed, leaving bankruptcy and swindled investors in the aftermath. But the Trumps would nevertheless walk away with millions of dollars in fees, and no losses. If and when any of those buildings actually opened, the Trumps would be compensated munificently to manage them.

The $500 million Trump project in Toronto, for example, went under after it was finally completed, even though Ivanka Trump had claimed publicly in 2009 that its units had "virtually sold out." In truth, less than 25 percent of the units had sold. Her father also lied for years about owning a personal stake in the project. In 2016, the developers filed for bankruptcy, just when Trump was preparing to accept the presidential nomination of the Republican Party. All the investors were wiped out except for the Trumps, whose multimillion-dollar profit was tarnished only slightly by seeing their name removed from the mostly empty tower.

According to the *Toronto Star*, which published a scorching investigation of the Trump deal, it was the only major construction project in the booming Canadian city to lose money during that decade. "I don't know why this failed and so many other projects were successful," an investor told the newspaper. "It is mind boggling to us." (The fact that Trump's original partner was a wanted fugitive, who had escaped across the northern border after pleading guilty to bankruptcy fraud and embezzlement in the United States, may not have helped.)

In Fort Lauderdale, Trump announced that a hotel-condominium project was "pretty much sold out" in April 2006, according to a broker who attended the presentation. That was far from true: the project was insolvent and the Trump name was taken off, but not before he collected his million-dollar fee. In lower Manhattan, the Trump SoHo had supposedly sold 60 percent of its units, as Ivanka declared in a press release, but in fact, only 15 percent had sold. Once again, a Trump-branded building went up, went bankrupt, and took down the Trump name.

In the wake of *The Apprentice*, monetizing the yokels who trusted in "Trump" became the updated business model of the Trump Organization. The show's most devoted viewers were the same kind of people whose dim perception and guileless enthusiasm had been exploited by generations of con men. The difference between those crooks and the protean Trump was how he deployed his name and fame to pursue not just a couple of swindles but a panoply of modern rackets.

For decades, consumer protection agencies have warned against get-rich-quick hucksters offering to divulge the "secrets" of successful investing in penny stocks, precious metals, real estate, or most recently in cryptocurrency and other blockchain assets. Conservatives are persistently targeted by these scammers, dating back to the gold-coin hustle promoted by Glenn Beck and assorted right-wing political celebrities—an abuse of trust that proved cruelly effective in relieving the elderly and vulnerable of their savings.

But it's not only the old and lonely (and reactionary) who get robbed at pen point in America; if it were, these crooked enterprises couldn't have grown nearly as rapidly as they did during recent years. In February

2023, the Federal Trade Commission estimated that consumers had lost $8.8 billion to investment rip-offs during the previous year, an increase of more than 30 percent over 2021. Private analysts have confirmed and augmented the FTC data, noting that the estimated loss to investment scams of all kinds was $94 million in 2018, but swelled enormously in the following years. They blamed at least some of that growth on social media, websites, mobile apps, and other online outlets that have increasingly enabled con artists to find and engage their victims.

Among the most prolific of these rackets, according to the FTC, is the "real estate investment seminar scam," which continues to attract suckers across the country with promises of easy wealth. "Don't be convinced by ads with success stories of people saying how much money they made with little time, effort, and risk," the agency warned recently. "Or ads that feature celebrities praising the program." Celebrities like Donald J. Trump, real estate mogul and television star, who pioneered the real estate seminar swindle in 2005, under the very fancy brand of Trump University.

At the zenith of his *Apprentice* fame in 2004, Trump met with an entrepreneur named Michael Sexton, who proposed that he lend his name, for a fat fee, to a for-profit real estate seminar. Instead, Trump took an ownership share of 93 percent and let Sexton and another partner run the business. In announcing his new venture, Trump insisted that he was so rich that he only wanted to make others wealthy. "If I had a choice of making lots of money or imparting lots of knowledge, I think I'd be as happy to impart knowledge as to make money," he said.

Trump University soon ran into trouble with authorities in New York, where it was established as a limited liability company, because even its name violated state law. Unlike most institutions of higher learning, it admitted anyone who could pay in full. And although it claimed to offer "graduate courses, post-graduate courses and doctoral courses," Trump U in fact had no charter and no license to offer classes or instruction of any kind. In response to warnings from the state education department, Sexton offered to stop selling classes in New York and find his customers elsewhere.

Billing itself as an "opportunity to learn from the master," the phony university depended wholly on Trump's allure in its advertising, with frequent references to *The Apprentice* and Trump himself boasting that he had personally overseen Trump U staffing. "My hand-picked instructors will share my techniques, which took my entire career to develop," promised a direct-mail solicitation bearing Trump's signature. Those instructors in turn suggested that Trump would appear at a seminar, claiming that he "often drops by" or "is going to be in town."

NONE OF THAT was remotely true, as he admitted years later when he was forced to testify in lawsuits filed by disgruntled students. He had contributed nothing to the course development, reviewed none of the curriculum or programs, selected none of the instructors, and never appeared at any of the seminars, which taught "no specific Donald Trump techniques or strategies," as a complaint brought by the New York attorney general alleged. They were not just swindled but insulted. Reporting on a Trump U seminar for the *Weekly Standard*, journalist Matt Labash noted: "At one seminar, attendees were told they'd get to have their picture taken with Trump. Instead, they ended up getting snapped with his cardboard cutout." The cardboard Trump's face flashed a telltale smirk.

Nor did the hapless students get even a taste of Trump's secret recipe for success. Most of the course material was cooked up by an outside firm that specialized in creating content for motivational speakers and time-share sales sharks—presumably because Trump U's business style so closely resembled those high-pressure hustles. Offering free seminars and weekend courses to draw in the marks, the Trump U staff immediately began to "upsell" attendees on yearlong seminars, mentoring, and other far more expensive options.

The staff received a "playbook" that omitted any mention of the coursework but featured page after page of tips on how to sell more Trump U courses to every student. They were urged to play the old Top 40 hit "For the Love of Money" at the start of each seminar. They were instructed to collect financial information on every attendee, and then to rank them in order of their ability to pay for more and more expensive courses.

And they were told to encourage students to take on credit-card debt to finance the exorbitantly priced "elite" course, which at $35,000 exceeded credit limits for most consumers. Anticipating that obstacle, the "university" gave instructors a detailed guide on coaching students to deceive their credit card lenders and obtain approval of additional credit for Trump U courses. The personal risk was justified, or so the teaching staff were primed to insist, by "projected income from your future real estate ventures."

When one conscience-stricken instructor refused to push a married couple into taking on so much burdensome debt, his bosses reprimanded him. And someone else signed them up—perhaps one of the "successful" instructors who had previously filed for bankruptcy. They were all paid on commission for inducing their pupils to purchase more and more expensive courses.

Trump U was such a blatantly bootleg operation that even its starstruck and gullible "alumni" came to realize they had been swindled. Among the most voluble and widely quoted was Richard Hewson, a New Jersey resident who took courses with his wife, Shelly, after first attending a free seminar and a three-day workshop, hoping to learn how to flip properties and get rich.

"We had paid over $20,000 for nothing, based on our belief in Donald Trump," Hewson said. "The whole thing was a scam." Robert Guillo, a seventy-five-year-old retiree, said he felt embarrassed "and very dumb" after paying $35,000 for scant instruction and a few how-to books he could have found in a library. "I feel the Donald Trump school scammed good and honest people in believing the school would help them in the real estate business," he told the Federal Trade Commission.

Thousands of complaints like theirs, filed under oath, eventually prompted action by state regulators and resulted in three major lawsuits—including class actions in a Southern California federal court claiming breach of contract, fraud, and bad faith misrepresentation against Trump University and Donald Trump personally, and a fraud action brought by New York State's then attorney general Eric Schneiderman in 2013, two years after Trump U had ceased operations. It was, said Schneiderman, "essentially a fraud from beginning to end."

Channeling his inner Roy Cohn, Trump attempted to bluster and bully his way out of the enormous liability he had created by ripping off his would-be acolytes. He had skimmed off millions of dollars during that process, according to Schneiderman's estimate, and angrily refused to surrender a penny. He sent out Alan Garten, counsel to the Trump Organization, to insist absurdly that the "university" had provided top value and high levels of satisfaction. He publicly vowed never to settle the complaints against him. He pursued extensive lawsuits against the plaintiffs, claiming that they had "defamed" him.

Dragging on for years, the Trump U litigation became an issue in the 2016 presidential election, when Trump attacked several of the plaintiffs by name in campaign speeches, a thuggish tactic designed to intimidate them. The evidence of chicanery amassed to prosecute those cases provoked the conservative *National Review* to publish an investigative report in February 2016 with a bluntly damning headline: "Yes, Trump University Was a Massive Scam."

AMONG THE MOST profitable and durable hustles in postmodern America is the multilevel marketing corporation. Often known by its initials, MLM is the pyramid-style business model first made famous (or infamous) by Amway, the mammoth global corporation that has generated billions for the far-right DeVos and Van Andel families of Michigan, their obscene wealth siphoned from the savings of hapless, would-be entrepreneurs who believed false promises of easy money.

The MLM phenomenon bills itself as "direct selling" to consumers, but in fact relies on every salesperson making a cash investment in the company and then recruiting more and more sellers, with heavy commissions paid at each stage up the chain of a corporate hierarchy. It is impossible for MLM recruits to make money unless they succeed in enrolling a legion of subordinates, which very few are able to accomplish; in reality, only a tiny percentage recover their original investment, let alone earn any substantial income. Rather than a traditional productive enterprise, based on invention or efficiency, the typical MLM more closely resembles a cult, with a strong scent of fraud. The rise of multilevel marketing, and the elevation of MLM billionaires like Jay Van Andel, who became chairman of the United States Chamber of Commerce, demonstrates an American vulnerability to hucksterism and deception that abetted Trump's rise to power.

In the decadent phase of the Trump Organization, at a time when the bogus cachet of its brand could attract thousands of rubes to a con like Trump University, multilevel marketing became an inevitable outlet for the charismatic star of *The Apprentice*. Here was a kind of business ideally suited to Donald Trump, where money could be taken from the admiring and unsuspecting, based on hollow promises and glittering illusions, without providing much of anything in return.

Not just greed but grim necessity motivated Trump's frantic pursuit of these opportunities for grift. As *The New York Times* eventually revealed, his tax returns from that period showed enormous losses incurred by the Trump Organization, even as he boasted that his company had grown "bigger than it ever was and stronger than it ever was." He was lying: before the first episode of *The Apprentice* aired, his personal tax return showed a loss of nearly $90 million for 2004. But in the years that followed, as he sold his reputation to hype anything from laundry detergent and mattresses to ties and underwear, Trump earned millions by endorsing not one but two MLM outfits almost simultaneously.

Robert L. FitzPatrick, the nation's most persistent and trenchant critic of multilevel marketing, has argued that Trump's experience in that shady sector created a "grassroots foundation" for his entrance into national politics. It was during a decade as the most prominent pitchman for the MLM companies he represented, according to FitzPatrick, that Trump honed his proficiency in the "Big Lie."

As a messianic spokesman for MLM, Trump stood for the first time before thousands of rapturous followers and got "an intoxicating taste for the cultish, large-spectacle politics he now practices." It was then that Trump began to transcend his image as a sharp dealmaker and to become a glorified figure promising financial opportunity, personal renewal, and salvation—even or especially in the throes of the Great Recession.

LIKE THE MAGA movement that would propel his political career, the huge and enduring MLM economic subculture is based on an alternative worldview—sustained not by facts or reality but by the need to belong and the will to believe. And the dismal true history of Trump's MLM ventures closely parallels the scandalous saga of Trump University during the years before he declared his presidential candidacy.

WHEN THE FOUNDERS of ACN, short for American Communications Network, first approached Donald Trump, flush with the success of *The Apprentice*, they had been in the dubious multilevel marketing business for decades. But his support for their venture, which began in 2005, permitted exponential growth like they had never seen before.

The ACN members, who are known as "independent business owners," paid a registration fee of $499, subject to annual renewal, for the right to sell company products such as videophones and services, including online access, telephone, gas, and electricity. But as multiple investigations by government regulators proved, the only way for those investors to earn any significant profit would be to recruit others and thus earn additional commissions—which only a very small number of them ever achieved. The rest tended to earn little or nothing, and many lost their entire investment, which included not just the initiation fee but thousands of dollars in additional fees for conferences, seminars, subscriptions, and renewals.

Enticed by Trump to join ACN, what none of its would-be entrepreneurs seemed to know was that he had been paid millions of dollars over the years for publicly praising the firm. At dozens of ACN rallies in cities across the country, in ACN publications and promotional videos, and perhaps most importantly on episodes of *The Apprentice* and *Celebrity Apprentice*, the self-proclaimed billionaire delivered a full-throated and unconditional validation of the company. Among the earliest instances was a 2005 video interview that featured Trump telling ACN cofounder Greg Provenzano why he had chosen to work with them.

"I am asked to do this, what you're doing with me, many, many times. And I turn down many, many different proposals." Then he added, "We do a lot of research on companies before we agree to do something like I'm doing for you, and ACN is a great company." In the years that followed, Trump would repeatedly claim that joining up as an ACN investor was virtually free of risk. "You have a great opportunity before you at ACN without any of the risks most entrepreneurs have to take," he said on the "ACN Opportunity Disc," a primary recruitment tool for the company. Among the most infamous incidents was Trump's promotion of the ACN videophone, which employed obsolete technology and could only make calls to other ACN videophones. (The company's insiders also owned the outfit that made the phones, so their profits were guaranteed.)

Over the decade that followed, Trump would continue to broadcast outlandish claims on behalf of ACN—and the company would secretly compensate him with nearly $9 million in payments, as his tax returns obtained by *The New York Times* ultimately revealed. Encouraged by those lucrative arrangements, which entailed little or no work beyond the ego-boosting rallies and interviews, he sought to expand into yet another MLM sector, the sale of vitamins and supplements.

In 2009, he entered into an agreement with Ideal Health, a firm that sold a multivitamin that supposedly improved the well-being of its customers—with results validated by a proprietary urine test. That test retailed for $139.95, and didn't include the $69.95 monthly price of the vitamins or the $99.95 cost of additional testing every six months. No credible health expert believed that the vitamins had any beneficial effect. But Trump couldn't resist the chance to fleece a new cohort of marks—and Ideal Health soon was rebranded as the Trump Network, with a deal that paid him for the use of his image and fervent promotional statements.

As Americans struggled in the wake of financial collapse, Trump made extravagant promises for his new MLM scheme. "The Trump

Network wants to give millions of people renewed hope," he said in an introductory video, "with an exciting plan to opt out of the recession." He told potential recruits that the network offered "something you can believe in—products that help make people healthier, an opportunity for you to make as much money as you want, based on your own efforts, and the training and support to help you succeed."

The truth was not quite so uplifting for those who signed up. After paying thousands of dollars for seminars and starter kits, very few of them recovered those outlays in actual sales. As one salesperson told the Federal Trade Commission, the Trump Network executives "kept tricking me into believing that I will make money just by selling more products and inviting more people, but the rate of return is so low. . . . In other words, they are scamming and deceiving people, making them believe that if they 'just hang in there' they will make money."

NOT ONLY DID very few of the recruits ever earn back the money they had invested in the Trump Network, but within two years, its original owners declared personal bankruptcy, and its parent firm was sold off in 2011 to another company. Trump's own tax returns, however, showed that he had walked off with at least $2.6 million for doing almost nothing.

Left behind were the thousands of suckers who had staked their money and faith on Trump's MLM ventures, believing that he would never lead them astray. No doubt they were stunned to hear him say in August 2015, just before he announced his candidacy for president, that he had never really been involved with ACN in any meaningful way.

"I do not know the company," he told reporters for *The Wall Street Journal*. "I know nothing about the company other than the people who run the company. I'm not familiar with what they do or how they go about doing that, and I make that clear in my speeches."

TRUMP DIDN'T ENTIRELY escape the legal consequences of the scam rampage that had preceded his presidential campaign. In the wake of his historically narrow Electoral College victory—achieved despite a stinging defeat in the popular vote by Hillary Clinton—the president-elect settled the lawsuits brought against Trump University. Dropping his repeated vows to fight the charges in court until the very end, he agreed to pay $25 million in restitution to the plaintiffs, a result that ultimately compensated most of them for more than 80 percent of the fees they had paid.

Two years later, New York attorney general Letitia James, successor to Eric Schneiderman, brought an action against the Trumps alleging that the Trump Foundation was "little more than a checkbook to serve Mr. Trump's business and political interests" and had perpetrated "a shocking pattern of illegality." By the end of 2018, Trump's lawyers agreed to close down the sham charity, refrain from engaging in any such phony charitable activities in New York State, and to pay the remaining $2 million in its accounts to several bona fide charitable organizations, including Children's Aid, Meals on Wheels, the United Negro College Fund, the United Way, and the US Holocaust Memorial Museum.

But justice was not so easily won by the victims of his multilevel marketing ventures, who brought a federal class-action lawsuit in 2018 against the Trump Organization and Donald, Ivanka, Eric, and Donald Trump Jr. in 2018, alleging fraud, deception, and unfair trade practices. Brought by four anonymous investors who claimed that they had lost thousands of dollars because they had been deceived by Trump's promotion of the pyramid scheme, the lawsuit dragged on for years. In May 2023, following depositions of the three Trump children, they were dismissed as defendants because, as the plaintiffs' attorney noted, their father was in fact "the architect, principal actor and largest beneficiary of the fraudulent scheme to endorse and promote ACN in exchange for secret payments"—with a trial expected to occur in 2024.

13

A Predatory Presidency

Donald Trump was never fit to serve as president, a truism even he seemed to comprehend during the 2016 campaign. It seemed at first to be a mere exercise in bluster that his own advisers privately conceded was more likely to establish a lucrative media brand than to achieve a political victory. And yet in a fateful fluke, he won the Electoral College by a fraction of 1 percent in each of three crucial Rust Belt states, despite losing the national popular vote by nearly three million ballots.

For the remnant of honest Republicans and conservatives shocked by the sudden ascent of this morally repellent man, it was consoling to believe that his presidency would be a temporary infection rather than a chronic and perhaps fatal malady. The 2016 primary contest had revealed a depth of rot in their party and movement that was understandably difficult to contemplate, let alone confront. During the primaries, Trump had amply demonstrated his own depravity and cynicism, but his irresistible rise—and the rapid capitulation of many of his harshest Republican critics—showed how little those character defects mattered.

It's worth recalling that his Republican primary opponents seized on the story of Trump University, hoping his mistreatment of its defrauded victims would repel conservative voters. Early in the campaign, Marco Rubio had released press statements proclaiming that "Trump

University Is an Absolute Scam," with details of the class-action lawsuits and profiles of the "veterans, seniors, and unemployed Americans" who had complained of being cheated. "Trump University was a con job," declared the Florida senator, "and we cannot allow a con artist to become the Republican nominee for president of the United States."

During the CNN primary debate in February 2016, both Rubio and Ted Cruz had pummeled the front-runner over Trump U, with the Texas senator warning that Trump might be called as a witness in fraud litigation before Election Day. The Cruz campaign then issued satirical "Certificates of Deception," marked with a Trump University crest. Both Trump rivals were encouraged when Google searches for "Trump University" spiked a couple of times during that debate. Two weeks later, Trump soared to seven victories on Super Tuesday and essentially secured the nomination.

What Rubio, Cruz, and every other Republican learned that night was how few of their party's voters cared whether Trump was a crook. His victories proved that hate drove politics on the right, not morality or even ideology. Before Election Day, nearly every conservative who had denounced him as a narcissistic fraudster would crawl like "servile puppies," as Cruz put it, acknowledging him as their master. His political triumph completed the transmogrification of the American Right into a shameless hustle, devoid of principle and fully devoted to exploitation.

On the first day of his presidency, Donald Trump stood up in front of the United States Capitol—where he would instigate mob violence four years later—and swore to uphold the Constitution. Assembled to hear his inaugural address was a crowd much smaller than that which had shown up to welcome his predecessor in January 2009. The mood set by his words was surly as Trump spoke of "American carnage" and the depredations of "the establishment."

Leaving the dais after the inaugural, former president George W. Bush turned to Hillary Clinton, the former secretary of state and Democratic presidential nominee narrowly defeated by Trump—who had dutifully attended the inauguration despite his ceaseless threats to incarcerate her—and muttered, "That was some weird shit."

Weird indeed, yet still darkly amusing to anyone who had observed the real Donald Trump in action or knew what he and his minions had been up to as his inauguration approached. At a moment when most new presidents seek a unifying theme, Trump struck the same resentful tone that had mobilized millions of angry Americans to support his campaign. Gazing balefully on the rather sparse crowd that lingered on the Mall below the Capitol steps, Trump again appealed to their sense of grievance, as if poised to enact justice against the grasping denizens of the place he always called "the swamp."

"For too long," he declared, "a small group in our nation's capital has reaped the rewards of government while the people have borne the cost. Washington flourished, but the people did not share in its wealth. . . . The establishment protected itself but not the citizens of our country. Their victories have not been your victories. Their triumphs have not been your triumphs. And while they celebrated in our nation's capital, there was little to celebrate for struggling families all across our land. That all changes starting right here and right now. Because this moment is your moment. It belongs to you. . . . The forgotten men and women of our country will be forgotten no longer."

Lurking beneath those populist promises, on that very historic day, was the usual deceit practiced by Trump and his seedy milieu. In the weeks since Election Day 2016, the president-elect and those around him had seen the opportunities presented by the inauguration and taken them, as a Tammany boss once phrased it. The Trump inaugural committee, headed by a developer and lobbyist named Tom Barrack, had raised $107 million, more than twice as much as the amount raised and spent for Barack Obama's inaugural festivities eight years earlier—mostly in checks for a million dollars or more from individuals and companies who wanted the new administration to do (or undo) something for them.

Exactly who those donors were and what they desired would come under scrutiny by prosecutors and the press. What became glaringly obvious to experienced observers after that first glitzy evening of gala receptions and balls was how suspiciously little bang the Trump gang had gotten for their big bucks. What had happened to all that greasy money?

The organizers of recent inaugurations found the Trump event's finances mystifying. "It's inexplicable to me," said Greg Jenkins, a former Bush White House aide who had handled the 2001 inauguration. "They had a third of the staff and a quarter of the events and they [raised] at least twice as much as we did," he told reporters for ProPublica, the investigative reporting website. "So there's the obvious question: Where did it go? I don't know." Steve Kerrigan, the official who had overseen both Obama inaugurations, was equally puzzled: "We literally did two inaugurations for less than the cost of that."

In October 2017, a coalition of national public interest organizations, including Common Cause, Democracy 21, and Public Citizen, the nonprofit founded by Ralph Nader, sent a letter to Trump and his inaugural committee asking for a full accounting of its receipts and expenditures. Among other oddities noted in the letter was that "Trump's inauguration shaped up to be a relatively low-key affair. Obama's 2009 inauguration stretched over five days, involving 10 official balls and hosted a record public attendance. Trump's inauguration lasted three days, involved three official balls, and hosted a much smaller crowd."

The same questions persisted months later in January 2018, when a reporter for *USA Today* asked billionaire Trump crony Tom Barrack, who chaired the inaugural committee, whether he could provide a full accounting yet, one year after the event. "We must decline comment at this time," said a Barrack spokeswoman.

Inauspicious as this mysterious evaporation of millions of dollars might seem, given Trump's promises to "drain the swamp" of corruption, it wasn't too surprising given whom he had put in charge. With gangland ties dating back to his mob lawyer Roy Cohn, and the unsavory business practices that had become synonymous with his name, Trump habitually cultivated a certain element—meaning the kind of grifters and skimmers who perhaps ought not to be entrusted with a fund of over $100 million.

The ProPublica investigation pointed toward three Trump inaugural officials with exceptionally dubious records. At the top was inaugural deputy chairman Rick Gates, a longtime Republican operative and close associate of former campaign manager Paul Manafort—whom he had first met while working as an intern for the unsavory Black, Manafort, Stone, and Kelly consulting firm. Like Manafort, Gates eventually was sent to prison by Special Counsel Robert Mueller in the Russian influence probe; as part of a plea deal, he finally confessed to dozens of financial crimes, including the gross inflation of his expenses to steal hundreds of thousands of dollars from Manafort. When Mueller's prosecutors asked Gates under oath whether he had submitted expenses to the Trump inaugural committee, too, he replied, "It's possible."

That admission only occurred years later. But lobbyist and businessman Elliott Broidy, the inaugural committee's financial cochair, already had a rap sheet dating back to a 2002 bribery conviction in New York State, where he had secretly paid public officials to invest employee pension funds in his private equity firm. Broidy had pleaded down to a misdemeanor by cooperating with prosecutors to send the state comptroller and several other officials to prison, while avoiding incarceration himself.

Even that close call failed to deter Broidy's criming. Having raised millions for the Trump campaign, the lobbyist exploited his perch on the inaugural committee to promote various crooked foreign clients, notably including a Congolese warlord and a Romanian politician, previously convicted of corruption, who got his photo taken with Trump at an inaugural eve party.

In due course, Broidy was implicated in a series of White House influence-peddling scandals. One involved an Emirati associate named George Nader, likewise a foreign lobbyist, who ended up in jail after being convicted of sex trafficking a minor and possession of child porn. Another involved Broidy's efforts to stall a Justice Department probe of Malaysian banking officials accused of embezzling billions of dollars. (Ultimately convicted of acting as an unregistered foreign agent and related money-laundering charges, Broidy accepted a pardon from Trump on January 20, 2021.)

As for the inaugural committee's treasurer, his résumé, too, should have set off alarms. Former KPMG partner Doug Ammerman had been named as an unindicted coconspirator in a massive 2005 tax fraud case brought by the government against the accounting giant. Although Ammerman wasn't charged in that case, independent experts told *The Wall Street Journal* that corporations would be ill advised to entrust him with any auditing responsibilities.

So perhaps nobody should have been too surprised to learn that millions from the Trump inauguration had been purloined, squandered, or siphoned away. Fully tracing the flows of cash proved difficult if not impossible because inauguration spending isn't subject to the disclosure, auditing, and controls that govern most public or corporate entities. What did become alarmingly clear, when accounting for roughly half of the funds became available, is how the new president's entourage bellied up to plunder the inauguration's swollen accounts.

Among the line items that initially provoked outrage was $26 million paid out to a company called WIS, set up just before the inauguration by Melania Trump's friend and New York event planner Stephanie Winston Wolkoff. The Trump spouse cut off their relationship after learning of that payment, which included a $1.6 million management fee that Steve Kerrigan, the Obama inaugural manager, described as "outrageous." Greg Jenkins, the Bush inaugural manager, scoffed, "I have never heard anybody getting that kind of fee associated with any inaugural, ever."

In the end, Wolkoff herself only took home a consulting fee of $484,000, having paid out nearly all of that $26 million to other event planners and companies. In taped conversations recorded by Michael Cohen, the former Trump lawyer who ended up in jail, she expressed suspicion and dismay over the behavior of Gates, Barrack, and others entrusted with inaugural responsibilities by the Trumps—who pretended that they knew nothing about how the inauguration had been run, when in fact they had been apprised daily about its planning and budgeting.

Continuous outbreaks of boodling and scamming worried Wolkoff, a political novice who had worked for years at *Vogue* magazine—

especially when she saw Barrack set up a "chairman's dinner" using inaugural funds to curry favor with foreign diplomats from Saudi Arabia, Qatar, and the United Arab Emirates, oil states where he did millions of dollars of business. She was troubled to watch Gates conducting business out of Donald Trump Jr.'s office in Trump Tower, ignoring any effort to police conflicts of interest involving the family. She questioned millions of dollars in payments from the inaugural committee to the Trump International Hotel, their property just down Pennsylvania Avenue from the White House—a gross conflict of interest that prefigured Donald Trump's ongoing effort as president to funnel public dollars to his company.

A television company associated with the former *Apprentice* producer Mark Burnett appeared to have billed up to $25 million for broadcasting the inauguration. Another $2 million was paid to Brad Parscale, the Trump campaign's digital media manager, for his effort to attract crowds to the Capitol Mall on Inauguration Day (a failure that led to the first embarrassing "scandal" for the Trump White House when press secretary Sean Spicer lied about the crowd size to reporters and senior adviser Kellyanne Conway then defended Spicer's presentation of "alternative facts.") As much as $10 million went for travel alone, with huge additional sums paid out for meals, lodging, and other costs, including such extraneous items as $10,000 in makeup for a single evening.

One indisputable fact about the inauguration stood out when all the glitz had faded. Of the $107 million total raised from fat cats and corporations, no more than $67 million in audited expenditures could be traced, which meant that $40 million had simply disappeared. Despite strenuous investigation by federal authorities—including Justice Department subpoenas to the inaugural committee—what happened to those funds was never determined.

The only effort to hold the Trumps accountable for the misuse of inaugural funds that achieved any traction at all came in the form of a civil lawsuit by Karl Racine, the attorney general of the District of Columbia. As the district's top law enforcement official, Racine had the power to enforce laws affecting nonprofit entities like the inaugural committee. He sued both the Trump Organization and the Trump inaugural committee for enriching the Trumps with nonprofit money used to rent space at the Trump International Hotel. Racine argued that the Trumps had grabbed more than $1 million by overcharging the inaugural committee for those facilities.

But his lawsuit, settled in May 2022, recovered only $750,000 and allowed the Trumps to maintain their innocence; indeed, they crowed over the fact that an insurance company had covered most of the litigation and settlement costs, which they termed "modest." Once more, Donald Trump's wealth, power, and political influence had shielded him from the consequences of his grifting.

It was Wolkoff, Melania's former friend and the chief witness for Racine's lawsuit, who sounded most disappointed by the outcome. Months earlier, she had predicted, "The world's about to learn how Trump's inner circle—with Trump's full knowledge—took advantage of the presidential inauguration. Everything they did was all about self-dealing." When the settlement was announced, she told The Daily Beast, "I'm just so shattered. It's awful, it's unjust, it's absurd. . . . They stole so much. The self-dealing. The perjury. They know all about it."

THE STYLE OF arrogant deception that had shaped Trump's life also defined his presidency from the beginning, when the new commander in chief instructed White House staff to lie about the crowd size at his depressing inauguration. Spicer, Conway, and their White House colleagues found themselves obliged to lie constantly, as the ensuing four years mocked Trump's vow to "drain the swamp." His campaign had been inspired and run by Roger Stone and Paul Manafort, Republican operatives whose long careers were emblematic of Washington corruption; indeed, they could fairly be counted among the original swamp creatures. And as soon became clear, there were many more like them waiting to pounce on the opportunities for grift and graft that a Trump administration would offer.

As with Trump's own corruption, the scope and frequency of amoral behavior at the highest levels of government were overwhelming. Said

Walter Shaub, who headed the Office of Government Ethics until he quit in disgust after several months of Trump, "We're seeing a level of ethics problems we just haven't seen" in previous administrations. While prior presidents pushed their own appointees to stay within ethical boundaries, he said, "We're discovering that you can't always count on that if you have a president who doesn't care about ethics rules."

Whether in the White House or in his cabinet, Trump surrounded himself with individuals whose self-serving instinct and disdain for ethics mirrored his own. Those traits were on full display at the first Trump cabinet meeting, where the president seized the chance to praise himself grandiloquently on camera for a "record-setting pace" of achievement, although he had yet to sign a single piece of major legislation. Then, before the doors of the cabinet room closed to the media, he invited each of his appointees to make "a statement."

What that meant, as immediately became clear, was a short speech *praising him*, with each of his appointees burbling in turn about the "honor . . . great honor . . . greater honor . . . privilege . . . greatest privilege" of serving him. "We thank you for the opportunity and the blessing to serve your agenda," squeaked Reince Priebus, the White House chief of staff who would soon endure the humiliation of an *Apprentice*-style dismissal via Twitter. Only General James Mattis, chairman of the Joint Chiefs of Staff, eschewed this groveling—the kind of tribute demanded by a primitive despot and an intolerable insult to the dignity of any reputable American official.

But these were not very reputable individuals, as each would demonstrate during Trump's presidency.

"Drain the swamp," a slogan that Trump acknowledged had no meaning to him, might have suggested a desire to clean up Washington's legal graft and systemic corruption. His choices to head crucial departments and agencies, however, only strengthened the grip of corporate power over government.

Indeed, Trump appeared to welcome the naked conflicts of interest that previous administrations had avoided or at least concealed. He named a pharma executive to oversee health care, a Big Oil lobbyist to head the Interior Department, a former coal industry lobbyist to head the Environmental Protection Agency, a weapons industry lobbyist at the Defense Department, a telecommunications industry lawyer to chair the Federal Communications Commission, and a former Goldman Sachs partner to run the Treasury Department. In all, Trump named almost three hundred lobbyists to important federal positions, supposedly "regulating" the industries they had protected; that was four times as many as Obama had ever hired.

Mick Mulvaney, who served as Trump's budget director, head of the Consumer Financial Protection Bureau (CFPB), and one of several White House chiefs of staff, summed up the administration's insolently corrupt atmosphere when he spoke to a group of banking lobbyists. "If you are a lobbyist who never gave us money, I did not talk to you," he said, recalling his days in Congress. "If you are a lobbyist who gave us money, I might talk to you." Mulvaney hadn't elevated his ethical standards when he went to the White House. A few months earlier, his agency had quietly canceled a CFPB probe of a payday lending firm that had regularly donated to his campaigns.

While his arrogant money-grubbing enraged Democrats and embarrassed colleagues, Mulvaney's candor reflected a bipartisan reality in American politics. In the corridors of the Trump administration, however, it was easy to stumble across far more rapacious characters, enmeshed in a culture of grifting that pervasive on the Republican right. They swiftly found ways to exploit the offices he had entrusted to them.

Housing secretary Ben Carson, the former neurosurgeon and right-wing celebrity who had endorsed Trump after dropping out of the 2016 primary, made headlines with the purchase of a $31,000 dining set for his office—an act of wretched excess that he tried to blame on his wife. Treasury secretary Steven Mnuchin, who had served as Trump's campaign finance chair, spent hundreds of thousands of tax dollars on military flights for himself and his (third) wife, including a trip to view an eclipse in Kentucky. He tried to get military transportation for their honeymoon in France and Italy, a request that was rebuffed.

Health and Human Services secretary Tom Price spent more than a million dollars on private charter and military jet transport for himself and his wife, including trips to Europe and Africa (and he was forced to resign by the White House after only seven months in office). Seema Verma, who headed the Center for Medicare & Medicaid Services, became known solely for squandering nearly $5 million on outside public relations consultants she had hired to get her profiled in magazines and wangle awards to improve her image (while she urged budget cuts for poor Medicaid patients, including children). For some unknown reason, Verma also awarded a $500,000 no-bid contract to a consulting company owned by Ben Carson's daughter-in-law.

They were all outperformed by EPA chief Scott Pruitt, a former Oklahoma legislator noted for soliciting favors from lobbyists, whose routinely scandalous conduct shocked Washington's most jaded observers. Surrounding himself with a huge security detail at a cost of $4.5 million, he proceeded to spend still more millions of taxpayer dollars on first-class and charter flights, as well as trips on military aircraft and luxury hotel accommodations. (His predecessors had almost always flown economy.)

When he wasn't traveling, Pruitt rented a Capitol Hill flat for $50 a night, far below market value, from lobbyists representing a Canadian energy producer, whose proposal to expand a tar sands pipeline he coincidentally approved. When he wasn't hindering his agency's statutory regulation of polluters, Pruitt kept busy seeking employment for his wife; he sent entreaties on her behalf to major corporations and Republican donors, including the boss of the Chick-fil-A fried chicken chain. Flagged early on by officials in his agency as a radioactive ethics risk, he became the target of multiple investigations—and set up a "legal defense fund" to solicit contributions from lobbyists and others to defend him. He finally had to resign in July 2018.

Interior secretary Ryan Zinke somehow outlasted Pruitt by a few months, although he, too, had to resign in the wake of metastasizing scandals. Zinke squandered $140,000 on a new set of fancy doors for his office, $200,000 on flagpoles to raise a special banner celebrating his presence in the Interior Department headquarters, and thousands more on charter flights, helicopter trips, and private aircraft for political trips.

Two of the scandals brought Zinke dangerously close to federal indictments—the first over a land deal involving his wife and the oil services giant Halliburton, and the second over his interference with a Connecticut tribal casino license opposed by MGM Grand. Evidently fearful of further investigation, he left office following a Trump tweet that announced his departure in late 2018.

When such small-time peculators drew enough negative media and prosecutorial attention, Trump dumped them. He appeared to believe that great wealth conferred wisdom or at least competence, however, no matter how it had been acquired.

For instance, a conspicuous absence of any relevant credentials had posed no obstacle to Secretary of Education Betsy DeVos, the ultra-right heiress from Michigan, whose unfitness for that position was amply exposed during her confirmation hearings. Her family billions derived from Amway, the scandal-ridden multilevel marketing behemoth that the Trump Network had aimed to imitate. (Trump's first choice for Treasury secretary, the multibillionaire corporate raider Carl Icahn, was then embroiled in a decade of financial warfare over Herbalife, a major multilevel marketing outfit and alleged pyramid scheme.)

Trump's cabinet also featured at least one world-class rogue, the octogenarian Commerce secretary Wilbur Ross. Sometimes called the "king of bankruptcy," he specialized in "turning around" distressed companies and had developed a relationship with Trump that dated back to the spectacular failure of the president's Atlantic City casino hotels.

Like Trump, Ross pretended to be a billionaire despite falling short of that status by hundreds of millions of dollars. Unlike Trump, Ross had promised during Senate confirmation hearings to divest his own enormously complex portfolio of corporate and financial holdings, a pledge that won praise. But his professed transparency proved to be a mirage, and after taking office, he was caught lying repeatedly about his supposed divestments. His omissions and deceptions were so extensive that the usually placid Office of Government Ethics delivered an extraordinary rebuke by refusing to certify his 2018 financial disclosure documents.

What could be detected from even his limited and unverified disclosures was a series of questionable dealings with foreign banks and shipping firms, which had brought him into financial proximity to hostile authoritarian regimes. The most notable of these shady outfits was Navigator Holdings, a natural-gas shipping company that included Vladimir Putin's son-in-law as a director. Ross held on to that investment while he negotiated a deal to "facilitate" the export of liquefied natural gas produced in the United States to China. When he learned that *The New York Times* was preparing to publish a negative story on his Navigator investment, Ross shorted the company's stock—and made an additional profit when he cleared the position a few days after that story came out.

His failure to divest shares in major corporations provoked the watchdogs at Citizens for Responsibility and Ethics in Washington to demand a criminal investigation of Ross. Within weeks after he took office at the Commerce Department, CREW complained that he had "participated in a series of meetings with CEOs of Boeing, Chevron Corporation, Greenbrier Companies, and the International Automotive Components (IAC) Group at a time when they were lobbying his agency and other parts of the government on trade issues and policy matters impacting the companies. At the time of these meetings, Secretary Ross or his wife held financial interests in each of these companies despite his previous pledge to divest from approximately 80 potentially problematic holdings."

Executives who had worked at his company, W. L. Ross, told *Forbes* magazine in 2019 that he had refused to pay workers at his house in the Hamptons and reneged on a million-dollar charity pledge. During his tenure at the Commerce Department, former business associates filed lawsuits against Ross, alleging that he had swindled them out of huge sums—siphoning off a few million here or there—through improper charges and fees. The total amount that he had misappropriated, they said, came to nearly $120 million.

"If even half of the accusations are legitimate," *Forbes* concluded, "the current United States secretary of commerce could rank among the biggest grifters in American history."

SETTING THE TONE was the grifter in chief, who often whined that he had lost money as president and made an annual show of donating his presidential salary back to the Treasury. Independent analysts calculated that giving back $400,000 annually amounted to less than 0.1 percent of the $1.6 billion he had received as income during his presidency. Rather than divest his business interests to prevent any perception of greed or misconduct, Trump had openly leveraged the office to promote his private interests not once but continuously.

So persistent was his self-dealing that reporters had difficulty keeping track of the ways he had profited—and of his specific violations of the Constitution's foreign emoluments clause, which forbids the president and other federal officials from receiving anything of value from a foreign government or interest unless approved by Congress.

TRUMP'S INITIAL PROMISE to "leave my great business" in the hands of his adult children also proved entirely hollow. Soon it became obvious how Trump would instead use his power to promote and enrich the Trump Organization, precisely the kind of tainted arrangement feared by the nation's founders. He spent one out of every three days on visits to his luxury resorts, hotels, or golf courses, at a cost of millions to taxpayers. He used public resources to promote those developments on scores of occasions. He directed millions of public dollars to his enterprises in the US and around the world. And he accepted millions of dollars poured into his hotels and resorts by foreign governments and other foreign entities as they sought favors from his administration.

Just down Pennsylvania Avenue from the White House stood the premier symbol of this unprecedented executive avarice—the Trump International Hotel, a historic edifice that formerly housed Washington's Old Post Office. Leased from the federal government, the property's timely reopening as a Trump hotel occurred in 2016, and with his inauguration, it swiftly became a glitzy hangout for lobbyists both foreign and domestic, as well as visiting heads of state, congressional Republicans, and anyone else seeking favorable treatment from Trump. Although the hotel had projected a $2 million loss during the first four months of 2017, its revenues soared—thanks to room rates far above average for Washington—and the Trump International booked a $2 million profit.

That appeared to be a triumph of constitutionally prohibited marketing. One week after Election Day in 2016, Trump International invited hundreds of foreign diplomats to a promotional event at the hotel, with hors d'oeuvres and Trump-branded champagne. Within days of his inauguration, the Saudi government's representatives purchased five hundred nights at Trump International—a direct violation of the foreign emoluments clause, and only one of many such incidents.

The Saudi room scandal was merely a passing liaison in the orgy of venality hosted by the Trump White House, reminiscent of autocratic regimes in places like the Philippines, Ukraine, or the Congo—and unlike anything previously seen in this country. It was worse than the Reagan administration, once the high-water mark of Washington malfeasance.

The disgrace extended to his children, raised in the shadow of Trump's greed and mendacity. Daughter Ivanka, hired as a "senior adviser" in her father's White House along with her husband, Jared Kushner, got into the grifting spirit as early as the 2016 Republican convention, when she merchandised her own dress on Twitter after delivering a speech (she had an Ivanka Trump purse and shoes to match). She registered more than two dozen foreign trademarks during the Trump administration and reported as much as $640 million in outside income to her and her husband. Like his father-in-law, Kushner pretended to divest himself of conflicts of interest involving his own family's massive real estate holdings, but in fact profited hugely from his role in both domestic and foreign policy. Despite the advice of ethics advisers, he maintained an investment in a firm called Cadre that sold investments in federal Opportunity Zones, with his shares doubling in value from $25 million to $50 million.

When the House Ways and Means Committee obtained and then released several years of Trump's taxes in December 2022—despite his strenuous legal efforts to keep them secret—the sheer scale of his profiteering began to emerge. Analysis of those documents, along with investigative reports and official disclosures, suggested that Trump had kept his struggling business empire afloat by exploiting his office. During those four years, he reported more than $1.6 billion in personal income exceeding his $400,000 government salary.

He derived much of that revenue from the resorts and golf courses he visited most often, including Mar-a-Lago, his winter home resort and club in Palm Beach, Florida, his Trump National Golf Club outside Washington, his Trump Doral resort in Miami, and his summer home and club in Bedminster, New Jersey. All the clubs had hiked their membership fees after he became the Republican presidential nominee in 2016, with Mar-a-Lago's annual fee doubling to $200,000 in 2017.

He had visited those properties nearly four hundred times as president, while government agencies, the Republican National Committee, Republican members of Congress, and right-wing organizations of all kinds booked rooms at his resorts under all sorts of pretexts. Trump had even ordered his ambassador to the United Kingdom, pharmaceutical heir Robert Wood Johnson, to pressure London into relocating the British Open at Doonbeg, his golf resort in Scotland.

This unrelenting drive to maximize money flowing into his properties from every conceivable source finally led Trump to overreach. With the G7 summit of the top industrialized nations scheduled to occur in the United States in 2020, he proposed to host the meeting at his Doral resort. Explaining the plan at a White House press conference, Mulvaney, his chief of staff, insisted that the Doral was "perfect for our needs," despite its dilapidated condition and security concerns raised by the Secret Service. (Eight years earlier, President Obama had hosted G7 leaders at Camp David, where nobody made a private profit.) It was a choice that potentially involved the expenditure of hundreds of millions of dollars by the US government and the other six nations.

The normalization of corruption had gone so far that Senator Marco Rubio—a onetime Trump critic who had denounced Trump University as a scam and Trump himself as a "con man"—wouldn't condemn the outrageous Doral bid. "Anything that draws a major event like that to Florida is not something I would discourage," Rubio said blandly as ferocious protest erupted from Democrats, good government watchdogs, and a handful of Republicans, including some who had tried until then to wave off Trump's incessant self-dealing.

But as he faced the threat of impeachment for the first time, Trump needed every vote. With a whining tweet, he backed off: "I thought I was doing something very good for our country by using Trump National Doral, in Miami, for hosting the G-7 leaders," touting its amenities. "But, as usual, the Hostile Media & their Democrat Partners went CRAZY! Therefore, based on both Media & Democrat Crazed and Irrational Hostility, we will no longer consider Trump National Doral, Miami, as the Host Site for the G-7 in 2020."

The summit was held again at Camp David instead.

Hundreds of millions of dollars sloshed into the accounts of the Trumps and Kushners while they occupied the White House, pretending to serve the public as they gorged on the spoils of office. Scarcely a single Republican official and very few conservatives took exception to this sickening spectacle. Many more would ignore, excuse, or defend the ongoing heist. Which no doubt encouraged the even more outrageous acts of plunder they would commit within months after Trump left office.

14

Guns, Walls, and the Culture of Impunity

Grifting, pilfering, and outright looting were endemic on the American Right long before Donald Trump's ascent to power. Exploiting the ignorant was always profitable, and modern information technology had made such fleecing feasible on a mass scale at very low cost. But Trump also changed the game in fundamental ways. His overt displays of bigotry and cruelty, applauded by adoring crowds, meant that such expressions were far more likely to be accepted—and rewarded—on the right. Having long escaped any substantive sanction for his self-serving behavior and unbridled rapacity, he set an example that others of his ilk eagerly followed.

If he got away with everything, no matter how appalling, why should anyone ever be held accountable?

Trump's reign as the dominant figure in the Republican Party and the right-wing movement (which could no longer be described accurately as conservative) fostered what their political forebears would have called an extremely "permissive" atmosphere. Almost nothing was out of bounds anymore. Early in his political career, Trump had said that he could shoot someone on Fifth Avenue and not lose a single voter—and for him, that monstrous boast may well have been true. Even if other right-wing leaders didn't have a license to kill, they behaved as if they had a license to steal.

Nowhere was the decay of conservative morality more plainly visible than in the scandals that beset the National Rifle Association—the largest, wealthiest, and most powerful grassroots organization on the right. Founded in the late nineteenth century by former Union Army generals seeking to improve marksmanship and gun safety in America, the once staid and responsible NRA has devolved over the decades into a menacingly extreme outfit that promotes fringe ideologies, divisive partisanship, and paranoid fantasies. Its increasing hostility to government and law enforcement exhibited the worst aspects of Trumpian populism well before the ascent of that movement's avatar.

Unsurprisingly, the gun lobby spent more on the 2016 presidential campaign than ever before, committing as much as $55 million to elect Trump and a Republican Congress. That year, the NRA's "dark money" operation, the Institute for Legislative Action, poured as much money into a single election cycle as it had in every election dating back to 1992 combined, according to OpenSecrets.org, the nation's top political-money-tracking organization. It was an unprecedented triumph and an enormous setback for gun safety.

Seemingly at the zenith of influence during Trump's presidency, however, the NRA suddenly began to implode. Targeted by investigations and litigation brought by Democratic law enforcement officials in New York and California, its leaders turned on each other, exposing spectacularly nefarious practices that had led the organization toward ruin.

Compounding the pressure from those hostile forces was an internal rift that had opened up when NRA CEO Wayne LaPierre hired a brash New York attorney named William Brewer as the organization's principal outside counsel. LaPierre had signed the controversial lawyer even after Angus McQueen, the gun lobby's powerful longtime public relations and media consultant, had warned him against engaging Brewer—who also happened to be McQueen's cordially despised son-in-law.

Brewer had returned the insult when he ordered unsparing audits of all NRA contractors—notably including Ackerman McQueen, his father-in-law's Oklahoma City firm, which had received tens of millions in NRA contracts. Soon Ackerman McQueen mounted a campaign to resist those audits both in court and by mounting a secret coup attempt against LaPierre. Amid the ensuing confrontation, disturbing facts inevitably emerged about the NRA's financial condition, including instances of massive waste, greed, and misuse of resources on all sides.

On the eve of the NRA's 2019 convention in Indianapolis—featuring a keynote address by Trump—those hostilities burst into an embarrassing public showdown between LaPierre and the group's titular president, the Iran-Contra grifter and right-wing "hero" Oliver North. Acting as the cat's-paw of Ackerman McQueen, which had been paying him lavishly under the table, North tried to quietly blackmail LaPierre into resigning with threats to reveal the NRA leadership's financial misconduct. In a dramatic rebuke at the convention, LaPierre pushed back by revealing the blackmail scheme and ejecting North from the presidency.

Until then, LaPierre's bureaucracy and the Ackerman McQueen firm had worked in tandem, siphoning off millions of dollars in questionable expenditures and inflated salaries for decades. Their dueling leaks to media outlets revealed that the NRA was on the cusp of bankruptcy, despite raising over $300 million annually, and that its huge treasure chest had been squandered with abandon by its most prominent leaders.

It was under the tutelage of Ackerman McQueen, after all, that the meek and bespectacled lobbyist LaPierre had been reshaped into a macho advocate of the Second Amendment and an outspoken champion of the populist right. "We're not here to be popular at Beltway cocktail parties," he told the media in blustering interviews. But his proclaimed affinity for the common man didn't inhibit LaPierre's elite appetites—specifically, his taste for luxury aviation, costly designer apparel, and high-end vacations, among other indulgences.

Despite annual compensation as high as $5 million, including deferred payments, the NRA boss had glommed a fantastic array of perks that sparked furious indignation among the organization's largely rural and working-class membership. According to New York attorney general Letitia James's heavily documented lawsuit, he had spent tens of millions of dollars on personal trips and expenditures for himself and a handful of others, including his wife and niece. He had abused the tax-exempt nonprofit NRA, said James, as "a personal piggy bank." Her complaint showed precisely how LaPierre and his top lieutenants had "instituted a culture of self-dealing, mismanagement, and negligent oversight. . . . They overrode and evaded internal controls to allow themselves, their families, favored board members, employees, and vendors to benefit through reimbursed expenses, related party transactions, excess compensation, side deals, and waste of charitable assets without regard to the NRA's best interests."

Among the hundreds of improper expenditures attributed to LaPierre were multiple vacations in the Caribbean and safaris in Africa; over $300,000 in suits, including several purchased at the Ermenegildo Zegna store in Beverly Hills; and a series of private jet excursions that included a $15,000 flight to pick up the husband of LaPierre's niece in Nebraska so that he could babysit their daughter in Las Vegas. (On another occasion, LaPierre authorized a $79,000 flight from Washington to Orlando with his family, with a Nebraska stopover.)

LaPierre and his family took Bahamas vacation trips on a 108-foot yacht, complete with waterslide, from an NRA contractor who had received tens of millions of dollars in payments from the organization. After Trump appointed LaPierre's wife, Susan, to the board of the National Parks Foundation, the NRA booked $150,000 in charter flights for the couple to attend foundation events. LaPierre expensed over $100,000 for membership fees in a fancy Washington, DC, golf club and spent tens of thousands more on expensive Christmas gifts from luxury retailers Neiman Marcus and Bergdorf Goodman. His cronies were not as extravagant, but they, too, reaped the illicit spoils.

As scandal engulfed the NRA, factional loyalties frayed, and the double-dealing leaders turned against each other. The most prominent defector was LaPierre's top lieutenant, Josh Powell, a former business executive with scant qualifications, who had been awarded an eye-popping salary of $850,000 a year (plus a $30,000 contract for his wife). In a tell-all book he wrote after LaPierre fired him, Powell recalled, "I began asking myself who was more corrupt, me or Wayne?" He later told National Public Radio that the NRA was in "a death spiral," with its finances "in shambles" because the group had become an arm of "the grifter culture of Conservative Inc." He wasn't wrong: a leaked internal document on the NRA's financial condition showed three years of increasing deficits and a freeze on contributions to employee pensions while spending ballooned on "travel and entertainment," the category that covered the top officials' pillage.

With rather belated remorse, Powell also acknowledged that the NRA leadership had profited heavily by encouraging a paranoid and hostile outlook among its members to pull in donations. The NRA, he said, had created and popularized a mythological threat of federal gun confiscations, while depicting law enforcement officials as jackbooted thugs. Its multipronged media machine—ranging from magazines and newsletters to social media, advertising, and for a while its own streaming TV channel—had even promoted rhetoric anticipating a second civil war.

The gun lobby's divisive and hateful propaganda drove firearm sales, which in turn attracted massive donations from both foreign and domestic weapons manufacturers that replenished its coffers. Its turn toward extremism proved to be highly profitable, especially for its crooked leadership—although membership remained static and many of its members were repelled by its pugnacious image.

Yet despite the alienation of many gun owners and the undeniable scandals that had tarnished LaPierre and his clique, accountability remained elusive. In his quest to avoid the consequences of his misconduct, the NRA boss filed for bankruptcy protection in Texas, where a federal judge rejected this "shocking" ploy in May 2021, saying it had no legitimate purpose. He had not consulted the organization's board or many of its top officials.

James's effort to dissolve the organization was frustrated when a New York judge ruled against her in May 2022. When the trial of *People of the State of New York vs. National Rifle Association, Wayne LaPierre et al.* was about to begin in January 2024, the gun lobby boss suddenly announced that he would resign, supposedly owing to his poor health. Among the first witnesses at trial was Oliver North, the former NRA president, who testified at length about the organization's rampant self-dealing. Under oath he also recalled what LaPierre had told him about the enormous sums paid to the Brewer law firm.

"Brewer is the reason why I am not going to spend the rest of my life in an orange jumpsuit," North said LaPierre had told him. He may have been right. Although LaPierre and other NRA officials were found guilty of fraud and ordered to pay millions in damages, none of them would be going to prison as a consequence of James's lawsuit.

Unsurprisingly, Republican politicians and right-wing media outlets had remained largely silent in the face of the NRA's corruption and angrily criticized James instead for launching a "politically motivated" lawsuit. Their acquiescence typified a culture on the right that scorned responsibility, transparency, and even basic honesty.

WHILE THE TRUMP era saw declining concern on the right with public policy—marked by the Republican Party's bizarre decision at the 2020 convention to dispense with its platform altogether—one or two actual ideas did seem to thrill the base.

What stirred the most enthusiasm among Trump fanatics was the notion of constructing an impenetrable "wall" along the southern border. While it was never a plausible scheme, for a wide range of geographic, political, engineering, and economic reasons, that never dampened the zeal of its supporters. The predictable response was a surge of greed that culminated in swindle, scandal, and ultimately the prosecution of the guilty parties. Yet even that denouement only proved again how indulgently the Right treats its worst miscreants, especially those with a connection to its Dear Leader.

Early on the morning of August 20, 2020, a Coast Guard vessel intercepted the *Lady May*, a 107-foot superyacht off the Connecticut coast in Long Island Sound. Heavily armed Coast Guard officers boarded and swept the yacht for weapons, followed swiftly by federal agents carrying an arrest warrant for Stephen K. Bannon, a guest of his political patron Guo Wengui. Simultaneous raids by agents in Florida and Colorado nabbed Bannon's associates Timothy Shea, Andrew Badolato, and Brian

Kolfage. All four had been indicted in the Southern District of New York and charged with wire fraud, money laundering, and conspiracy, among other felonies.

They stood accused of stealing millions of dollars raised online for a heavily publicized crowdfunding effort to finance construction of a barrier along the Mexican border, known to its duped supporters as "We Build the Wall."

The swindle started up in December 2018, when Kolfage, an air force veteran who had lost both legs and a hand while serving in Iraq, created a GoFundMe page with the stated intention of donating funds to Trump's border wall. Although Trump had vowed repeatedly that Mexico would pay for constructing it, that proved to be as vaporous as most of his promises, and the Democratic takeover of the House in the previous month's midterm elections didn't bode well for federal funding either. In the vacuum left by those circumstances, Kolfage saw a major business opportunity.

By then, the triple-amputee airman already was a veteran of both right-wing politics and online scams. Promoting inflammatory conspiracy theories and racist memes—he once insulted President Barack Obama as "a half-breed"—Kolfage started a Facebook page called Right-Wing News, which then sprouted a series of affiliated sites with names like Freedom Daily, Keep America First, and Trump Republic. Those sites used fake accounts and clickbait to drive traffic to Kolfage's websites. At the time, he told associates that the sites were earning him as much as $200,000 per month, but Facebook eventually took them down in a sweeping removal of abusive pages that pretended to be "forums for legitimate political debate" while actually serving as "ad farms." (He responded with another abortive online fundraising effort, titled Fight4FreeSpeech.) Facebook ultimately banned Kolfage.

He had also exploited the sympathy evoked by his wartime sacrifice for an entirely separate swindle: a "mentoring service" that featured him and his wife, a model named Ashley, that supposedly delivered counseling and comfort to veterans suffering from similarly terrible injuries in military hospitals across the country. They called this outfit the Wounded Warrior Mentoring Engagement Program. In Facebook posts, Kolfage said his group worked with disabled veterans at Walter Reed and Brooke Army Medical Centers and the Landstuhl military medical center in Germany.

When media outlets later asked what Brian and Ashley Kolfage had done for those veterans, however, the answer from every hospital spokesperson was the same—nothing. The Kolfages had neither shown up to provide "mentoring" services nor had they made any donations to provide such care. In fact, the Wounded Warrior Mentoring Engagement Program never existed as a nonprofit entity or in any form, except as a phantom buzz phrase. He never explained to donors what had happened to their money, which amounted to at least $15,000.

Though he had carefully cultivated his image as a public-spirited conservative voice, Kolfage left a very different impression in private. His own former employees told BuzzFeed in 2019 that he was a vicious and manipulative fabricator, motivated by personal greed.

Kolfage's border-wall fundraising campaign, titled "We the People Will Build the Wall," aimed to raise a billion dollars for the project, drew instant national media attention, and brought in a startling $17 million during its first week and another $8 million soon thereafter. It was among the most successful GoFundMe pages ever established, but executives at the online fundraising website quickly contacted Kolfage about taking it down because of concern about his plans for the money.

At that point, he contacted Bannon and Andrew Badolato—a dubious Sarasota businessman with long-standing ties to the Trump adviser as well as organized crime connections and multiple bankruptcies—who took over the operation and established We Build the Wall as a tax-exempt nonprofit group. They also brought on Timothy Shea, a Colorado business executive, and his wife, Amanda, who had written for Kolfage's scam websites.

The explosive success of the fundraising campaign depended heavily on its association with Trumpism and the president's inner circle, although he seemed hesitant to offer a full-throated endorsement of We Build the Wall. (He is often suspicious of associates seeking to use his name to profit, a privilege he mostly reserves for himself and his family.) When the indictments came down, he scrambled to dissociate himself from the scandal, saying the whole thing was a plot to "make me look bad."

But many of the then president's closest associates, including his two older sons and Chad Wolf, his Homeland Security secretary, had let their names and images be used to promote the project. Donald Trump Jr. had shown up with fiancée Kimberly Guilfoyle at We Build the Wall events and described the project as "private enterprise at its finest"—a remark that would soon prove to be painfully ironic.

The premise of We Build the Wall's fundraising was a pledge that "every penny" donated would go toward construction and not a cent to its founder and operators, who were all described as "volunteers." Kolfage, Bannon, and their associates offered the same guarantee repeatedly in the organization's social media as well as in press statements and media appearances. Donor solicitations approved by Bannon and Badolato reiterated the identical message: nobody would take a salary, and all the money would finance the wall.

The organization's bylaws, often quoted by Kolfage, Bannon, and their associates, specifically forbade any compensation for its officers and board members. In text messages unearthed by prosecutors, Bannon and Badolato discussed the importance of that altruistic narrative, with Badolato gloating that it would drive donations, remove "all self-interest taint" and "give Kolfage sainthood."

As Kolfage himself declared on social media, "I made a promise that I would NEVER take a penny, 100% of fundraising through donations will only go towards the wall. 100% means 100%, right? Board won't see any of that money!" Bannon, who served as the outfit's board chair, echoed that assurance in interviews and public appearances. "We're a volunteer organization," he said. And Shea's wife Amanda, a right-wing social media influencer, contrasted We Build the Wall with federal agencies that she suggested were untrustworthy. "As we all know, the government is not great stewards of people's money, and it could just be misappropriated in little ways and whatever, and we don't want that to happen; that's not our purpose," she told a TV interviewer.

These smooth assurances evidently impressed hundreds of thousands of Americans who forwarded small amounts to We Build the

Wall. "Donors took notice of this core narrative," according to prosecutors, "and told Brian Kolfage . . . that it mattered to them. Some of those donors wrote directly to Kolfage that they did not have a lot of money and were skeptical of online fundraising campaigns, but they were giving what they could because they trusted Kolfage would keep his word about how those donations would be spent."

Nothing about We Build the Wall's spin was true—as revealed in the lengthy and detailed indictment filed by federal prosecutors in New York in August 2020.

The eight-count indictment followed an investigation that began almost two years earlier in Florida, when consumer complaints about We Build the Wall's fundraising reached the office of Nikki Fried, a Democrat who had been elected as the state agriculture commissioner, whose department includes a "consumer services" division. The organization had never registered with the state of Florida, as its nonprofit status required it to do, had only one director on its board, and appeared to be flouting the laws governing charitable organizations. After determining that We Build the Wall appeared to be engaged in criminal activity, Fried referred the investigation to federal authorities.

The postal investigators who ran the federal probe found a complex scheme designed to disguise ongoing embezzlement by all four of the defendants. Under Bannon's direction, they agreed to transfer huge sums from We Build the Wall to another nonprofit that he controlled known as Citizens of the American Republic—a dark-money operation that promoted "economic nationalism," anti-immigrant xenophobia, and Trumpian propaganda through films and podcasts.

ProPublica reported that Citizens of the American Republic had collected $4.5 million in 2018 from unidentified persons. Its IRS filing showed $250,000 in loans and payments to Bannon's "documentary" film business, $850,000 for travel expenses, $40,000 in payments to Bannon's nephew, Sean, $20,000 in payments to his sister, Mary Meredith, and more than a million dollars in payments to various vendors for unexplained reasons. Bannon's "nonprofit," already scammy in its own operations, became a vehicle to implement the border wall scam.

The Bannon dark-money outfit paid out huge sums to Kolfage,

beginning with a transfer of $100,000 and then subsequent transfers of $20,000 a month. Bannon and his coconspirators used additional methods to conceal their embezzlement, including "fake invoices and sham 'vendor' arrangements," according to federal prosecutors. Shea created a shell company, which he falsely listed as a "social media" vendor to We Build the Wall and then used to funnel money to himself and Kolfage.

Text messages recovered by prosecutors showed Bannon and Badolato discussing the scheme. On January 15, 2019, not long after they took over the management of We Build the Wall, Bannon sent a text to Badolato that said, "[No] deals I don't approve; and I pay [Brian Kolfage] so what's to worry," according to the indictment. The following week, he asked Badolato how Citizens of the American Republic would be repaid for advancing money to Kolfage, texting, "We need wire of cash to [CAR]."

It was all set up so that, as Kolfage urged in a text message to Badolato, the flow of payments remained "confidential" and disclosed only on a "need to know" basis.

The wiring of cash between the two nonprofit entities began the following month, according to federal and state indictments of Bannon. On February 4, 2019, he ordered a wire transfer of $250,000 from We Build the Wall to Citizens of the American Republic, and then a week later arranged a wire transfer of $100,000 to Kolfage. He had kept $150,000 in his nonprofit's bank account. The next day, on February 12, talking with a media outlet about his work for We Build the Wall, Bannon said, "I did this kind of as a volunteer."

"Kind of as a volunteer," except not really, because federal investigators found that Bannon had taken donor money for his own benefit. The indictment charged that Citizens of the American Republic (identified in the charging document as "Nonprofit-1") had received over $1 million from We Build the Wall, and that after deducting the money paid to Kolfage, Bannon had pocketed "a substantial portion of those donor funds for personal uses and expenses" unrelated to the wall project.

Badolato and Shea had profited personally from the scam, too, although they hadn't taken as much money as Bannon or Kolfage. According to the federal indictment, each of the defendants had "received hundreds of thousands of dollars in donor funds from We Build the Wall, which they used to pay for a variety of personal expenses including, among other things, travel, hotels, consumer goods, and personal credit card debts." Shea reportedly pocketed as much as $180,000.

The prosecutors offered a catalog of Kolfage's more extravagant purchases, which included a Range Rover luxury sport utility vehicle, a golf cart, jewelry, cosmetic surgery, and home renovations. He, too, had used the stolen funds for tax and credit card payments. But his biggest splurge was *Warfighter*, a Jupiter Marine fishing and pleasure craft with four-hundred-horsepower outboard engines that he flaunted on social media and in a July 4 Trump boat parade on a Florida waterway—six weeks before he, Bannon, Badolato, and Shea were busted.

While this looting proceeded, two smallish sections of private border wall or fence went up in New Mexico and Texas with funding from We Build the Wall. But when builder Tommy Fisher sought more money from the group to continue, none was forthcoming, and he broke ties with them. While their website said that a stretch of one hundred miles was "ready to be built," fewer than five miles of border barrier were ever erected. Still the site boasted, "Promises Made, Promises Kept."

THE CONSPIRATORS MAINTAINED their blustering front even after the August 2020 indictments and arrests. When he posted bail, Bannon publicly insisted that his indictment was a government "fiasco" and a "political hit job," intended to "stop people who want to build the wall." Kolfage echoed his patron's aggressive denial with the right-wing framing that would become all too familiar under the Biden administration, denouncing the indictment as "a witch hunt" undertaken by a "weaponized judicial system" seeking to jail Trump supporters.

While some on the right treated the case as the embarrassing disgrace that it was, others echoed Bannon's absurd defense. On Fox News, Lou Dobbs called the prosecution a "deep state plot," and Jenna Ellis—

the Trump campaign lawyer who would later plead guilty to a felony for participating in Trump's 2020 coup plot—declared on Twitter that this was "yet another malicious political prosecution." (Bannon, Kolfage, and their media enablers all neglected to explain why the Trump Justice Department would persecute the president's supporters.)

All four defendants initially pleaded not guilty. After their lawyers were apprised of the copious evidence against them, Kolfage and Badolato entered into negotiations with the Justice Department, and in April 2022, both men agreed to plead guilty to one count of conspiracy to commit wire fraud. Kolfage also pleaded guilty to separate tax and wire fraud charges filed in the Northern District of Florida. Before accepting the plea deal, US judge Analisa Torres allowed each defendant to make a statement and then required them to fully acknowledge what they had done.

"I knew what I was doing was wrong and a crime," said Kolfage. The judge asked whether he had publicly promised that "100 percent" of donations would be used to build the wall. "That is correct," he replied. And despite that promise, had he instead secretly schemed with others to "keep a large sum of money" for himself? "That is correct," he said again. The judge asked Badolato whether he knew that Kolfage was stealing the donations. "Yes, I did, and I helped facilitate it," he confessed. "I knew this was wrong and I'm terribly, terribly sorry for what I did and I humbly beg the court for mercy." On the day after their court appearance, Kolfage arrogantly posted a story on the Trump-oriented microblogging site Gettr that praised him for building more border wall than Obama or Biden. As for his guilty plea, Kolfage's post said, "They Michael Flynn'd me," evidently to suggest that he wasn't really culpable for his crimes.

The disabled veteran's pugnacious posturing turned out to be a mistake, as he discovered several months later, when the judge sentenced him to four years and three months behind bars and Badolato to only three years. Their codefendant Shea, convicted at trial in October 2021 after the jury heard his counsel argue they had done nothing wrong, was sentenced to five years.

The most revealing moment of this saga had occurred months earlier, during the final hours of the Trump administration, when Donald Trump had bestowed a pardon on Steve Bannon that protected him from the consequences of his crimes.

Despite a heated debate within the White House over whether to give a very unusual preemptive pardon to Bannon, Trump surprised and angered some of his own advisers when he signed the papers. The news of Trump's clemency for Bannon infuriated Roger Stone, who had previously received a pardon undoing his conviction for perjury and obstruction of justice in Special Counsel Robert Mueller's probe of Russian interference in the 2016 election. Stone told friends that he thought the rival adviser had "blackmailed" Trump. And in an angry outburst captured on video by filmmakers producing a documentary about him, Stone cursed Bannon—who had testified against him at trial—as a "grifter scumbag."

It was a classic pot-insults-kettle moment. By accepting their pardons, both of those flawed human vessels had essentially admitted guilt, according to Supreme Court jurisprudence. But the conviction of Bannon's coconspirators and then his pardon in no way affected his influence on the right. The indictments and guilty pleas had left no reasonable doubt that this top Trump adviser, who had managed the 2016 campaign and continued to advise him, had stolen up to a million dollars from the America First faithful.

Yet just as the National Rifle Association and its leadership had escaped any meaningful reproach on the right, so did Bannon. Republican members of Congress kept seeking the approval and endorsement of the NRA, remaining silent about the endless chiseling of funds by Wayne LaPierre and his cronies. In the same vein, many of those same Republican figures continued to make their way to the recording studio in Bannon's Capitol Hill town house to appear on his popular *War Room* podcast, including New York representative Elise Stefanik, the third-ranking member of the House GOP leadership. Far from being ostracized by House Republicans, Bannon freely intervened in congressional affairs, stoking the rebellion that ended the short tenure of Speaker Kevin McCarthy in October 2023.

Nor did Bannon's disgrace hinder his incessant grifting. On the same podcast where he hosted Representative Matt Gaetz of Florida and Representative Nancy Mace of South Carolina to talk about McCarthy's ouster and succession, he urged listeners to sign up for his latest sponsor, a company marketing gold-backed retirement accounts.

Like Trump himself, both Bannon and LaPierre are being held accountable for their transgressions. The lawsuit against the NRA by New York attorney general Letitia James result resulted in multimillion-dollar financial penalties on the gun lobby and its officials, and Bannon has been indicted on the same charges for which Trump pardoned him. He may also face imprisonment for contempt of Congress, stemming from his refusal to testify before the House Select Committee on the January 6 insurrection.

If Bannon and LaPierre ultimately are held to account, however, it will only happen because prosecutors—one of them an elected Democrat, the other appointed by a Democratic president—have pursued them doggedly for years. Following the example of Trump, who has shunned neither Bannon nor the NRA, leading figures on the right treat them as if their gross misconduct had never occurred, let alone been exposed in awful detail. *Grifting* may be too mild a term for the embezzlement, self-dealing, and outright theft they have perpetrated, but in the Trump era, such miscreants cruise along with impunity—a measure of their movement's deep and perhaps irreparable corruption.

Whether elderly scammers like Bannon and Stone ever pay for their crimes or not, a new generation of political con men is already far along the grimy trail they blazed. The outstanding example is a young man named Charlie Kirk, cofounder of Turning Point USA, the right-wing youth organization that has grown into an enormous conglomerate by attaching itself to the Trump machine.

With chapters on hundreds of college campuses, TPUSA is ostensibly a nonprofit group (with an attached political action committee). Its politics are on the far right of Trumpism, with a troubling tendency to encourage white nationalism, anti-gay bigotry, and other extremist and hateful ideologies. But hiding behind its tax exemption and its stated "charitable" purposes is a business that has proved highly lucrative for Kirk, who at age thirty finally may be aging out of the movement's "youth" contingent.

In October 2023, an Associated Press investigation of TPUSA's finances found that the group has raised "roughly a quarter-billion dollars" over the past seven years—much of which has been spent not to educate young conservatives but on "cultivating conservative influencers and hosting glitzy events" (which included a lavish wedding for Kirk at a Scottsdale, Arizona, resort). Kirk's personal compensation has soared from $27,000 to over $400,000, and he owns three luxury properties, including a beachside condo on the Gulf Coast and a new "Spanish-style mansion" on a Phoenix golf course worth nearly $5 million. The AP report also revealed that the organization has doled out more than $15 million to companies controlled by TPUSA insiders and their cronies.

Kirk's ambitions have not abated even though he has outgrown the movement's "youth" wing. For the 2024 campaign, he vowed to raise $108 million for "get out the vote" activities in the swing states of Arizona, Georgia, and Wisconsin—an amount far in excess of what any experienced political organizer believes could be wisely spent on such an effort.

Young Charlie dropped out of junior college and never earned a degree, but he honed his vocation with the most grizzled grifters of our time. He will go far.

15

Is the Big Lie the Biggest Grift?

Long after the proof of Donald Trump's ignominious defeat in the 2020 presidential race had been firmly established in every legal and political forum, he would continue to insist that he was the victim of "a rigged election" and "a fraud on the American public." More than sixty courts, up to the United States Supreme Court, many overseen by judges whom Trump had appointed, rejected that claim outright, and yet he continues to insist that he "won the election, by a lot."

It was a conscious falsehood that he and his cronies had conspired to foist on the public before a single vote was cast. He would promulgate that lie on every available platform, presumably for the rest of his life, because it had become not only the central theme of his political identity but a multimillion-dollar stream of unregulated revenue.

Almost immediately, the Big Lie ballooned into a monstrous grift, so large that it dwarfed all the previous "conservative" scams by an order of magnitude. But it was rooted in the familiar paranoid attitudes of the American Right—a mindset impervious to facts and logic that Trump exploited with a ferocity that overshadowed previous generations of right-wing hustlers. All those earlier versions of agitation for profit looked quaint and almost innocent compared with his propaganda operation, which had incited a violent and deadly assault on the United States Capitol.

Trump reshaped a toxic political culture into a live threat to the American republic.

Dramatic as that threat was, with lives lost and hundreds injured, his MAGA movement was, at the same time, just another tacky Trump enterprise, another ruse to separate the susceptible rubes from their money. Trump's dissembling became so obvious that even *The Wall Street Journal*, whose editorial page had long echoed or excused his mendacities, turned away in disgust. "Mr. Trump betrayed his supporters by conning them on January 6," scolded the paper's editorial board, "and he is still doing it." He was "conning his supporters," the Murdoch-owned daily huffed, and he would never stop.

A grift is, by definition, a conscious act. Every grifter knows that he or she is promoting a falsehood (or a series of falsehoods) with intent to swindle a mark (or a whole population of marks). In the parlance of prosecutors—who would find ample reason to scrutinize Trump's postpresidential scams—that consciousness of acting in bad faith is known as *mens rea*, the Latin phrase that means "guilty mind" in legal parlance.

Although political observers have often suggested that Trump truly believes his own lies, or persuades himself that they are true, the evidence shows that he has always known the ugly truth. Like his amoral mentor Roy Cohn, who schooled him in this belligerent style of deception a half century ago, his only principle is escaping accountability for his actions. To confront Trump over his lies is to encounter a commitment to falsehood so persistent and determined as to be maddening, or to appear mad itself.

That is why attorney general William Barr, who had dutifully investigated the myriad allegations of voter fraud and ballot stuffing after the 2020 election, said that he questioned the president's state of mind when Trump stubbornly refused to acknowledge the truth.

"I thought, boy . . . he's become detached from reality, if he really believed this stuff," Barr told the House Select Committee on the January 6 insurrection. The attorney general soon realized, however, that Trump was not insane but merely insincere. "On the other hand," Barr's taped testimony continued, "when I went into this and would tell him how crazy some of these allegations were, there was never an indication of interest in what the actual facts are."

As Barr came to understand, Trump didn't care about the truth and rejected any information that contradicted his self-serving narrative. He remained immovable no matter who tried to persuade him to acknowledge that he had lost the election—including nearly all his own top administration and campaign officials, from Barr and ranking Justice Department officials to his White House chief of staff, campaign manager and deputy campaign manager, his White House counsel and deputy counsel, as well as that long parade of federal judges, state judges, and state election officials, most of them Republicans.

None of those judicial decisions directly addressed Trump's state of mind until October 2022, when US judge David Carter handed down a scathing opinion that accused the former president himself of purposely misleading the court about alleged election fraud in Georgia. Citing emails between Trump and campaign attorney John Eastman (who at this writing appears likely to forfeit his law license in California), the judge found that the former president had knowingly signed a document he knew to be false in furtherance of a crime—namely, the conspiracy to prevent the congressional certification of Joe Biden's Electoral College victory.

Eastman had sought to conceal those emails, citing attorney-client privilege, but Judge Carter disclosed them as evidence of a criminal fraud, which voided the privilege. Included was a warning message sent by Eastman to Trump and his attorneys in December 2021: "Although the President signed a verification for [the state court filing] back on December 1, he has since been made aware that some of the allegations (and evidence proffered by the experts) has been inaccurate. For him to sign a new verification with that knowledge (and incorporation by reference) would not be accurate."

As the judge noted, despite Eastman's word of caution, the former president had persisted in raising the same mendacious assertions in federal court. "President Trump, moreover, signed a verification swearing under oath that the incorporated, inaccurate numbers are true and correct—or believed to be true and correct—to the best of his knowledge and belief. The emails show that President Trump knew that the specific numbers of voter fraud were wrong but continued to tout those numbers, both in court and to the public. The Court finds that these emails are sufficiently related to and in furtherance of a conspiracy to defraud the United States."

It was a crime based on a lie consciously repeated by Trump.

By then corroborating evidence of Trump's calculated duplicity had emerged in the form of a tape recording of Steve Bannon—the far-right swindler, pardoned by Trump, who had advised him in both his presidential campaigns and in the White House. Published by *Mother Jones*, the tape revealed that Trump always planned to claim victory on Election Night, regardless of the verified results and the final vote count.

On the evening of October 31, four days before the election, Bannon secretly confided that plan to a group of his political cronies gathered in his town house on Capitol Hill. Most of those present were associates of businessman Guo Wengui, a wealthy Chinese exile and sponsor of Bannon's political activities (who would be arrested by the FBI in 2023 for fraud and money laundering). When Bannon was arrested in 2020 by federal agents in connection with his We Build the Wall fraud scheme—the crime for which Trump later pardoned him—he was aboard a superyacht owned by Guo.

At the Halloween meeting, Bannon offered a detailed prediction of what would happen on and after Election Night that turned out to be remarkably precise. "What Trump's gonna do is just declare victory. Right? He's gonna declare victory. But that doesn't mean he's a winner," Bannon said with a laugh. "He's just gonna *say* he's a winner." The votes of Republicans who mostly voted in person would be tallied immediately, creating the illusion of a Trump lead, explained Bannon, which would likely be erased by Democratic mail-in ballots that take longer to count. Denouncing those votes as "fraud," Trump would cite his early lead in key states and pronounce himself the victor.

"At 10 or 11 o'clock, Trump's gonna walk in the Oval [Office], tweet out, 'I'm the winner. Game over. Suck on that.'"

The additional time required to tally mail ballots, Bannon said, imposed "a natural disadvantage" on Democrats. "And Trump's going to take advantage of it. That's our strategy. He's gonna declare himself a winner." Bannon foresaw that the upshot of such a strategy—and of Trump stigmatizing Democratic votes as fraudulent—was likely to be partisan violence. (As a key Trump strategist, he again predicted violence on the day before the January 6 insurrection.) His uncannily accurate projection of Trump's conduct on Election Night—despite advice from White House lawyers and campaign advisers to forgo any such premature pronouncements—showcased the calculating mendacity of both Bannon and his boss.

In many respects, the decision to mount a Big Lie campaign to overturn the 2020 election was simply another iteration of Trump's everyday propensity for self-serving falsehood, but it was more than that. What made this instance different from the thousands of documented lies he had uttered publicly was the scale and consequence of the Big Lie—and the enormous sums of money that he raked in from it. That rip-off compounded the many offenses perpetrated by Trump and his cronies in the aftermath of the election, with fundraising abuses that veered into apparent criminality.

THE EARLIEST SIGNAL of Trump's plan to profit from the Big Lie came shortly after Election Day when Jared Kushner—who had overseen the 2020 campaign's digital strategy—told the staffers who had overseen online fundraising that he wanted a new daily financial tracker for the Trump Make America Great Again Committee. Known internally as TMAGAC, pronounced "T-Magic," this joint committee had directed fundraising proceeds to both the Trump campaign and the Republican National Committee, using staff and consultants tied to both organizations.

The purpose, explained Kushner, was to monitor cash flow because they aimed to continue raising money after the election and also because Trump planned to launch a new political action committee called Save America PAC. When Kushner sent that message, the campaign had just seen three of its best fundraising days, on November

4, November 5, and November 6, with over $100 million arriving in response to shrill appeals warning that Democrats were "stealing the White House" and urging patriotic Americans to donate to Trump's Official Election Defense Fund.

Yet while the Save America PAC opened for business and began to deposit millions of dollars in its new accounts (with daily reports sent to Kushner detailing those receipts), that Official Election Defense Fund never got a dollar—because it never existed. As one of the campaign fundraisers later explained under oath, the touted fund was only "a marketing tactic." The share of funds previously allocated to the Trump campaign would, under Kushner's purview, flow instead into Save America from November 9 onward.

As a leadership PAC, however, Save America could not spend more than $5,000 under federal election law to contest the 2020 election or seek recounts—in other words, it could not legally spend more than a tiny fraction for the purposes claimed in its advertising. In fact, Save America spent not a dime in 2020 on election-related expenses.

Every day from Election Day 2020 until the January 6, 2021, assault on the Capitol, TMAGAC and its vendors sent scores of emails and text messages to the millions of Trump supporters on its lists, exhorting them to "join the Trump army" and "fight the Liberal Mob" that was driving their idol from the White House. Denouncing Democrats repeatedly for "trying to steal the election," those hysterical messages warned that if Biden took office, he would be an "illegitimate president." Only their donations could "uncover" and "stop" the rampant voter fraud that had deprived Trump of victory.

As the House Select Committee investigators learned, those same messages also reached millions of Americans across the online portals where Trump supporters were organizing, at the tweeted behest of Trump himself, to come to a "wild" January 6 protest in Washington, DC, against congressional certification of Biden's victory in the Electoral College. And those messages appeared, too, on the platforms where the most militant MAGA forces were promoting and plotting violence at the Capitol—and sharing links to the Official Election Defense Fund.

Like Trump himself, the TMAGAC staffers and vendors knew that the rhetoric of their fundraising and organizing appeals was politically extreme and extremely untruthful. All of them admitted that they had seen no evidence of significant fraud in even a single state, let alone a "stolen election." But as the chief copywriter said, when asked why TMAGAC persistently referred to Biden as "illegitimate," those stylistic flourishes ensured "effective" fundraising. After a young RNC staffer named Ethan Katz refused to write an email pitch making the false claim that Trump had won Pennsylvania he was fired.

Intimidated by Trump and profiting heavily from his grift, the Republican National Committee leadership, including chairwoman Ronna Romney McDaniel, "knew that President Trump was lying to the American people," as the House Select Committee's report noted. The RNC's response was merely to tinker around the edges of the fundraising copy, never to fundamentally challenge the message that pervaded TMAGAC's postelection fundraising copy—the Big Lie. After Trump brusquely dumped her as RNC chair in early 2024, McDaniel moved to a new sinecure as a Republican "political analyst" at NBC News, which agreed to pay her $300,000 per year. Appearing on the network's *Meet the Press* Sunday flagship broadcast, McDaniel admitted for the first time that Biden had won the 2020 election "fair and square." But the announcement of her hiring provoked an on-air revolt by many of the network's top journalists. MSNBC host Rachel Maddow compared it to bringing a mob boss into the district attorney's office. Four days later, the network dropped McDaniel.

Despite feeble bleats of dissent from such figures as Senate majority leader Mitch McConnell—who declared his acceptance of Biden's victory and at first excoriated Trump and the January 6 mob—the Republican Party had been indelibly corrupted. From the election to the insurrection, Trump and his subservient Republican partners banked a total of $255.4 million, a record-setting haul by nearly any measure. Online ads and email appeals—as many as twenty-five per day—pitched for funds to fight the nonexistent election fraud, drawing in at least two million individual donations in a few weeks.

The Save America PAC drew much of its revenue from the accounts of donors who kept giving whether they knew it or not, thanks to an automatic "recurring donation" button that Trump had digitally checked without their consent. Half of the funds went to the Republican National Committee, another substantial share went to paying off the campaign debts of Trump-Pence 2020, and about $80 million was transferred to Save America. Those millions would become immediately available to Trump for his personal use, to pay for travel and hotel costs (and would later be tapped to cover his exploding personal legal expenses as both federal and state prosecutors investigated his alleged crimes).

Rather than "election defense," hundreds of thousands of dollars funneled through Save America went to Trump's lackeys and cronies, including former White House chief of staff Mark Meadows, with additional sums paid to firms associated with them. A right-wing nonprofit, the Conservative Partnership Institute, where Meadows had landed, received $1 million. An even further rightward nonprofit, the America First Policy Institute, run by former Trump adviser Stephen Miller, got another million dollars. More than $2 million was spent on "legal consulting," evidently to pay lawyers representing witnesses who testified before the House Select Committee. Save America also spent more than $300,000 at Trump hotels and clubs, including Mar-a-Lago in Palm Beach, where Trump resides during the winter months.

And the Save America PAC paid almost $100,000 to fashion designer Hervé Pierre Braillard, who dressed Melania Trump when she was First Lady and created her January 2017 inaugural gown. His payment was described as "strategy consulting."

In the months that followed the 2020 election, Trump and his campaign were hardly alone in attempting to contest his defeat by Joe Biden—or in seeking to skim dishonest profits from the frustration of his followers. A major Republican donor in North Carolina discovered this postelection scamming the hard way.

Fredric Eshelman, who had devoted millions of dollars to the Trump cause, decided that he wanted to finance efforts to uncover voter fraud in major cities. His advisers introduced Eshelman to Catherine Engelbrecht, a former Tea Party activist from Texas who had founded an organization called True the Vote, which promoted the false idea that voter fraud is rampant and that Democrats—principally minority voters—are the culprits.

With publicity from right-wing media, especially *The Wall Street Journal* and Fox News, her nonprofit had been pushing that partisan canard for more than a decade when she heard from Eshelman and his advisers. So convincing did he find her in their brief phone call that after twenty minutes, the wealthy donor said he was "in for two"—meaning $2 million.

His pledge inspired Engelbrecht to fashion an ambitious $7.5 million program, which she dubbed Validate the Vote, to find election whistleblowers, gather and analyze data, and pursue lawsuits to overturn Biden's victories in seven battleground states. Until that day, True the Vote had never raised more than $1.8 million in a single year for its "election integrity" programs.

Very little of what Engelbrecht promised Eshelman in that conversation ever materialized. Her group's prominent Republican attorney, James Bopp, filed lawsuits against the 2020 election results in only four states, not seven—and then, astonishingly, withdrew all of the litigation a few days later without any court action. According to a series of articles later published by The Intercept and Type Investigations, True the Vote blamed its sudden legal retreat on "an excruciating series of events that will one day be known, but now is not the time to air." Bopp's explanation was equally murky and didn't account for his Indianapolis law firm billing nearly $800,000 for those aborted lawsuits.

Enraged by this bait-and-switch routine, Eshelman filed suit to recover $2.5 million in donations, claiming that True the Vote had swindled him. "True the Vote failed, in every way, to make use of my donation to investigate and either prove or disprove election fraud, as agreed upon, and failed to respond to my requests for information about how the funds were spent," his spokesman said, accusing the group of "deceptive practices."

The lawsuit identified Gregg Phillips, a former Texas public official and True the Vote board member, as the mastermind of a plot with

Engelbrecht to abscond with funds intended for the "fraud" investigation. Phillips had gained some notoriety in 2016 by claiming he could prove that Hillary Clinton had received millions of illegal immigrant votes, which supposedly provided her popular vote margin over Trump.

He never offered any proof of that assertion, despite fervent declarations on CNN and other platforms that he would. (Phillips and Engelbrecht later claimed that it would have cost "hundreds of millions" to prove their claims about illegal voting, and they had just failed to raise enough funds to complete their investigation.)

Eshelman's lawsuit against True the Vote tagged Phillips as Engelbrecht's secret paramour and accused him of creating an outfit named OPSEC Group LLC to move money from the nonprofit into other accounts. He had taken at least $750,000 personally from True the Vote for "research contracts."

When pressed on what its work had accomplished, True the Vote cited "whistleblower testimony and information which has led to four indictments so far in Arizona, federal investigations in Nevada and Georgia, and investigations by Michigan officials"—but those purported probes led nowhere. What eventually emerged was a pattern of financial manipulation by Engelbrecht that included hundreds of thousands of dollars in illicit personal loans to her from the nonprofit—and the concealment of those transactions and other questionable payments via falsified tax returns.

Sadly for Eshelman, his lawsuit was thrown out of federal court because his lawyers couldn't prove that his donations were "conditional" on any results. He didn't get far in Texas state courts either. But the swindled donor had the ironic satisfaction of watching his legal nemesis Bopp sue True the Vote for failing to pay more than $1 million in *his* legal bills. Engelbrecht countersued Bopp, charging that he had committed fraud and provided substandard legal services. "We were shocked they responded this way. They did nothing but praise our work," the right-wing lawyer told ProPublica, which had investigated the activities of True the Vote. "This is what unscrupulous people will do when they try to avoid the repayment of debt."

Just as appalling as the shady behavior of Engelbrecht and Phillips was the discovery that prominent right-wing activists had long been aware of their dishonesty, without ever warning the public. In August 2020, at a closed meeting of the Council for National Policy—the umbrella coalition that serves as the Far Right's most important network—two longtime supporters of True the Vote vehemently cautioned the donors present against any further funding.

Former *Wall Street Journal* columnist John Fund, who had been among the group's earliest endorsers, expressed deep disappointment in Engelbrecht, whom he still considered "a friend." Saying she had "gone astray" and "hooked up with the wrong associates," he added, "I would not give her a penny." Trump lawyer Cleta Mitchell, a veteran of Republican and right-wing campaigns, echoed Fund, who sat next to her. "Don't look so shocked," she said, addressing someone in their small audience. "It's true."

Those quiet caveats did nothing to deter Engelbrecht and Phillips, who found a new way to monetize the Big Lie despite their failure to produce any results for Eshelman. During the summer of 2021, they persuaded Dinesh D'Souza, the far-right author, conspiracy theorist, and filmmaker, that they could prove Democrats had "harvested" hundreds of thousands of voters to "stuff" ballot boxes, using geolocation tracking data. Salem Media Group agreed to finance and promote the film, a low-budget documentary called *2000 Mules*, a racially charged title that echoed the slang term for criminals transporting narcotics illegally across US borders.

The Associated Press, National Public Radio, and numerous other mainstream news outlets found that D'Souza's film misused data and fabricated evidence. Former attorney general William Barr noted specifically in congressional testimony that he was "unimpressed" by *2000 Mules*, which he said proved nothing. When Georgia secretary of state Brad Raffensperger, a Republican, investigated one of the film's few identified instances of alleged ballot stuffing, he found no wrongdoing at all. The Arizona attorney general's office, then run by Republican Mark Brnovich, urged the federal government to investigate True the

Vote for refusing to turn over purported evidence of voter fraud to its investigators.

Major right-wing media outlets, including *National Review* and *The Wall Street Journal*, panned the vaguely sourced and amateurish production. On The Washington Free Beacon website, conservative journalist Eli Lake ripped D'Souza for being "like Trump, willing to peddle innuendo and insinuation and pretend it's proof of electoral larceny because he knows there are millions of people who just want to hear someone tell them what they think they already know." None of this ought to have surprised anyone: D'Souza had a long, checkered professional history that included a 2014 guilty plea on charges involving federal campaign finance fraud. Trump had pardoned him four years later.

Boosted to its target audience with a premiere at Mar-a-Lago featuring Trump himself—who hailed it online and in person as "the greatest & most impactful documentary of our time"—D'Souza's film reached millions of viewers and raked in proceeds from streaming sales, estimated at well over $10 million by Salem Media. Some of that money would go toward litigation, because the film's hostile reviews included at least one defamation lawsuit against the producers, seeking damages for false accusations of voter fraud against innocent individuals.

Always remaining in character, Engelbrecht and Phillips turned their attention to an entirely different "nonprofit" grift later that year. On Trump's Truth Social site, the pair claimed to be raising $25 million to operate a mobile hospital service in war-ravaged Ukraine. According to an investigation by ProPublica, they told gullible online donors that the so-called Freedom Hospital already was helping "old folks, women and kids near the fight receive healthcare." Like their voter-fraud evidence, however, the "hospital" simply never materialized. When reporters asked about the phantom medical facility, Engelbrecht and Phillips said they had refunded all the donations and abandoned the project. But ProPublica found that Phillips had continued to raise funds months after it had supposedly folded.

Having turned Trump's election defeat into a financial bonanza, his fundraisers swiftly learned to monetize every event or incident that could be portrayed as an attack on him.

During the first six months of 2022, donations slowed to a mere $36 million, or about $200,000 per day, down from $50 million during the second half of 2021. But on August 8, the FBI raided Mar-a-Lago in a search for the hundreds of classified documents that Trump had withheld illegally from the National Archives and Records Administration. What would have been a damning story for any other politician turned on a fresh money spigot for Trump, whose PAC fired off more than a hundred emails seeking money from supporters outraged by the FBI "break-in," as he called it. As in the days following the election, his excitable fans vented their anger by sending still more money to the billionaire. Save America's daily take climbed back to a million dollars in each of the two days following the raid.

No doubt with that lucrative episode in mind, Trump then rushed to announce his own impending indictment by the Manhattan district attorney. Well before District Attorney Alvin Bragg issued a press release on the tax and fraud charges arising from the secret 2020 hush payoff to adult film star Stormy Daniels, Trump himself warned on Truth Social that he was about to be arrested. The ensuing storm of publicity saw donations crest again to a million dollars a day. And as soon as Bragg's grand jury handed down the actual charges, Trump's operation began hawking pricey $47 T-shirts proclaiming I STAND WITH PRESIDENT TRUMP.

Over the years, Trump had developed an unlimited appetite for fundraising by any means necessary, no matter how questionable or tacky. Beyond the usual campaign-style speeches to support his PAC, he signed a reported multimillion-dollar contract with a private outfit, the American Freedom Tour, to make appearances in venues around the country atop a bill of right-wing speakers and performers. Designed to appeal to "disappointed voters who love President Trump," the tour's roster included Donald Trump Jr., right-wing pundits Candace Owens and Dan Bongino, the election-denial fabulist Dinesh D'Souza, and gun-fetish guitarist Ted Nugent.

Appropriately enough, the tour's impresario was Brian Forte, a motivational-speaking hustler who had declared bankruptcy four times amid a cascade of lawsuits and business failures. His latest enterprise was not much different, with missed payments, angry investors, canceled tour dates, and eventually another bankruptcy looming after about six months. But the tour's failure scarcely mattered to Trump, who reportedly had taken his share of the proceeds up front. He was always ready to mount a fresh grift.

Just before Christmas 2022, Trump previewed a "major announcement," which, to the dismay of his savvier advisers, turned out to be a new venture in the sale of non-fungible tokens. Better known as NFTs, these investments exist only in digital form, their unique identities recorded on blockchains—the same distributed and encrypted databases that form the basis of all cryptocurrencies. The NFTs marketed by Trump included a heroic image of him, in the style of a baseball card with comic-book art. Their debut instantly provoked widespread mockery for poor quality and unpresidential tackiness. "AMERICA NEEDS A SUPERHERO," blared the promotion on his Truth Social platform.

At that juncture, even Steve Bannon couldn't suppress his disgust. The pardoned fraudster led a chorus of Trump allies who urged the former president to immediately fire those responsible for this aesthetic travesty. "I can't watch this again. Make it stop!" Bannon moaned on his *War Room* podcast.

The timing seemed unfortunate, too, so soon after the collapse of the FTX cryptocurrency exchange and the cascading crash of related assets (including NFTs). Yet none of those caveats seemed to discourage the MAGA crowd, as eager dupes scooped up hundreds of Trump NFTs for $99 each within hours, earning him a cool $1.5 million for items with no inherent value.

According to Trump—who had offered a dinner with him at Mar-a-Lago to anyone who purchased forty-seven of the cards—his true purpose was to help his supporters get rich. "People love to collect baseball cards, but why settle for that when you can collect the greatest trading card in history?" he brayed in a video posted to his Instagram account.

The company selling them included a disclaimer that the NFTs were for entertainment only, not investment.

Their warning proved all too prescient the following April, when Trump issued a second series of NFTs: a series of images that depicted the draft-dodging hero in camo gear, as an Elvis-style rocker strumming a guitar, as George Washington crossing the Delaware, as a biker, and, more true to life, serving up burgers and dogs at a barbecue. "I find the Trump NFTs absolutely fascinating in their ugliness," snapped reviewer Luke Savage. "They're a pastiche drawn from the blandest stock images, stripped of all specificity. Just a kitsch and empty iconography of money, Americana, and machismo—all for images that only exist in the digital ether."

Within six hours after their issuance, Trump bragged that "Series 2" had sold out, claiming he had earned $4.6 million. He also lauded himself for maintaining the initial price at $99 each. "I hope everyone notices, & I'm sure the Fake News won't, that I'm leaving the price of the Trading Cards the same as last time, even though they are selling for MANY TIMES MORE & sold out almost immediately, because I want my fans & supporters to make money, and have fun doing it," he wrote on Truth Social. "I could have raised the price MUCH HIGHER, & I believe it still would have sold well, with a lot more money coming to me, but I didn't choose to do so. I WILL BE GIVEN NO 'NICE GUY' CREDIT?"

The Independent trashed Trump's boast after observing that the value of the second NFT series had plunged on the OpenSea trading platform and sales appeared anemic. As the price fluctuated, only he and his partners were certain to make any profit—and in fact, his issuance of the second set of cards had only driven down the value of the earlier edition.

TRUMP'S INNATE PROPENSITY for grift suffused everything he touched in his post-presidency, including his digital tokens, his election-denial crusade, his MAGA rallies, his paid speeches, and of course his campaign to regain the White House in 2024. In the normal course of Trump business, his tendency to scam his partners and skirt the law inevitably tainted Truth Social, sometimes called TRUTH, the social media platform that he had used to promote his various endeavors, feuds, and alarms ever since his unceremonious ejection from Twitter after the January 6 insurrection.

Getting bounced from Twitter in 2020 had deeply irked Trump, who had amassed nearly ninety million followers on the site, and he had quickly seized on the chance to establish an ambitious new venue with a name that ironically echoed *Pravda*, the Kremlin's premier propaganda organ, which means "truth" in Russian.

Behind that enterprise were Will Wilkerson, a West Coast radio producer, and a trio of former "losers" on *The Apprentice*—Wes Moss, Andy Litinsky, and a Miami lawyer named Brad Cohen. The group of would-be entrepreneurs approached Trump in the weeks after his Twitter ouster, proposing to build a new social media platform within a much larger business to be known as Trump Media and Technology Group.

"Trump's New Media Empire," as they framed it, could encompass documentary films, online payment firms and servers, as well as social media—and Trump would own 90 percent of the company, without producing much more than the garrulous, agitated, subliterate, and sometimes incoherent posting that had succeeded for him on Twitter. They all believed his name alone would guarantee success.

But reputable investment bankers wanted no truck with Trump in the wake of his attempted coup and the deadly violence he had instigated. As an alternative, his partners brought in Patrick Orlando, a Florida financier who offered a new and nontraditional idea. Orlando said he could raise a billion dollars or more for Trump Media through a corporate shell he controlled known as Digital World Acquisition. A faddish Wall Street instrument known as a "special purpose acquisition corporation," or SPAC, Digital World Acquisition would enable Trump Media to "go public" and offer shares.

Merging Trump Media with Orlando's SPAC would allow the new

company to offer its shares outside the usual highly regulated process of an initial public offering. Their SPAC could bypass the normal auditing and vetting that accompany a typical IPO and present the most optimistic and speculative expectations to investors. Operating outside normal capital markets, the deal would also—in theory, at least—close very quickly.

True to form, the slide presentation shown to potential Trump Media investors was sketchy. The presentation claimed to anticipate billions of dollars from streaming and podcasting as well as social media, without naming any specific products or employees. A New York University business professor who saw the Trump Media slideshow described it to *The Washington Post* as "hilarious."

What raised eyebrows even higher, on close examination, was the deal's sponsorship by Arc Capital, an obscure financial firm lurking behind several of Orlando's SPAC companies. Based in Shanghai, and apparently tied to the Chinese government, Arc had repeatedly run afoul of the Securities and Exchange Commission (SEC) with dodgy practices that regulators regarded as deceptive. On at least three occasions, the SEC had enjoined companies floated by Arc from selling shares due to "material misstatements and omissions" in their registration documents.

It was, in short, a business with ample running space for Trump's habitual dodgy practices.

When Digital World rolled out its initial public offering in October 2021, touting its eventual merger with Trump Media, the company raised $300 million, with the prospect of another billion when the merger was completed. The family's grifting instinct had surfaced even before the IPO, when both Eric Trump and Donald Trump Jr. showed up to demand large stakes in the firm, despite contributing nothing to its creation and launch.

As millions flowed in from the IPO, Trump himself contacted Litinsky, one of the original partners, asking that he turn over some of his hard-earned shares, then worth millions on paper, to Melania Trump—and pay the resulting federal gift tax himself. After Litinsky rebuffed the same stickup several times, Trump dumped him from the company's board. At the same time, he placed loyal stooges on the board, including Don Jr., former representative Devin Nunes, a California Republican, and Kash Patel, a former Nunes aide. He named Nunes, who had no relevant corporate experience, as the new chief executive officer.

No doubt the dream that Trump Media would someday compete with infotainment behemoths like Disney and Amazon had excited Trump's avarice. But the Presidents' Day launch of TRUTH, a Twitter imitation, was entertainment of a kind that the company's founders hadn't anticipated. The site crashed on its first day, provoking mirth and mockery across the internet, and failed to function adequately for weeks afterward. Its early burst of popularity among Trump's base quickly turned to ashes, with repeated technical outages curtailing any viral spread of its app. The likelihood of success swiftly receded.

By April, the Business Insider website mocked TRUTH as "a conservative ghost town . . . overrun by bots," while *The Washington Post* reported that it was "falling apart." Would-be subscribers found themselves on long waiting lists—and despite promises from Nunes and Trump that the site would accumulate fifty million subscribers within a year, its users never reached more than five million, a faint shadow of the eighty-eight million Trump followers at his Twitter peak.

Trump's ill treatment of the *Apprentice* veterans and their team landed Trump Media in deep trouble before the SPAC merger could close. In August 2022, Will Wilkerson, the company's vice president for operations and one of its four founders, packed up a cache of 150,000 documents—including texts, emails, photos, and audio recordings—and took them to the SEC. Wilkerson filed those documents along with a complaint that Trump Media had made "fraudulent misrepresentations . . . in violation of federal securities laws" and became an official federally protected whistleblower. He also told his story (and shared his documents) with a reporter for *The Washington Post*, where his account of Trump's temper tantrums, blackmail schemes, and the suspicions and feuding he provoked exploded over his company like a bombshell.

AMONG THE QUESTIONS probed by the Justice Department, according to *The Guardian*, is whether "a relation of an ally of Russian president Vladimir Putin" laundered roughly $8 million into Trump Media during 2021 and 2022 from a murky trust account at a Caribbean bank. Before the subpoenas arrived from New York, both Trump and Don Jr., as well as Nunes and Patel, had jumped ship and resigned from the Trump Media board.

The company was in a steep decline, with its website traffic slowing and its debt growing to more than $17 million. The Digital World board had dismissed Patrick Orlando and, in an April 2023 filing with the SEC, warned that unless it completed the merger with Trump Media by early June or received another extension, the entire deal would have to be "terminated."

"It could be an interesting and somewhat fitting end for Trump's SPAC: that it ends in failure and liquidation and sticks its shareholders—presumably many or most of whom are his political supporters—with the bill," said Michael Ohlrogge, a law professor at New York University who studies companies like Digital World.

Yet the Trump Media saga didn't end in an abrupt liquidation, and instead persisted into the election year as Trump began his third presidential campaign. Although the company's founders filed two lawsuits over his efforts to dilute their shares, neither the SEC nor the courts prevented the Digital World merger with Trump Media in late March 2024.

With its listing on the NASDAQ stock index, the company's paper value soared to over $8 billion, a major "liquidity event" for Trump himself at a moment when he sorely needed funds to cover mounting legal liabilities from federal and state prosecutions and civil judgments. Unable to sell or even borrow against his $3 billion-plus in shares for six months, he was suddenly a billionaire again—at least in theory.

The flaw still lay in the actual value of Trump Media, a failing digital venture with no plausible path to stem its ongoing financial losses, estimated at nearly $50 million. Its stock prospectus not only acknowledged that the pending lawsuits could lead to bankruptcy but noted that the company had simply declined to provide the most basic information about its finances and operations, including the number of

Truth Social's active users and ad impressions. The newly public company owed the early surge in its share price, according to analysts like Fox Business Channel's Charles Gasparino, to its status as a "meme stock," whose valuation depends on "vibes"—and, in this case, the devotion of small retail shareholders who idolize Trump. Gasparino warned that the former president, anticipating an inevitable decline, is likely to "dump" many of his shares.

That could leave his eager fans in the same embarrassing position as the believers who once put their faith in Trump Hotels and Casino Resorts, which went public at a billion-dollar valuation in 1995 and then went bankrupt nine years later, after losing hundreds of millions of dollars. Trump walked off with $44 million from that debacle while his investors lost everything. The Trump Hotels stock sported the same ticker symbol later bequeathed to Trump Media—the initials DJT.

As he campaigned for president, continuing to loot the Republican base with constant demands for money, fresh revelations of grifting by Trump's offspring appeared regularly. Before leaving the White House, the former president had directed the Treasury Department to continue his adult children's Secret Service protection for six months, at a cost to taxpayers of at least $1.7 million.

Meanwhile, Don Jr. set up an online store, selling cheesy Trump-branded merchandise that he insisted was "made in the USA," but had in fact been manufactured in China, often the target of Junior's bitterest xenophobic tirades online. The younger Donald also became an online salesman for a dubious meat-merchandising outfit, which had lost its Better Business Bureau accreditation in 2021.

Overshadowing that petty pelf was Jared Kushner's big post–White House score—a $2 billion investment in Affinity Partners, his newly minted private equity firm, from the Saudi Public Investment Fund. Advisers to the fund had warned that Jared and his business partners were "inexperienced" and charging an "excessive" fee, while the Saudi government would shoulder "the bulk of the investment and risk" in the deal—and in summary that the Kushner investment firm was "unsatisfactory in all aspects."

Reinforcing the impression of corrupt motives on all sides, Crown Prince Mohammed bin Salman approved the deal anyway, presumably in appreciation of Kushner's unwavering support for his blood-soaked and repressive rule, in particular the grisly murder of the dissident journalist and *Washington Post* columnist Jamal Khashoggi, which the Trump White House had waved away. A Washington University law professor specializing in ethics remarked that "the reason this smells so bad is that there is all sorts of evidence [Kushner] did not receive this on the merits."

Kushner and former Treasury secretary Steven Mnuchin had spent the final weeks of the Trump administration jetting around the Middle East on the public dime arranging this scheme, which had also resulted in over a billion dollars for Mnuchin's own fund—while pretending to raise billions for investment in poorer countries.

The Saudi investment in Affinity Partners echoed a dubious deal involving the government of Qatar early in the Trump administration. In the spring of 2018, the Kushner family obtained a massive bailout of their very big and very unprofitable Midtown Manhattan tower at 666 Fifth Avenue, which had come uncomfortably close to bankrupting their company. Their financial savior was Brookfield Asset Management, a firm bankrolled by the Qatar Investment Authority, whose intervention came at a fraught moment when Jared Kushner oversaw US policy toward Qatar, then in conflict with Saudi Arabia and its Gulf neighbors. Eventually, after the rescue of 666 Fifth Avenue, Kushner brokered an agreement that lifted an economic blockade of Qatar.

Unsurprisingly, both Qatar and the United Arab Emirates joined the Saudis in greasing Kushner's investment fund in 2022, with investments estimated at $200 million from each nation's wealth fund. At roughly the same time, the Trump Organization was booking profits from deals with Saudi investors, both through the LIV Golf tour sponsored by the Public Investment Fund in Riyadh and a multibillion-dollar real estate project in the tiny Gulf kingdom of Oman.

Every dictator in the region wants to maintain a close relationship with Trump, just in case—and the only way to keep him friendly, as they know too well, is to grease him and his family.

THE FRENETIC AND often lawless money-grubbing of the Trumps and their imitators was worse than unseemly. And yet by the time that the forty-fifth president left office under a cloud of unprecedented disgrace, nobody was surprised by his grasping. Trump had transformed the Republican Party flagship (which participated openly in his postpresidential scamming) and the conservative movement into shell operations whose substantive messages were subordinated to his cult—and his corrupt demands.

Both party and movement had long since abandoned any commitment to policy or philosophy, focusing instead on grievance messaging to motivate a very specific group of voters—and not incidentally, to siphon money from their accounts as often as possible. The Republicans could no longer bother with a campaign platform. Their issue positions and political messages, all based on conspiracy theories, were designed to instigate paranoia and hatred, those inchoate forces which, as Roger Stone had observed decades earlier, truly drove the American Right. His boldest political competitors were those, such as Florida governor Ron DeSantis, who strained to outbid his demonization of gays, transsexuals, and everyone else who didn't fit their bitter redefinition of "American."

Devolving toward a kitsch style of fascism, embroidered with pseudo-religious frippery, Trump's version of "Republican conservatism" was not so different from past outbursts of right-wing extremism in this country. The difference was that in his Republican Party—and what now masqueraded as the conservative movement—there was so little space for anything else.

Negative polarization has so deeply distorted the nation's political and moral standards that Donald Trump could be convicted of multiple felonies and perhaps still be elected president for the second time. Whatever happens to Trump, the fate of American conservatism and the Republican Party that he has disfigured so deeply already seems fixed—or "rigged," as he might put it. The industrial production of falsehood and fraud will grind on shamelessly, with or without him, overseen by entrepreneurs who understand that substance and commitment carry no sales value in a political culture dominated by noisemaking, grandstanding, and malice.

Nothing illustrated the howling emptiness on the right as starkly as the farcical leadership struggles within the House Republican conference that overshadowed the 118th Congress. Elected as Speaker after fifteen protracted rounds of voting, California's Kevin McCarthy found himself perched on a trap door that was set to spring open as soon as a single member signed a "motion to vacate" against him. He fell victim to that inevitable doom after just nine months, simply because he had dared to compromise with Democrats and the White House to keep the government funded.

The far-right faction that deposed McCarthy had no program or policy, only a hatred of government and a yearning for the spectacle of shutdown. Having rejected McCarthy, the partisan placeholder admired mainly for his fundraising prowess, his hard-right antagonists attempted to replace him with their own Rep. Jim Jordan of Ohio, a frothing loudmouth who has quite literally never passed a single bill in his eight terms on Capitol Hill.

Despite that utter failure as a legislator, Jordan entered the contest for speaker with an enthusiastic endorsement from Trump, whose January 2021 coup attempt the Ohioan had plotted and promoted relentlessly. But the abrasive Jordan carried excess baggage, including an alleged failure to report rampant sexual abuse of students that had occurred decades ago, while he was on the coaching staff of Ohio State University's wrestling team. Attempts by Jordan and his supporters to bully his GOP colleagues into supporting him for speaker, fronting a campaign that included intimidating calls from Fox News personalities and even death threats against the recalcitrant, only made matters worse. He lost votes in each of three successive roll-call votes before abandoning his bid for power.

Yet Jordan's flameout didn't result in a course correction by House Republicans. Instead, they unanimously elected Rep. Mike Johnson, an obscure politician from Louisiana with only four terms and no leadership experience. It was an inexplicable choice, except that unlike Jordan, Johnson displayed a friendly face and an inoffensive demeanor.

Behind Johnson's smile, however, lurked an unwavering devotion to the most fanatical wing of the religious Right, known as "Christian nationalists," whose urge to return to eighteenth-century hierarchies and values he had articulated enthusiastically as a lawyer and podcaster. He believed that public authorities, operating to enforce the will of God, had the duty to outlaw not only homosexuality and abortion but contraception and any sexual activity outside heterosexual marriage.

There had to be exceptions, of course—such as the case of Texas Judge Paul Pressler, a ranking figure in the Southern Baptist Convention and a Johnson mentor who had appointed him dean of a Louisiana law school named after Pressler himself. That appointment didn't last long, as the fledgling school fell apart amid accusations of financial misconduct and lack of academic rigor. Several years later, Pressler was sued in Texas courts in a civil case that eventually came to include allegations of assault and abuse by several men, with some saying that the incidents dated back to their childhood.

Subsequent revelations in court documents and press reports showed that the allegations against Pressler had emerged as early as 1978, when he was expelled from a Houston church for sexual misconduct. What also emerged was that Pressler's law partner, a Houston attorney who led the Harris County Republican Party for twelve years, had known of harassment and assault allegations against Pressler since 2004 and had lied publicly to cover up the scandal.

Like the Falwells, Billy James Hargis, Paula White, and many other evangelical celebrities who preceded him, Johnson felt no moral scruple against such deceptions, despite his constant invocation of Biblical morality. After all, he had lied publicly about the 2020 election. He had even adopted Sidney Powell's tall tale about Dominion Voting Systems and its supposed origins in a Venezuelan Communist scheme to control US elections. The "tell" came on the day after Johnson's election as speaker, when he attempted to erase from the Web all of the radio podcasts that showcased his extreme and, in some instances, quite bizarre but firmly held opinions. (He takes as a matter of faith that the Earth has existed for only six thousand years, not four or five billion, and that Noah's Ark cruised the flooded planet in antiquity with a cargo of creatures that included dinosaurs.)

Nicknamed "MAGA Mike" for his sycophantic devotion to Trump, Johnson plainly understands the need for vehement and constant denial. Following press reports on the cultish worldview he and his wife share, the new speaker told Fox host Sean Hannity that "I don't even remember" some of the harsh rhetoric he has uttered about gays and lesbians.

Until his elevation, Johnson's wife, Kelly, has pursued her own small-time grift as a "Christian" counselor. That meant advising individuals and families how to "drive out the demons" that cause homosexuality, which she and her husband equate with bestiality and incest. Her business, Onward Christian Counseling, purported to soothe the anguish of its clients using a method based on the ancient Greek theory of four human "temperaments"—as interpreted more recently by the far-right Christian author Tim LaHaye. In fact, she is a "certified temperament counselor," according to her website. But business may have dropped off since she took down that site the day after her husband became speaker.

Even as the most reactionary faction consolidated its command of the House, the remnant of reality-based Republicans in the Senate found themselves isolated in their own party—not solely because of Trump's enmity, but because they are regularly vilified by the Internet-based arbiters who control political discourse on the right. The razing of the Republican Party as a policymaking and governing entity will only leave conservative voters more confused, atomized, and vulnerable to deception. Success in Congress is no longer measured by the passage of landmark legislation, but by social media followers and millions of dollars raised online. Deep stupidity, ignorance, and grubby cynicism in no way handicap a Republican legislator, as demonstrated by the stellar careers of Marjorie Taylor Greene and Lauren Boebert.

Beyond Capitol Hill, Trump's acolytes and imitators are likewise poised to dominate whatever is left of conservatism. The most influential figures display little interest in ideas or policy, and indeed scorn academic and intellectual achievement. College dropout Charlie Kirk, leader of Turning Point USA, the largest youth organization on the right, openly derided higher education as a "scam" and urged his peers to "start a business" instead. And indeed TPUSA, his "nonprofit" business, has reaped millions for Kirk and his cronies.

The galaxy of conspiracy-mongers and con artists that includes Alex Jones, Steve Bannon, and literally dozens of like-minded crooks is as expansive as the Internet itself. The QAnon cult, which has proved invulnerable to failed predictions and even criminal misconduct by its promoters, has reached far beyond the limits of the Tea Party or the old John Birch Society, with nearly one in four Republicans sharing its credence in a fantastical sex-trafficking mafia run by a global cabal of Satanic pedophiles who control government, finance, entertainment, and the mainstream media. The cult continued to grow after Trump left the White House, a cataclysmic event that should have disabused followers of their illusions, and yet appeared to have the opposite effect.

The protean nature of the right-wing grift allowed figures ostensibly on the left to engage and profit—such as Robert F. Kennedy Jr., who had earned millions of dollars from anti-vaccine propaganda during the COVID-19 pandemic before declaring his candidacy for president in 2023. Proud heir to the legendary liberal political dynasty, Kennedy had long since transferred much of his allegiance to the far right, where he found a receptive (and easily duped) audience for the conspiracy theories behind his crusade against vaccination.

Until he seemed to potentially threaten Trump as an independent candidate, Kennedy's challenge to President Joe Biden was hyped by the likes of Bannon and Hannity and promoted incessantly on Fox News and across the far right's cable and internet platforms. Pulling donations mostly from right-wing Republicans, Kennedy's campaign raised millions of dollars—while he, like Trump, refused to disclose his own income tax returns. His fundraising prowess showed what fortunes could be minted in the angry and irrational "horseshoe" milieu where the extremes of left and right combine.

Whether fake left or hard right, however, the machinery of deception that reproduces such credulous cohorts keeps expanding in still more extreme directions. With or without Trump, the American right rewards political swindlers who possess a knack for exploitation and a lack of any hobbling conscience, while rejecting anyone who insists on facts and truth. Yes, there really is a sucker born, or created, every minute—and there is a pernicious ideology that will thrive so long as that process endures.

ACKNOWLEDGMENTS

In a tense political moment, writing a book about the darker aspects of American political culture means risking not only rebuttal but retribution—(as a certain former president and his flunkeys recklessly suggest almost every day). So I want to state clearly that my appreciation of those who helped me to conceive, create, and publish this book doesn't implicate any of them in its contents. I'm pleased to share any credit, but I insist on keeping the blame for myself.

That said, I owe profound thanks to Pete Wolverton, my editor at St. Martin's Press, who has seen this book through from the beginning with patience and kindness as well as valuable guidance. My thanks as well to the now-retired Thomas Dunne, who published *The Hunting of the President*, *Big Lies*, and *It Can Happen Here*, for advancing the launch of this project. I also appreciate the contributions of editorial assistant Claire Cheek, copy editors Sara Robb and Chris Ensey, designer Kelly Too, cover designer Young Lim, production editor Ken Silver, publicity manager Joe Rinaldi, marketing manager Michelle Cashman, and Joshua M. Rubins of Duane Morris LLP for his thoughtful legal review of the text. For nearly three decades, I've had the great good fortune to be represented by my friends Andrew Wylie and Jeffrey Posternak of the Wylie Agency, where I also wish to thank Tucker Smith.

I owe a debt of gratitude to my colleagues at Type Media Center, including Taya McCormick-Grobow, Kristine Bruch, Andrea Bott,

Cassi Feldman, and Jeffrey Kusama-Hinte, and I'm most thankful for generous fellowship support from Danny, Tom, and Nancy Meyer; Cecilia Johnson and John S. Johnson; Susan Blaustein and Alan Berlow; and the Mai Family Foundation.

Much of this book was written on the second floor of the Nantucket Atheneum, where I found a quiet, cool, and pleasant place to write on many days when others were frolicking at the beach. It is a truly wonderful library and a cornerstone of island life that has served people there for nearly two centuries. I'm very grateful to its staff and trustees.

I appreciate everyone who has assisted me as editor in chief of *The National Memo*, including Shakil Hossain, Rose Samoy, Chibueze Godwin, and Atunu Sarker. I've also enjoyed gracious support from Jan Ritch-Frel of Independent Media Institute, Roxanne Cooper of *AlterNet,* the editors at Creators Syndicate, *Daily Kos, Media Matters*, and our friends Jeff Danziger, Lucian K. Truscott IV, Gene Lyons, Chandra Bozelko, Nina Burleigh, Mary C. Curtis, David Cay Johnston, Jonathan Alter, Peter Dreier, Paul Starr, Claire Bond Potter, Jane Mayer, and a host of others whose contributions have graced our pages.

Sidney Blumenthal has been my close friend since our earliest days in journalism. He also happens to be one of America's sharpest political analysts and a talented editor. I'm lucky that he made the time to read and comment on draft chapters of *The Longest Con*.

Special thanks are likewise due to George T. Conway III, for contributing the foreword—and for being open to a friendship despite our contrasting opinions (and contentious history) generous. His attitude gives me hope that our country will again someday enjoy an environment of reason, humor, and magnanimity.

Friends and family have provided encouragement and assistance in so many ways during the years that I worked on this book, including Ann and Graham Gund, Barbara Landreth, Symmie Newhouse, Julie Conason, Marc and Sherri Feigen, Jay and Nancy Nichols, Clara Bingham and Joe Finnerty, Sally Horchow and John Seitz, John Sexton, Michael Tomasky, Richard Yeselson, Mary Pat Bonner, David Frum, David Brock, Andrew Karsch, Wes Enzinna, Eli Clifton, Fran Barrett, Christopher Ruddy, Sarah Posner, Rick Perlstein, Agnes Gund, Anne Hess and Craig

Kaplan, David Neiwert, William Bastone, Charles Bagli, Andrea Bernstein, Arthur Browne, Jim Callaghan, David Cay Johnston, Tom Robbins, and Tricia Romano.

Every day, I still miss Gail Furman and Martin Rosenblatt, my dear friends who are gone, and my late mentor and friend Wayne Barrett, whose spirit inspires me constantly.

And then at last there is my family, who sacrificed so much as I spent days away from them when we wanted to be together: our children Edward and Eleanor, both of whom fill me with such happiness and pride, and my adored wife, Elizabeth Wagley, who has made my life possible and promising. This book was her idea and I trust it meets with her approval.

—December 2023

NOTES ON SOURCES

1. The Role Model

Richard H. Rovere, *Senator Joe McCarthy,* Harper Torchbooks, 1959.

Roy Cohn, *McCarthy,* New American Library, 1968.

Larry Tye, *Demagogue: The Life and Long Shadow of Joe McCarthy,* Houghton Mifflin Harcourt, 2020.

Nicholas von Hoffman, *Citizen Cohn,* Doubleday, 1988.

Murray Kempton, *Rebellions, Perversities, and Main Events,* Crown, 1994.

Donald J. Trump and Tony Schwartz, *Trump: The Art of the Deal,* Random House, 1987.

Julia Child, The Association for Diplomatic Studies and Training Foreign Affairs Oral History Project, interview with Jewell Fenzi, July 7, 1991 (https://adst.org/oral-history/fascinating-figures/a-movable-feast/).

Ben Bradlee, *A Good Life: Newspapering and Other Adventures,* Simon & Schuster, 1995.

William Lambert, "The Hotshot One-Man Roy Cohn Lobby," *LIFE,* September 5, 1969.

Ken Auletta, "Don't Mess with Roy Cohn," *Esquire,* December 5, 1978.

Joe Conason, "Where There's a Will, There's a Way: Marie Lambert Brings Patronage Back to Surrogate's Court," *The Village Voice,* February 5, 1979.

Jim Callaghan, "'Fixers,' Mob Guys Profited: Ameruso Let DOT Go Corrupt," *The Chief,* June 1, 2006.

Steven R. Weisman, "Several Hundred Friends Salute Roy Cohn, a Lawyer for 25 Years," *The New York Times,* November 30, 1973.

Eleanor Randolph, "William Safire, Right to the Core," *The Washington Post,* August 24, 1987.

Jack Anderson and Dale Van Atta, "NIH Treats Roy Cohn with AIDS Drug," *The Washington Post,* August 4, 1986.

Wayne Barrett, "Roy Cohn's Cash Clients Crash," *The Village Voice,* March 29, 1983.

Wayne Barrett, *Trump: The Deals and the Downfall*, HarperCollins, 1992.
Jeffrey Toobin, "The Dirty Trickster," *The New Yorker*, June 2, 2008.
Interview with former New York *Daily News* editor Arthur Browne, November 3, 2021.

2. The Profits of Paranoia

Sen. Joseph R. McCarthy, "America's Retreat from Victory," Senate Floor Speech (later published as booklet), June 14, 1951.

Hubert Villeneuve, *Teaching Anticommunism: Fred C. Schwarz, the Christian Anti-Communism Crusade and American Postwar Conservatism*, McGill-Queen's University Press, 2020.

Markku Ruotsila, *Fighting Fundamentalist: Carl McIntire and the Politicization of American Fundamentalism*, Oxford University Press, 2015.

Lee Roy Chapman, "The Strange Love of Dr. Billy James Hargis," *This Land* podcast, November 1, 2012.

Anne Constable, Richard Walker, and Tom Carter, "The Sins of Billy James," *Time*, February 16, 1976.

Daniel K. Williams, *God's Own Party: The Making of the Christian Right*, Oxford University Press, 2012.

Thomas Wayne Dehanas, "America's Modern Day Messiah: Billy James Hargis and His Christian Crusade—A Case Study in Extremism," MA thesis, Oklahoma State University, 1964.

Sasha Issenberg, "The Wild Road Trip That Launched the Populist Conservative Movement," *Smithsonian*, September 2018.

Peter Adams, *The Insurrectionist: Major General Edwin A. Walker and the Birth of the Deep State Conspiracy*, Louisiana State University Press, 2023.

Roger Mudd, "Case History of a Rumor" on Operation Water Moccasin, *CBS Reports*, November 13, 1963.

Sanford J. Ungar, "Ideology: The Christian Anti-Communism Crusade," *The Atlantic*, June 1974.

FBI HQ file 62–69602, #297, memo on Fred Schwarz from FBI Chief Inspector William C. Sullivan to Assistant Director Alan H. Belmont, March 13, 1961 (Ernie Lazar FOIA collection on archive.org).

3. "Experts" and Patrioteers

"G.O.P. 'Right Wing' Attacks Regime; President, Dulles and State Department Assailed at Chicago Meetings," *The New York Times*, February 12, 1956.

FBI HQ file 62–104576, #50, memo re Edgar Bundy to FBI Assistant Director William C. Sullivan, August 11, 1961(Ernie Lazar FOIA collection on archive.org).

FBI HQ file 62–104576, #26X, Edgar Bundy letter to FBI Director J. Edgar Hoover, February 27, 1961; FBI HQ file 62–104576, #26X3, Hoover reply to Bundy, in Sullivan memo to Assistant to the Director Alan H. Belmont (Ernie Lazar FOIA collection on archive.org).

FBI HQ file 62–104576, #27X, memo from Sullivan to Belmont re incoming Bundy letter, March 17, 1961 (Ernie Lazar FOIA collection on archive.org).

FBI HQ file 62–104576, #26X3, Sullivan memo to Belmont, March 6, 1961 (Ernie Lazar FOIA collection on archive.org).

FBI HQ file 62–102576, #125, memo on Dan Smoot from FBI Special Agent Donald C. Morrell to Deputy Associate Director Cartha DeLoach, November 8, 1962 (Ernie Lazar FOIA collection on archive.org).

Ernie Lazar, report on the John Birch Society, 2019 (Ernie Lazar FOIA collection on archive.org).

4. The Wizard of Id

Donald Janson, "Rightists Buoyed by the Election," *The New York Times*, November 23, 1964.

Richard A. Viguerie and David Franke, *America's Right Turn: How Conservatives Used New and Alternative Media to Take Power*, Taylor Trade Publishing, 2004.

Alan Pell Crawford, *Thunder on the Right: The New Right and the Politics of Resentment*, New American Library, 1980.

Whitney Strub, "Meet the Spiritual Forefather of Conservatives' War on Women," Salon.com, April 13, 2014.

N. J. O'Shaughnessy, "High Priesthood, Low Priestcraft: The Role of Political Consultants," *European Journal of Marketing*, February 1, 1990.

Nicole Hemmer, *Messengers of the Right: Conservative Media and the Transformation of American Politics*, University of Pennsylvania Press, 2016.

5. Nixon's Avaricious Avengers

J. Anthony Lukas, *Nightmare: The Underside of the Nixon Years*, Viking, 1976.

Stanley Kutler, *The Wars of Watergate: The Last Crisis of Richard Nixon*, Knopf, 1990.

Alan Pell Crawford, "Twilight of the Right," *The American Conservative*, February 26, 2014.

Daniel Schlozman and Sam Rosenfeld, "The Long New Right and the World It Made," paper for the American Political Science Association meetings, version of January 2019.

George Lardner Jr., "On Tape, Nixon Outlines 1971 'Deal' to Settle Antitrust Case Against ITT," *The Washington Post*, January 4, 1997.

Lou Cannon, "Tapping the Little Guy," *The Washington Post*, March 6, 1977.

Ronald Radosh, "Phyllis Schlafly, Mrs. America, Was a Secret Member of the John Birch Society," The Daily Beast, April 20, 2020.

Myra McPherson, "The New Right Brigade," *The Washington Post*, August 10, 1980.

Joseph E. Cantor, "Political Action Committees: Their Evolution, Growth, and Implications for the Political System," Congressional Research Service, November 6, 1981, updated April 30, 1984.

Craig Shirley, "Not Just Good at National Politics, But the Best," *National Review*, January 26, 2017.

Elizabeth Kastor, "The Cautious Closet of the Gay Conservative," *The Washington Post*, May 11, 1987.

Eleanor Clift, "Arthur Finkelstein, the Hypocrite Gay Consultant Who Kept Electing Right-Wing Homophobes," The Daily Beast, August 26, 2017.

6. Feeding the "Conservative" Hogs

William Greider, "The Education of David Stockman," *The Atlantic,* December 1981.

Stephanie Mansfield, "The Rise and Gall of Roger Stone," *The Washington Post,* June 16, 1986.

Manuel Roig-Franzia, "The Swamp Builders," *The Washington Post,* November 29, 2018.

Franklin Foer, "The Quiet American," Slate.com, April 28, 2016.

Thomas Byrne Edsall, "Profit and Presidential Politics," *The Washington Post,* August 12, 1989.

Jeffrey Toobin, "The Dirty Trickster," *The New Yorker,* May 23, 2008.

Ed Pilkington and Dominic Rushe, "News Corp Faces Global Investigation into Bribery," *The Guardian,* July 18, 2011.

Art Levine, "Publicists of the Damned," *Spy,* February 1992.

Michael Isikoff, "Bush Aides' Lobbying Debated," *The Washington Post,* September 9, 1988.

Brian Ross, "Cocaine Islands," *NBC Evening News,* April 30, 1987.

Ronald Reagan, "Remarks Following Discussions with President Mobutu Sese Seko," December 9, 1986, Ronald Reagan Presidential Library and Museum Archives.

Tom Kertscher, "Many More Criminal Indictments Under Trump, Reagan and Nixon Than Under Obama, Clinton and Carter," PolitiFact, January 9, 2020.

Philip Shenon, "The McKay Report: An Ambiguous Conclusion to a 14-Month Investigation," *The New York Times,* July 19, 1988.

"EPA Officials 'Violated Trust' by 'Manipulating the Superfund,'" excerpts from House Energy oversight subcommittee report on the Environmental Protection Agency controversy, *The Washington Post,* August 31, 1984.

Lawrence E. Walsh et al., *Final Report of the Independent Counsel for Iran/Contra Matters,* US General Services Administration, June 4, 1993.

Lawrence E. Walsh, *Firewall: The Iran-Contra Controversy and Cover-up,* W. W. Norton, 1997.

Joe Conason, James Ridgeway, and Murray Waas, "What the Iran-Contra Report Leaves Out," *The Village Voice,* December 1, 1987.

William J. Eaton, "GOP Consultant Admits Using Influence to Obtain HUD Grant but Defends Action," *Los Angeles Times,* June 21, 1989.

Gwen Ifill, "Foggy Recollections, Contradictions Mark Testimony of 3 in HUD Probe," *The Washington Post,* July 17, 1989.

Frank E. Hagan, "From HUD to Iran-Contra: Crime During the Reagan Administration," paper presented at the American Society of Criminology meetings, November 4, 1992, New Orleans, Louisiana (under a grant from the U.S. Department of Justice).

Malcolm Byrne, editor, "Oliver North's Checkered Iran-Contra Record," National Security Archive Briefing Book, May 16, 2018.

Kenneth P. Vogel, "Paul Manafort's Wild and Lucrative Philippine Adventure," *Politico,* June 10, 2016.

Tom McCarthy, "Paul Manafort: How Decades of Serving Dictators Led to Role as Trump's Go-To Guy," *The Guardian*, October 30, 2017.

William Raspberry, "Cut Off Aid to UNITA," *The Washington Post*, September 12, 1990.

Steven Rosenfeld, "Donald Trump's Number One Goon: Top Campaign Adviser tied to Arms Dealers, Warlords, Dictators and Oligarchs," Salon.com, May 26, 2016.

Jane Mayer, "The Secret Papers of Lee Atwater, Who Invented the Scurrilous Tactics That Trump Normalized," *The New Yorker*, May 6, 2021.

Jon Schwarz, "Farewell to P.J. O'Rourke, America's Only (Semi-)Funny Conservative," The Intercept, February 16, 2022.

7. Profits (and Prophets) Without Honor

Dirk Smillie, *Falwell Inc.: Inside a Religious, Political, Educational, and Business Empire*, St. Martin's Press, 2008.

David John Marley, "Ronald Reagan and the Splintering of the Christian Right," *Journal of Church and State*, Autumn 2006.

David Grann, "Robespierre of the Right," *The New Republic*, October 27, 1997.

Laura Sessions Stepp, "IRS Probes Evangelists' Operations," *The Washington Post*, December 10, 1988.

Susan Antilla, "Investors Had Faith; U.S. Didn't," *The New York Times*, June 3, 1992.

Cody Lowe, "Liberty Saved by the Faith—and Money—of Two Men," *The Roanoke Times*, February 6, 1995.

Wayne King, "Falwell Quits as Moral Majority Head," *The New York Times*, November 4, 1987.

Joe Conason and Gene Lyons, *The Hunting of the President: The Ten-Year Campaign to Destroy Bill and Hillary Clinton*, St. Martin's Press, 2000.

8. Let Us Prey

Joe Conason, *It Can Happen Here: Authoritarian Peril in the Age of Bush*, St. Martin's Press, 2007.

Dana Milbank, "Religious Right Finds Its Center in Oval Office," *The Washington Post*, December 24, 2001.

"An Evolving Faith: Does the President Believe He Has a Divine Mandate?" Beliefnet .com, February 2003.

Jeffrey Toobin, "Ashcroft's Ascent," *The New Yorker*, April 7, 2002.

Joe Conason, "The Religious Right's Quiet Revival: Pat Robertson's Christian Coalition," *The Nation*, May 17, 1992.

Bill Sizemore, "Robertson Charity Misled Donors About Africa Work," *The Virginian-Pilot*, July 10, 1999.

David Kuo, *Tempting Faith: An Inside Story of Political Seduction*, Free Press, 2006.

Ron Suskind, "Why Are These Men Laughing?" and "The DiIulio Letter to Ron Suskind," *Esquire*, January 2003.

Sarah Posner, "The Devil Stole Rod Parsley's Money," *Religion Dispatches*, December 20, 2009.

Sarah Posner, *God's Profits: Faith, Fraud, and the Republican Crusade for Values Voters*, Polipoint Press, 2008.

Joe Conason, "The GOP's Spreading Plague," Salon.com, September 30, 2005.

Sean Flynn, "The Sins of Ralph Reed," *GQ*, July 11, 2006.

Matthew Continetti, "Scandal Season: The Long Strange Trip of David Safavian," *The Weekly Standard*, October 10, 2005.

Tucker Carlson, "What I Sold at the Revolution: Grover Norquist Joins the Club," *The New Republic*, June 9, 1997.

Lee Fang, "Big Pharma Funds 'Independent' Advocacy Groups Attacking Drug-Price Reduction Bill," The Intercept, August 10, 2017.

Susan Schmidt and James V. Grimaldi, "Nonprofit Groups Funneled Money for Abramoff: Funds Flowed to Lobbying Campaigns," *The Washington Post*, June 25, 2006.

9. Spilling the Tea Party

Stephanie Mencimer, "Tea Party Patriots Investigated: They Use You and Abuse You," *Mother Jones*, February 14, 2011; "Tea Party Patriots Investigated: Don't Ask, Don't Tell," February 15, 2011; "Tea Party Patriots Investigated: The Tax-Dodging Moneyman," February 16, 2011.

Stephanie Mencimer, "How a Feud Between Two Tea Party Leaders Helped Lay the Groundwork for the Capitol Insurrection," *Mother Jones*, February 19, 2021.

Stephanie Mencimer, "Remember the Tea Party? It's Still Raising Millions in Dark Money," *Mother Jones*, May/June 2021.

Andy Kroll, "Powerful Tea Party Group's Internal Docs Leak," *Mother Jones*, January 4, 2013.

Doug Mataconis, "Have Conservatives Finally Had Enough Of Sarah Palin?" OutsidetheBeltway.com, September 7, 2011.

Joe Conason, "'Dysfunctional' Too Polite to Describe Tea Party Congress," The National Memo, July 22, 2011.

Adele M. Stan, "Tea Party, Inc.," Type Investigations/AlterNet, October 25, 2010.

Kenneth P. Vogel, "Inside the Dick Armey, Freedomworks Split," *Politico*, December 4, 2012.

Conor Friedersdorf, "Attacking Sarah Palin from the Right," *The Atlantic*, May 27, 2011.

"Tea Party Nationalism: A Critical Examination of the Tea Party Movement," Institute for Research and Education on Human Rights, Fall 2010.

Suzanne Goldenberg, "Tea Party movement: Billionaire Koch Brothers Who Helped It Grow," *The Guardian*, October 13, 2010.

Zachary Roth, "Tea Party Convention Organizer Used 'Our Passion for the Movement to Build His Start-Up'" TalkingPointsMemo.com, January 13, 2010.

Kenneth P. Vogel, "Sarah Palin's Tea Party Raises Eyebrows," *Politico*, January 8, 2010.

Chabeli Carrazana, "Founder of Tea Party Nation Has Been Disbarred for Trying to Scam Timeshare Owners," *Orlando Sentinel*, September 27, 2018.

Janie Lorber and Eric Lipton, "G.O.P. Insider Fuels Tea Party and Suspicion," *The New York Times*, September 18, 2010.

Paul H. Jossey, "How We Killed the Tea Party," *Politico*, August 14, 2016.

10. How Not to Get Rich Quick (or Cure Cancer, Ever)

Ariel Edwards-Levy, "Polls Find Most Republicans Say 2020 Election Was Stolen and Roughly One-Quarter Embrace QAnon Conspiracies," CNN.com, May 28, 2021.

Sander van der Linden et al., "The Paranoid Style in American Politics Revisited: An Ideological Asymmetry in Conspiratorial Thinking," *Political Psychology,* Vol. 42, Number 1, 2021.

Philip Bump, "Conspiracy Theories Are Common on the Right—but Few Republicans Adhere to All of Them," *The Washington Post,* July 19, 2021.

Securities and Exchange Commission v. Agora, Inc. et al., amended complaint, Civil Action No. MJG03CV1042, US District Court for the District of Maryland, November 14, 2003.

James Dale Davidson, *Who Murdered Vince Foster? And Why the Biggest Political Scandal in History Is Also the Biggest Financial Story of Our Lifetimes,* Strategic Investment, 1996.

James Dale Davidson and William Rees-Mogg, *The Great Reckoning: How the World Will Change in the Depression of the Nineties,* Sidgwick, 1992.

James Dale Davidson, *The Plague of the Black Debt: How to Survive the Coming Depression,* Strategic Investment Limited Partnership, 1993.

James Dale Davidson and Lord William Rees-Mogg, with a new introduction by Peter Thiel, *The Sovereign Individual: How to Survive and Thrive During the Collapse of the Welfare State,* Simon & Schuster, 2020.

Susan Schmidt, "Two Years After Foster's Death, Conspiracy Theories Thrive," *The Washington Post,* July 4, 1995.

Steve Kornacki, "What Newt Still Won't Admit," Salon.com, December 10, 2012.

Tim Murphy, "How This Company—and Mike Huckabee—Cashed In by Scaring Conservatives," *Mother Jones,* November/December 2015.

"Stansberry Research Announces the SEC Injunction Against the Company Has Been Vacated," press release, Stansberry Research, February 24, 2020.

Stephen Janis, "Man found dead at Belvedere worked at company that had SEC complaint," *Washington Examiner,* June 1, 2006.

Lauren Kranc, "Where Is Frank Porter Stansberry of Netflix's Unsolved Mysteries Now?" *Esquire,* July 7, 2020.

Eric Hananoki, "Meet Tobin Smith: The Dubious Stock Pitchman Fired from Fox News," MediaMatters.org, June 19, 2013.

Securities and Exchange Commission v. Members Service Corporation et al., Civil Action No. 97 CV 01146 (HHK), litigation release, August 11, 1999.

Eric Hananoki, "Fox Gives Show to SEC-Fined Analyst Who Was Paid to Push Now Worthless Stocks," MediaMatters.org, May 20, 2014.

Terry Krepel, "Beck's Golden Ticket: Gold Sellers Stayed Loyal While Other Advertisers Fled," MediaMatters.org, June 29, 2011.

Alexander Zaitchik, *Common Nonsense: Glenn Beck and the Triumph of Ignorance,* Wiley, 2010.

Hanna Kozlowska and Jeremy B. Merrill, "The New 'Wolf of Wall Street' Is an influencer Who Sells Gold to Republican Seniors," Quartz.com, November 18, 2019.

11. In Very Bad Faith

Gabriel Sherman, "Inside Jerry Falwell Jr.'s Unlikely Rise and Precipitous Fall at Liberty University," *Vanity Fair,* January 24, 2022.

Jack Stripling, "An Online Kingdom Come," *The Chronicle of Higher Education,* February 23, 2015.

Alec MacGillis, "How Liberty University Built a Billion-Dollar Empire Online," *The New York Times Magazine*/ProPublica, April 17, 2018.

Michael Rothfeld, Rob Berry, and Joe Palazzolo, "Cohen Hired IT Firm to Rig Early CNBC, Drudge Polls to Favor Trump," *The Wall Street Journal,* January 17, 2019.

Rod Dreher, "Adventures in Christian Grift," *The American Conservative,* September 12, 2019.

Chris Lehmann, "Jerry Falwell Jr.'s Filthy Predatory Finances," *The New Republic,* August 25, 2020.

David Halperin, "Falwell, Trump's Favorite College President, Pioneered the Scam Non-Profit College," RepublicReport.org, September 9, 2019.

Aram Roston and Joshua Schneyer, "Exclusive: Falwell Steered Liberty University Land Deal Benefiting His Personal Trainer," Reuters, August 27, 2019.

Aram Roston, "Business Partner of Falwells Says affair with Evangelical Power Couple Spanned Seven Years," Reuters, August 4, 2020.

Giancarlo Granda and Mark Ebner, "Inside the Jerry Falwell Love Triangle: Pool Boy Tells All," *Rolling Stone,* October 15, 2022.

Brandon Ambrosino, "'Someone's Gotta Tell the Freakin' Truth': Falwell's Aides Break Their Silence," *Politico,* September 9, 2019.

Brandon Ambrosino and Michael Stratford, "Falwell's Son Out as VP at Liberty University," *Politico,* April 14, 2021.

Complaint, *Nonbelief Relief, Inc., v. David J. Kautter, IRS Acting Commissioner,* US District Court for the District of Columbia, Civil Action No. 18-CV-2347, October 11, 2018.

Jacqueline L. Salmon, "GOP Senator Investigates Spending at Several TV Ministries," *The Washington Post,* November 7, 2007.

Mary L. Trump, *Too Much and Never Enough: How My Family Created the World's Most Dangerous Man,* Simon & Schuster, 2020.

James Barron, "Overlooked Influences on Donald Trump: A Famous Minister and His Church," *The New York Times,* September 5, 2016.

Eli Yokley, "Ted Cruz Wins Values Voters Summit Straw Poll Again," *Roll Call,* September 25, 2015.

Sarah Posner, "Televangelist Who Prayed with Trump Says It Wasn't Endorsement," *Religion Dispatches,* October 7, 2015.

Sarah Posner, "Kenneth Copeland's Protectors," *Religion Dispatches,* November 18, 2013.

Sarah Posner, *Unholy: How White Christian Nationalists Powered the Trump Presidency and the Devastating Legacy They Left Behind,* Random House, 2021.

Jacqueline L. Salmon, "GOP Senator Investigates Spending at Several TV Ministries," *The Washington Post,* November 7, 2007.

Mary L. Trump, *Too Much and Never Enough: How My Family Created the World's Most Dangerous Man*, Simon & Schuster, 2020.

James Barron, "Overlooked Influences on Donald Trump: A Famous Minister and His Church," *The New York Times*, September 5, 2016.

Eli Yokley, "Ted Cruz Wins Values Voters Summit Straw Poll Again," *Roll Call*, September 25, 2015.

Mark I. Pinsky, "Apopka Preacher Paula White and Presidential Nominee Donald Trump Are a Match Made in Alt-Right Heaven," *Orlando Weekly*, October 19, 2016.

Frederick Clarkson, "Beneath the 'Wacky' Paula White Video Is a Dark and Deeply Undemocratic World Propping Up the President," *Religion Dispatches*, November 17, 2020.

Mark I. Pinsky, "At Trump's Right Hand," *Harvard Divinity School Bulletin*, Spring/Summer 2020.

Bonnie Kristian, "Why Televangelist Paula White Is the Perfect Trump Administration Hire," *The Week*, November 1, 2019.

Harry Bruinius, "How Donald Trump Has Found Common Ground with Televangelists," *The Christian Science Monitor*, October 2, 2015.

Complaint, *Nonbelief Relief, Inc., v. David J. Kautter, IRS Acting Commissioner*, US District Court for the District of Columbia, Civil Action No. 18-CV-2347, October 11, 2018.

12. The King of the Con Men

Wayne Barrett, "The Dirty Deal That Helped Make Donald Trump," *The Village Voice*, February 26, 1979.

Susan Mulcahy, "Confessions of a Trump Tabloid Scribe," *Politico*, May/June 2016.

Jane Mayer, "Donald Trump's Ghostwriter Tells All," *The New Yorker*, July 18, 2016.

Robert Slater, *No Such Thing As Over-Exposure: Inside the Life and Celebrity of Donald Trump*, Prentice-Hall, 2005.

David A. Farenthold, "Trump Foundation Promised Millions to Charity. We Found Less Than $10,000 Over 7 Years," *The Washington Post*, June 28, 2016.

Joe Conason, "That Negative Image of the Clinton Foundation Is Owed to a Plan Run by None Other Than Steve Bannon," Salon.com, December 19, 2018.

Maggie Haberman, *Confidence Man: The Making of Donald Trump and the Breaking of America*, Penguin Press, 2022.

David Segal, "What Donald Trump's Plaza Deal Reveals About His White House Bid," *The New York Times*, January 16, 2016.

Patrick Radden Keefe, "How Mark Burnett Resurrected Donald Trump as an Icon of American Success," *The New Yorker*, December 27, 2018.

Katherine Sullivan and Heather Vogell, "Here Are the Trump Projects Where Ivanka and Her Dad Misled Buyers," ProPublica, October 17, 2018.

Michael Lewis, "Toronto Condo Buyers May Target Donald Trump to Recoup Losses," *Toronto Star*, November 6, 2016.

Robert Cribb et al., "How Every Investor Lost Money on Trump Tower Toronto (but Donald Trump Made Millions Anyway)," *Toronto Star*, October 21, 2017.

Nikki Ekstein, "The Trump Soho Hotel Was Struggling to Survive, Then Dropped Its Name," Bloomberg News, October 27, 2019.

Jillian Kay Melchior, "Did Donald Trump Run a Scam University?" *National Review,* July 16, 2015.

Maggie Severns, "Tales from the Trump University Legal Vault," *Politico,* March 3, 2016.

Ian Tuttle, "Yes, Trump University Was a Massive Scam," *National Review,* February 26, 2016.

Katie Reilly, "Ted Cruz Is Giving Out a Trump University 'Certificate of Deception,'" *Time,* March 3, 2016.

John Cassidy, "Trump University: It's Worse Than You Think," *The New Yorker,* June 2, 2016.

Robert L. FitzPatrick and Joyce K. Reynolds, *False Profits: Seeking Financial and Spiritual Deliverance in Multi-Level Marketing and Pyramid Schemes,* Herald Press, 1997.

Yelena Dzhanova, "Inside Trump's Ties to the Multi-Level Marketing Company That Gave Him $8.8 Million When He Was Approaching Financial Ruin," *Business Insider,* October 21, 2020.

Mike McIntire, Russ Buettner, and Susanne Craig, "How Reality-TV Fame Handed Donald Trump a $427 Million Lifeline," *The New York Times,* September 28, 2020.

Ana Swanson, "The Trump Network Sought to Make People Rich, but Left Behind Disappointment, *The Washington Post,* March 23, 2016.

Shane Goldmacher, "Trump Foundation Will Dissolve, Accused of 'Shocking Pattern of Illegality,'" *The New York Times,* December 18, 2018.

Josh Russell, "Pyramid Scheme Lawsuit Drops Claims Against Trump Children," Courthouse News Service, May 19, 2023.

13. A Predatory Presidency

Yashar Ali, "What George W. Bush Really Thought of Donald Trump's Inauguration," *New York* magazine, March 29, 2017.

Ilya Marritz and Justin Elliott, "Trump's Inauguration Paid Trump's Company—with Ivanka in the Middle," ProPublica/WNYC Radio, December 14, 2018.

Fredreka Schouten, "A Record $107 Million Was Raised for Trump's Inauguration. So Where Did It All Go? No One Will Say," *USA Today,* January 18, 2018.

Kenneth P. Vogel, "Elliott Broidy Pleads Guilty in Foreign Lobbying Case," *The New York Times,* October 20, 2020.

Associated Press, "Guilty Plea in Fraud Case Tied to New York Pension," December 4, 2009.

Desmond Butler and Tom LoBianco, "The Princes, the President, and the Fortune Seekers," Associated Press, May 21, 2018.

Jonathan Weil, "KPMG Probe Raises Concern Over Conflicts," *The Wall Street Journal,* December 28, 2005.

Maggie Haberman and Kenneth P. Vogel, "Trump Inaugural Committee Paid $26 Million to Firm of First Lady's Adviser," *The New York Times,* February 15, 2018.

Rebecca Davis O'Brien, Rebecca Ballhaus, and Aruna Viswanatha, "Trump Inauguration Spending Under Criminal Investigation by Federal Prosecutors," *The Wall Street Journal,* December 13, 2018.

John Santucci, Matthew Mosk, Allison Pecorin, and Benjamin Siegel, "President Donald Trump's Inaugural Fund Spent Lavishly at His DC Hotel, New Docs Show," *ABC News,* January 15, 2019.

Jonathan O'Connell, "D.C. Attorney General Sues Trump Inaugural Committee over $1 Million Booking at President's Hotel," *The Washington Post,* January 22, 2020.

Jose Pagliery, "'Shattered': How the Trump Family Won the D.C. Inauguration Case," The Daily Beast, May 5, 2022.

Lauren Gambino, "'Thank You for the Blessing': Cabinet Takes Turns Lavishing Trump with Praise," *The Guardian,* June 12, 2017.

Glenn Thrush, "Mulvaney, Watchdog Bureau's Leader, Advises Bankers on Ways to Curtail Agency," *The New York Times,* April 24, 2018.

Glenn Thrush, "Ben Carson's HUD Spends $31,000 on Dining Set for His Office," *The New York Times,* February 27, 2018.

Victoria Guida, "Mnuchin's Plane Travel Cost Taxpayers $1 Million, Documents Show," *Politico,* March 16, 2018.

Jim Lardner, "Mapping Corruption in Trump's Executive Branch," *The American Prospect,* April 9, 2020.

Juliet Eilperin, Brady Dennis, and Josh Dawsey, "Scott Pruitt Enlisted an EPA Aide to Help His Wife Find a Job—with Chick-fil-A," *The Washington Post,* June 5, 2018.

Emily Holden and Oliver Milman, "Embattled Interior Secretary Ryan Zinke Steps Down After Series of Scandals," *The Guardian,* December 15, 2018.

Colin Kalmbacher, "Trump-Era Interior Secretary Continued to Work on Private Land Development Deal in Montana While in Office and Then Lied About It: OIG Report," Law & Crime report, February 16, 2022.

Steven Mufson, "Wilbur Ross Owned Stock in a Company with Close Ties to Putin Associates. Now He's Facing Questions About What He Did with it," *The Washington Post,* June 20, 2018.

Timothy L. O'Brien, "Wilbur Ross, Trump's Elusive Swamp Creature," Bloomberg News, August 9, 2018.

"Request for Investigation of Criminal Conflicts of Interest and False Statements by Secretary of Commerce Wilbur L. Ross," Citizens for Responsibility and Ethics in Washington, August 16, 2018.

Dan Alexander, "New Details About Wilbur Ross' Business Point to Pattern of Grifting," *Forbes,* August 7, 2018.

Emily Stewart, "Trump Is 'Definitely Still Involved' in His Hotel Business, a New Report Says," Vox.com, December 30, 2017.

Chase Peterson-Withorn, "Trump Refuses to Divest Assets, Passes Control to Sons," *Forbes,* January 11, 2017.

Anita Kumar, "How Trump Fused His Business Empire to the Presidency," *Politico,* January 20, 2020.

Anita Kumar and Evan Semones, "After Backlash, Trump Says His Doral Resort Won't Host G-7 Summit," *Politico,* October 19, 2019.

Jordan Libowitz and Caitlin Moniz, "Jared and Ivanka Made Up to $640 Million in the White House," Citizens for Responsibility and Ethics in Washington, February 8, 2021.

Andrea Bernstein, *American Oligarchs: The Kushners, the Trumps, and the Marriage of Money and Power,* W. W. Norton, 2020.

Charlie Savage, Emily Cochrane, Stephanie Lai, and Alan Rappeport, "I.R.S. Didn't Audit Trump for 2 Years in Office, House Committee Says," *The New York Times,* December 21, 2022.

14. Guns, Walls, and the Culture of Impunity

National Rifle Association of America v. Ackerman McQueen, Inc., and Mercury Group, Inc., Circuit Court of Alexandria, Virginia, Civil Case C219001757.

National Rifle Association of America v. Oliver North, original complaint, Supreme Court of the State of New York, index number unassigned.

Interviews with William Brewer, Esq., and Travis Carter, New York City, June 2019.

Analysis of the 2018 NRA Consolidated Financial Statement, June 13, 2019, prepared by Ackerman McQueen and provided by William Brewer.

Peter Finn and Sari Horwitz, "Ackerman McQueen PR Firm Has Been Behind NRA's Provocative Ads for Decades," *The Washington Post,* February 13, 2013.

Michael Brice-Saddler, "NRA Ousts President Oliver North After Alleged Extortion Scheme Against Chief Executive," *The Washington Post,* April 19, 2019.

Cam Wolf, "The CEO of the NRA Spent Almost $300,000 on Suits," *GQ,* May 13, 2019.

David K. Li, "NRA's Wayne LaPierre Sought Refuge from Mass Shootings on a Friend's Luxury Yacht," *NBC News,* April 6, 2021.

Tim Mak, "The Weirdness of Wayne LaPierre, the NRA's Reluctant Leader," *Vanity Fair,* October 2021.

Letitia James, Attorney General of the State of New York, v. National Rifle Association of America, Inc., Wayne LaPierre, et al., verified complaint, Supreme Court of the State of New York, August 6, 2020.

Brian Mann, "Former Top NRA Exec Says Greed, Corruption Pushed Gun Group into 'Death Spiral,'" National Public Radio, September 4, 2020.

Joshua Powell, *Inside the NRA: A Tell-All Account of Corruption, Greed, and Paranoia within the Most Powerful Political Group in America,* Twelve Books, September 8, 2020.

Cydney Hargis, "NRATV Is Now Finished—But Here Are the Bigotry, Lies, and Hatred That the NRA Tolerated for Years," MediaMatters.org, June 26, 2019.

In re: National Rifle Association of America and Sea Girt LLC, Debtors, Chapter 11 Case No. 21–30085, Northern District of Texas, order granting motions to dismiss, May 11, 2021.

Jonathan Stempel, "Judge Blocks New York's Bid to Close NRA," Reuters, March 2, 2022.

Noah Lanard and Dan Friedman, "This Is the Very Expensive Yacht Steve Bannon Got Arrested On," *Mother Jones,* August 20, 2020.

U.S. Attorney for the Southern District of New York, "Leaders of 'We Build the Wall' Online Fundraising Campaign Charged with Defrauding Hundreds of Thousands of Donors," press release, August 20, 2020.

Emily Birnbaum, "Veteran Behind GoFundMe for Trump's Wall Allegedly Pocketed Money Meant for Wounded Veterans," The Hill, January 10, 2019.

Jeremy Schwartz and Perla Trevizo, "Veteran, War Hero, Defendant, Troll: Man Who

Raised Millions for Border Wall Uses Social Media to Attack His Detractors," The Texas Tribune/ProPublica, September 29, 2020.

Brandy Zadrozny and Ben Collins, "Behind the Viral #GoFundTheWall Fundraiser, a Rising Conservative Star and a Shadowy Email Harvesting Operation," *NBC News,* January 11, 2019.

Brianna Sacks, "'I Felt Dirty'": Former Employees of the Veteran Crowdfunding Trump's Wall Say He Pushed Fake News to Get Rich," BuzzFeed News, January 10, 2019.

Jose Pagliery, "Bannon Indictment Reveals Damning Texts on 'Build the Wall' Scheme," The Daily Beast, September 8, 2022.

Yeganeh Torbati, "Federal Prosecutors Have Steve Bannon's Murky Nonprofit in Their Sights," ProPublica, August 24, 2020.

Sarah N. Lynch, Andy Sullivan, and Brendan Pierson, "Steve Bannon, Key to Trump's Rise, Charged with Defrauding Border-Wall Supporters," Reuters, August 20, 2020.

Josh Russell, "Cohorts of Pardoned Steve Bannon Plead Guilty in Fundraising Scheme for Border Wall," Courthouse News Service, April 21, 2022.

Salvador Hernandez, "The Veteran Who Founded We Build the Wall Pleaded Guilty to Fraud and Agreed to Pay Back More Than $17 Million," BuzzFeed News, April 21, 2022.

Dalton Bennett and Jon Swaine, "The Roger Stone Tapes," *The Washington Post,* March 4, 2022.

Madeline Peltz, "McCarthy Rebels Flock to Steve Bannon's War Room to Beg for Cash," MediaMatters.org, October 4, 2023.

Brian Slodysko, "How Trump's MAGA Movement Helped a 29-Year-Old Activist Become a Millionaire," Associated Press, October 10, 2023.

15. Is the Big Lie the Biggest Grift?

"Conning His Supporters," *The Wall Street Journal* editorial board, June 10, 2022.

Final Report, Select Committee to Investigate the January 6th Attack on the United States Capitol, House Report 117–63, Government Printing Office, December 22, 2022.

Luke Broadwater and Alan Feuer, "Judge Says Trump Signed Statement with Data His Lawyers Told Him Was False," *The New York Times,* October 19, 2022.

Dean Cole and Katelyn Polantz, "Judge Preliminarily Finds Ex-Trump Attorney John Eastman Culpable in California Bar Disciplinary Case," CNN.com, November 3, 2023.

Dan Friedman, "Leaked Audio: Before Election Day, Bannon Said Trump Planned to Falsely Claim Victory," *Mother Jones,* July 12, 2022.

Mimi Swartz, "How True the Vote Fabricates Claims of Voter Fraud for Fun and Profit," *Texas Monthly,* August 22, 2022.

"Leaders of the Big Lie Movement Warn Donors Not to Fund Catherine Engelbrecht of True the Vote," Documented.net, May 31, 2022.

Cassandra Jaramillo, "She Helped Create the Big Lie. Records Suggest She Turned It into a Big Grift," Revealnews.org, June 8, 2022.

Cassandra Jaramillo, Lauren McGaughy, and Allie Morris, "Promoters of Election

Lies Also Hyped a Hospital for Ukraine. That Never Happened Either," *The Dallas Morning News*/ProPublica, January 23, 2023.

Richard Salame, "Was Election Denial Just a Get Rich Quick Scheme? Donors' Lawsuits Look for Answers," Type Investigations and The Intercept, February 6, 2021.

The Bopp Law Firm, P.C. v. True the Vote, Inc., US District Court, Southern District of Indiana, verified complaint, March 15, 2023.

David Marques, "Right-Wing Flop of the Year: Dinesh D'Souza's *2000 Mules*," *The New Republic*, December 28, 2022.

Danny Hakim and Alexandra Berzon, "A Big Lie in a New Package," *The New York Times*, May 29, 2022.

Ali Swenson, "Fact Focus: Gaping Holes in the Claim of 2K Ballot 'Mules,'" Associated Press, May 3, 2022.

Tom Dreisbach, "A Pro-Trump Film Suggests Its Data Are So Accurate, It Solved a Murder. That's False," National Public Radio, May 17, 2022.

Philip Bump, "The Team Behind '2000 Mules' Is Called Out for Deception. Again," *The Washington Post*, October 17, 2022.

Eli Lake, "Review: '2000 Mules,'" The Washington Free Beacon, May 27, 2022.

"*2000 Mules* Becomes the Most Successful Political Documentary in a Decade, Seen by 1 Million," Salem Media press release, May 12, 2022.

Nikki McCann Ramirez, "Trump Raises $4 Million in Indictment Cash Grab," *Rolling Stone*, March 31, 2023.

Josh Dawsey and Isaac Arnsdorf, "Trump's Paid Speeches Organizer Is Struggling Financially," *The Washington Post*, September 29, 2022.

Prem Thakker, "Even Trump's Allies Think His NFTs Are Dumb: 'I Can't Take This Anymore,'" *The New Republic*, December 16, 2022.

Lee Moran, "Donald Trump's New Trading Cards Go Viral for All the Wrong Reasons," HuffPost, April 19, 2023.

Margaret Hartmann, "Trump Wants 'Nice Guy' Credit for Not Gouging Prices on NFTs," *New York* magazine, April 19, 2023.

Ariana Baio, "Trump Boasts About Making $4.6M from NFT Cards That Actually Plummeted in Value," *The Independent*, April 19, 2023.

Drew Harwell, "Co-Founder of Trump's Media Company Details Truth Social's Bitter Infighting," *The Washington Post*, October 15, 2022.

Jonathan Swan, Kate Kelly, Maggie Haberman, and Mark Mazzetti, "Kushner Firm Got Hundreds of Millions from 2 Persian Gulf Nations," *The New York Times*, March 30, 2023.

INDEX

ABOUT THE AUTHOR

James Hamilton

JOE CONASON is an American journalist and commentator. He is editor in chief of *The National Memo,* a daily political newsletter, and a senior fellow at Type Media Center. His articles have appeared in many publications around the world, including *The New Republic, The Nation, The Guardian, Salon,* and *The Village Voice.* Two of his previous books, *The Hunting of the President* and *Big Lies,* were *New York Times* bestsellers.